DITA for Practitioners

Volume 1: Architecture and Technology

Eliot Kimber

D1501399

DITA for Practitioners Volume 1: Architecture and Technology

Copyright © 2012 Eliot Kimber

Credits

"DITA" and the DITA logo are used with permission from the OASIS open standards consortium.

Glossary of Aikido terms used by permission. Original source copyright © Stefan Stenudd, available at *http://www.stenudd.com*.

Disclaimer

Trademarks

XML Press
Laguna Hills, California
http://xmlpress.net

First Edition
ISBN: 978-1-937434-06-9

Acknowledgements

My thanks to all the reviewers of early drafts of this book—you provided invaluable feedback and encouragement and made this book much better than it otherwise would have been (if I had finished it at all). Most deep gratitude to my publisher and editor, Dick Hamilton, who both gave the time I needed to get this thing finished, who pushed me to finally put a fork in it, and who, in his role as editor, made numerous improvements to the text. And thanks to the DITA community and the DITA Technical Committee for making DITA the amazing technology that it is and for giving me the opportunity to contribute to it. Thanks also to my colleagues at RSI Content Solutions, who have fully supported my DITA-related activities. And thanks to the DITA Open Toolkit team for all the hard work they do to continuously improve our core DITA infrastructure.

And finally, love and thank you to my family for being so patient and supportive of my writing.

Preface

DITA for Practitioners is my attempt to capture as much of the DITA implementation how-to knowledge I have in my head as I can. There are a number of good books about how to *author* DITA content but few about how to implement, maintain, and extend DITA-based systems and solutions.

As a technology, DITA reflects many of the things SGML and XML practitioners and systems implementors have been doing or trying to do for more than twenty years: support modular writing and reuse, use hyperlinks in sophisticated ways, enable single source to multiple outputs, enable smooth and cost-effective interchange of content and processing, and generally support some of the most challenging requirements there are in the realm of document authoring, management, and publishing. DITA reflects person-centuries of experience with building these sorts of systems and, coming from IBM originally, reflects some of the most challenging requirements faced by any enterprise using XML for documentation.

That all serves to make DITA a powerful technology indeed. But it also makes DITA complicated, because it does a lot, and some of the things it does are very sophisticated. It also means that any single use of DITA will likely not need every feature of DITA. As with many powerful technologies, part of the challenge of applying DITA to a specific problem is figuring out what you don't need. Hopefully this book will help you answer that question as well as the "how do I do X?" questions that all DITA practitioners have.

As a how-to book, this book reflects opinion and practice as much as it does facts about the DITA standard. To that degree it is really a conversation about how best to apply DITA, not a prescriptive manual of how you *must* apply DITA. I heartily encourage feedback and discussion about anything I've said in this book. I will of course be updating and revising it as DITA evolves as a standard and as a body of supporting tools and knowledge. I need your help to make this book as good as it can be.

The main Web site for this book is *http://dita4practitioners.org*. Please go there for access to all the sample code and supporting artifacts used or mentioned in this book, as well as for discussion boards where you can provide feedback or engage other readers.

The DITA community's main online discussion group is the DITA Users Yahoo group, *http://tech.groups.yahoo.com/group/dita-users/*. If you are doing anything with DITA you should definitely subscribe. The DITA community is as supportive as any I've been involved with over the years. It is the go-to source for quick answers to any DITA-related question you might have.

I hope you enjoy your experience with DITA—my goal is to help make it as happy and productive as possible.

Eliot Kimber
Austin, Texas
April 2012.

Contents

List of Figures

List of Tables

1

Where Do I Start?

I often get asked the question "where do I start to learn DITA?" by people newly-tasked with implementing or supporting DITA-based systems. It's a hard question to answer because DITA has many aspects and dimensions, and no single book or website or white paper can hope to address them all.

The DITA specification, while it endeavors to be clear, is explicitly not a tutorial introduction to DITA but a formal specification. At the time of this writing most, if not all, of the DITA-related books focus on just one use of DITA and are primarily for authors using DITA, not practitioners implementing DITA. There is a lot of good practical information scattered about in various news groups, websites, and blog posts (most notably the *DITA Users Yahoo group*) but it has not, to date, been pulled into a single set of publications. So good question indeed—where to start?

This book is for people who are or will be involved in some way with the design, implementation, or support of DITA-based systems. This book is not primarily for authors. However, authors who want a deeper understanding of the technology they are using will find relevant sections, in particular *An Overview of the DITA Architecture* on page 179, which provides a general discussion of DITA features and how they are used.

As with most technologies, the knowledge required of users is quite different from the knowledge required of implementors.

Using This Book

This book provides an overview of the key architectural features of DITA, those things that distinguish it fundamentally from all other XML applications and standards. Even if, and especially if, you have worked with other XML applications before, read this section first. DITA does things quite differently from traditional XML practice. Therefore, if you are an experienced XML practitioner you will very likely be confused and surprised by DITA if you come to it without a guide.

Once you have read the overview you should then be prepared to read and understand the DITA specification.

Practitioners do need to understand *how* users use the system and why. Neither this book (nor any single source) can help you with that task in the general case because there are many ways to use DITA.

While many people associate DITA with modular, task-oriented, topic-based technical documentation, that is only one of an infinite number of useful ways to apply DITA to documents. There are an infinite number of possible useful writing *practices*, all of which DITA can support with equal facility.

Therefore, you must know which writing practice or practices your users want to use so you can figure out the best way to support those requirements through DITA technology (or even to determine if DITA technology is the most appropriate solution for your users).[1]

DITA for Practitioners is organized into two volumes:

- Volume 1 of *DITA for Practitioners* focuses on DITA as a technology: what is it about, how does it work, what are the core architectural concepts and features? It provides an in-depth exploration of DITA as a technology with a focus on how DITA works.

- Volume 2 of *DITA for Practitioners* focuses on the configuration, customization, and extension of DITA markup. It provides a tutorial introduction to the configuration and extension (specialization) of DITA vocabulary. The DITA configuration and specialization tutorials are also available online at *http://www.xiruss.org/tutorials/dita-specialization/*.

---

[1]   It almost always is, so it's a reasonably safe starting assumption, but there are rare cases where some other solution will be better.

Getting Started

So where to start?

Volume 1 is organized into two parts:

Part 1, End-to-End DITA processing, provides general information on processing DITA content using the DITA Open Toolkit and how-to information for extending and customizing the Open Toolkit. It also provides a detailed DITA authoring tutorial intended for practitioners. The authoring tutorial serves to introduce you to all the major features of DITA in the context of creating realistic DITA content.

Part 2, An Overview of the DITA Architecture, provides a general discussion of all the major features DITA, with a focus on how those features relate to the design and implementation of DITA systems. Part 2 can be useful for authors who want a deeper understanding of DITA, but it is not intended to be a guide to authoring.

If you are a hands-on person, you can dive right into the practical and start with Part 2, which begins with a tutorial introduction to end-to-end DITA using the OxygenXML editor and the DITA Open Toolkit. You can then move from there to the architectural overview.

Or you can start with the architectural overview and then do a deep dive into the DITA Architectural Specification before trying to do anything concrete.

For the markup and configuration tutorials, I recommend working through them in order, as they proceed in order of complexity and requirement.

Another consideration is the question of what specifically do you, as the DITA system implementor, actually need to get done:

- Are you enabling use of existing documents through a new system, or are you implementing a new system from scratch?
- Is this a non-XML-to-XML project or a migration of a legacy XML or SGML system to a DITA-based system?
- Have the tools already been chosen, or do you need to figure out what will work for you?
- Do you need to define new topic or map types?
- Is the primary task implementing a new output path for an existing body of documents?
- Are you implementing a DITA-supporting tool or product?

The goal of *DITA for Practitioners* is to support all these tasks as much as it can.

The DITA Standard

The Darwin Information Typing Architecture (DITA) is a standard published by OASIS (Organization for the Advancement of Structured Information Standards). The main OASIS site is *http://www.oasis-open.org/*. The main DITA standard page is *http://www.oasis-open.org/committees/tc_home.php?wg_abbrev=dita*. OASIS is organized into *technical committees*, so the group responsible for the DITA standard is the DITA Technical Committee (DITA TC).

OASIS is a not-for-profit consortium. You must be a representative of an OASIS member organization or an individual member of OASIS in order to participate in technical committees. This form of standards organization primarily serves to ensure that appropriate intellectual property protections are in place so that participants cannot submit proprietary technology to a standard and then later claim to have patents or other ownership of some part of the standard. All work products of the DITA Technical Committee are public, meaning you can track the activity of the DITA TC. DITA TC membership reflects a wide range of stakeholders, including DITA users, DITA tool vendors, and DITA-specialist consultants.

In addition to the DITA Technical Committee, DITA is also supported by the DITA Adoption Technical Committee, which develops materials to foster and support adoption of the DITA standard. Its primary work products are informational papers focusing on different aspects of DITA and how to use it effectively.

The chief architect of the DITA Standard is Michael Priestley of IBM.

At the time of writing, the DITA standard is at version 1.2, with version 1.3 under active development.

The DITA standard document is organized into two main parts, the Architectural Specification and the Language Reference.

The Architectural Specification defines the concepts, semantics, and syntax of the DITA application, while the Language Reference defines all of the element types and attributes that comprise the OASIS-defined DITA vocabulary. HTML, PDF, and Windows help versions of the DITA specification are available from the OASIS website. The DITA source of the DITA standard is also available from the OASIS website.

The Architectural Specification defines the basic rules for DITA, including the general structural rules for topics and maps. It specifies those aspects of document processing that are mandatory (address processing, metadata cascade, content referencing, conditional processing) and defines default or suggested behaviors for processing that is necessarily processor-specific or is largely or entirely a matter of rendition style. (This means that many aspects of DITA document processing are not, and cannot be, defined or mandated by the DITA standard—this can make it difficult to distinguish what parts of a given DITA system are defined by DITA the standard and what are simply how the particular system works.)

The Language Reference provides a reference entry for each element type and attribute defined in the DITA specification. It is the first place you should look for details on what elements or attributes are available and what the rules are for a given element or attribute.

The OASIS-defined DITA vocabulary has two parts:

- The base vocabulary, which defines the base element types and attributes from which all other conforming DITA vocabulary must be derived.
- Specializations that support specific use cases, such as the concept, task, and reference topic types used primarily in technical documentation. (If you are not familiar with the concept of DITA specialization, please read *Vocabulary Composition and Specialization* on page 183.)

All OASIS-defined specializations are standard but not mandatory, meaning that just because they are defined by OASIS, conforming DITA processors are not required to support them (although most do) and DITA users are not required to use any particular OASIS-defined specialization. However, as a matter of practice, you should use OASIS-defined vocabulary when the vocabulary is a close match to your requirements, simply to ensure ease of interoperation and interchange.

Note that you can't just say "the standard DITA vocabulary" or "the DITA vocabulary," because DITA is explicitly designed to be extended. Any conforming extension is part of the DITA vocabulary. In addition, other standards groups could standardize their own specialized DITA vocabulary modules. For example, an organization like the IDEAlliance, which primarily serves the publishing and printing industries and publishes many XML-based standards, could standardize DITA vocabulary modules for publishing usage. Such vocabularies would be just as standard as the OASIS-defined vocabulary, but they would not be part of the DITA standard as published by OASIS. That is, the DITA TC has no monopoly on standardizing conforming DITA specializations. It does have a monopoly on standardizing the DITA base vocabulary.

One implication of the extensible nature of DITA is that the DITA community is not dependent on the DITA TC to define all new or standardized vocabulary. That is, you don't have to necessarily wait for the TC to do something if you need new vocabulary as long as your requirements don't require new base types or architectural extensions to DITA. As DITA matures you should expect the DITA TC to focus almost entirely on the base DITA architecture and not on more specialized vocabulary, especially as the TC moves its focus in the future to DITA 2.0. You may, for example, see new OASIS Technical Committees formed specifically for the purpose of developing vertical or industry-specific DITA vocabularies. As separate TCs, rather than subcommittees of the DITA TC, they would not be required to synchronize their activities with the DITA TC.

You should familiarize yourself with the DITA specification, at least to the point where you know how to get to it for reference purposes. Once you are more familiar with DITA concepts and technology, I urge you to read through the Architectural Specification. In particular, you shouldn't blindly take my representation of the DITA architecture uncritically. Check it against your own understanding based on your own reading of the specification. Of course, I think my understanding is correct and reflected in this book, but DITA is sufficiently sophisticated that even those people intimately involved in its creation can get it wrong sometimes.

Finally, when discussing DITA as a standard, it is important to distinguish the DITA specification, which is the work of the DITA Technical Committee, from implementations of DITA, such as the DITA Open Toolkit or commercial products. There is no standard DITA implementation. While the DITA Open Toolkit is implemented primarily by IBM, and its development is closely coordinated with the DITA Technical Committee, The Open Toolkit is not "DITA," it is one of many implementations of DITA. In particular, you should not every say "DITA does X" or "DITA doesn't do X" when what you mean is "the Open Toolkit does X" or "the Open Toolkit doesn't do X."

A Brief History of the DITA Standard

The DITA Technical Committee was founded in 2003. The DITA 1.0 specification was donated by IBM to OASIS and was published largely without modification. DITA 1.1 was published 2007 and DITA 1.2 in December of 2010.

DITA was originally driven by IBM's internal requirements for, primarily, technical documentation, but it has evolved substantially since that initial donation to encompass a very wide scope of requirements indeed. The DITA core architecture is remarkably general considering its fairly narrow original requirements.

DITA's specialization facility reflects the fact that IBM is really a collection of disparate enterprises with competing requirements. Work that Don Day, Wayne Wohler, Simcha Gralla, and I did at IBM in the late 80's and early 90's to define a single SGML vocabulary to replace IBM's BookMaster GML application, which was used for almost all of IBM's product documentation, made it clear that a single all-encompassing document type would never work. It would simply be too large and too inflexible to adapt quickly to local requirements or new technologies.

We took the concept of "architectural forms," based on the HyTime standard developed by Charles Goldfarb and Steve Newcomb, and incorporated it into IBM ID Doc as a way of allowing local extension and customization without breaking interchange and interoperability. However, that aspect of IBM ID Doc got somewhat lost as it moved from its initial design into wider implementation and deployment at IBM.

I left IBM in 1994, but Don stayed and eventually helped adapt the IBM ID Doc modularity and extensibility ideas into what became DITA. But while IBM ID Doc reflected our old "big iron" way of thinking about standards, DITA reflected the new Web and XML approach, where simplicity was better. In many ways DITA succeeded because it found the simplest thing that would possibly work for a very challenging set of requirements.

Essential Background Knowledge for Those New to XML and DITA

Are you completely new to XML and DITA?

DITA is an XML application. That means that as a practitioner you must have a working knowledge of

- XML syntax and concepts.
- DTD syntax
- XML Schema (XSD) if you need to work with XSD-based vocabulary modules or document type shells

If you will be using, customizing, or extending the DITA Open Toolkit you must have at least:

- Some familiarity with the Apache Ant system, which is used to script the various Open Toolkit processes.
- A basic understanding of XSLT, although very simple tasks, like implementing HTML generation for new inline elements, requires only the most basic XSLT knowledge.
- Some CSS knowledge if you need to customize the HTML or EPUB presentation via CSS.
- A basic understanding of XSL Formatting Objects (XSL-FO) if you plan to customize or extend PDF generation.

Other XML technologies that you may need depending on the tools you're using include:

- XQuery, used by many XML repositories and database systems, such as MarkLogic and eXist.
- XProc, used to create XML processing pipelines.

Knowledge of Java or other programming languages is not normally required for most DITA implementation activities. This book assumes that you are primarily an XML technologist, not an application programmer. Key parts of the DITA Open Toolkit are implemented in Java, but all of the intentionally-extensible components use either XSLT or Ant.

In this book I assume that you have a basic working knowledge of XML, DTDs, and XSDs. Where I discuss using XSLT to implement DITA-specific processing, I assume you have a working knowledge of XSLT.

There is no shortage of good books and online resources on all the XML technologies and tools. The various online tutorials at sites like xml.com and w3schools.com can give you a good grounding in the basics. For XSLT, Mike Kay's and Ken Holman's books are the gold standard.

If you are starting from scratch, all of this can seem like a very high and steep learning curve. A complete DITA system has a lot of moving parts and involves a lot of different technologies. However, you can start fairly simply with just an XML editor like OxygenXML and the DITA Open Toolkit and make a lot of demonstrable progress before you have to dive more deeply.

The DITA community supports its own, primarily through the DITA Users Yahoo group. The group supports questions from both DITA authors and DITA implementors. Don't be afraid to ask questions there.

Essential Background Knowledge for Experienced SGML and XML Practitioners

Are you a seasoned XML or SGML practitioner?

Many people coming to DITA have been doing XML and—for some of us venerable types, SGML—for a long time.

If you are in this camp you have a challenge, which is essentially trying to forget a lot of what you thought was accepted best practice.

If you are like me, coming to DITA with no advanced warning or guidance, your initial reaction will likely be along the lines of "what the heck is going on here?"

The way DITA does things is, to a large degree, exactly opposite from the way many of us did things for going on twenty years. It completely changes the way you think about markup design, document type implementation, and system extension and deployment. This can be distressing, as I can attest to from personal experience. It took me a couple of years to come to understand that the DITA approach is actually much more effective and efficient than what I now think of as traditional XML practice.

I have also been through the experience of helping colleagues through the process of coming to a happy and productive relationship to DITA and DITA approaches to analysis, design, and implementation.

One goal of this book is to help you, as an experienced XML practitioner with a wealth of knowledge and experience, come as quickly as possible to an understanding of how to apply that knowledge and experience quickly and effectively without being slowed down by ways of thinking about things and doing things that simply will not work in a DITA environment.

The key to this is understanding that DITA imposes a small set of constraints that limit some markup design choices, but by so doing make everything else either easier or merely possible (in the case of blind interchange of content). If you are like me you will initially chafe at these constraints. My job in this book is to help you get past that.

I realize this sounds a bit evangelical or self helpy. All I can say is that I went through a truly transformative experience in coming to understand how DITA brings a novel approach to XML system design and implementation, an approach that works better than anything I've done in the past. I am excited about DITA technology because it makes me, and by extension my clients, so much more effective than we have ever been before.

This book is not titled "DITA in Anger," although I'm sure there are some people out there who would like to be (or are) writing that book. This book could be titled "DITA in Joy."

If you are reading this book because you are being forced to do some DITA stuff, I understand your position because I was there. You can use this book to find the specific technical details you need to get your job done. I've been there and will be there again, and I hope you find this book useful.

If you are reading this book because you have decided to "go DITA" because someone like me has convinced you that it has some merit then you can use this book to gain a deeper understanding of why DITA is the way it is.

Of course, at the end of the day, DITA is just a technology. It's not a religion, it's not a way of life. It's simply a clever and effective way of solving some challenging business and practical problems inherent in creating, managing, interchanging, and processing complex documents written by and intended for humans.

Essential Background Knowledge for Those With Prior DITA System Experience

Have you been working with DITA and DITA-supporting tools for a while now?

If you have been involved in the development or use of an older DITA-based system, one that predates DITA 1.2, you very likely had some painful experiences and ran up against a number of limitations in DITA 1.0 or 1.1.

DITA 1.2 goes a long way toward addressing most of the issues you likely had:

- The new constraint mechanism lets you configure content models to suit authors in a conforming way, avoiding the need for either specialization or non-conforming modification of the base DITA document types.
- The new keyref facility makes it possible to have element-to-element links (xrefs and conrefs) in topics that are used in different maps and generally makes linking manageable in a way it was not before.
- The new conref range and conref push features make content referencing more complete. With conref push you can impose new content onto topics you can't or shouldn't modify, simplifying many conditional processing use cases.
- The new `<bodydiv>` and `<sectiondiv>` elements provide a general base for specialization of arbitrary semantic structures within topic bodies. This allows you to model many things that could not be easily modeled before, especially content that might come from other sources.
- The new Machine Industry specializations provide elements needed by technical content that must conform to various national and international standards for hardware documentation.

- The extended glossary models better support sophisticated terminology markup, especially as needed for localization.
- The DITA 1.2 specification more clearly identifies which aspects of DITA are about writing practice and which parts are about data processing.
- The DITA 1.2 conformance clause makes it clearer what are and aren't conforming data and processors.

In addition, open source and commercial DITA tools have steadily improved and continue to improve. At the time of writing, the DITA Open Toolkit implements all DITA 1.2 features, and the commercial OxygenXML editor implements most DITA 1.2 features, including support for keys and key references. The community continues to develop better documentation and generally capture its collective knowledge in useful ways.

Essential Terminology

As with any technology, DITA has its own body of jargon and terminology conventions. This section defines those terms that have specific meanings in this book. In addition to these terms, you should be familiar with the terminology defined in the *DITA Architectural Specification* and in the XML specification. This book uses those terms as defined in those standards unless otherwise stated.

The term "DITA" is particularly problematic because it has so many meanings. By unqualified "DITA" or "the DITA standard," I mean the DITA specifications represented by the *DITA Architecture Specification* and the *DITA Language Reference* as published by OASIS. Those two documents define what DITA is in a formal, normative sense (that is, as a body of law).

By "DITA technology" I mean the DITA standard and all general-purpose DITA-aware software that supports it, including the DITA Open Toolkit and similar general-purpose DITA processors.

Additional terms:

XML document	In XML, a *document* is a *storage object* that contains the root element of an XML tree. A document may be stored as one or more *external parsed general entities*. The use of entities by an XML document requires the document to have a document type declaration, as it is the document type declaration that declares the entities. DITA does not use (or allow the use of) general entities.
entity	In XML, an *entity* is a named fragment of XML content. Entities may be *internal* or *external* and *general* or *parameter*. Parameter entities are used within document type declarations and are used to organize and parameterize DTD declarations. General entities are used within XML documents. Internal entities have *replacement text* that is specified as part of the entity declaration. External entities point to resources, where the resource contains the replacement text. Both internal and external entities are processed as though the entity replacement text had occurred where the entity reference occurred. That means, in particular, that there is no functional difference between an XML

document stored as a single storage object with no entities and one that uses entities to organize its storage—the parsed result is the same in both cases.

Because they are a syntactic feature, not a semantic feature, of XML, entities end up not being useful for managing reuse. In addition, because they require a document type declaration, they cannot be used with XML documents that do not have a DOCTYPE declaration.

DITA provides semantic, markup-based features, that satisfy the reuse and storage organization requirements entities were originally intended to satisfy.

resource   A unit of (nominally) physical storage, for example a file. DITA is an XML application and a Web application and therefore uses the Web model of resources as the unit of data access, rather than the "file," even though in most DITA systems resources are in fact files. But it is important to understand that DITA operates on resources, meaning things addressed by URIs, not on files. For example, in the context of a component management system, resources may not be files at all but objects managed in some type of database.

A resource may also be referred to as a *storage object*, meaning an addressable unit of physical storage.

For XML as used by DITA, a resource that contains XML is always an XML document because DITA does not use (and does not allow the use of) general XML entities for organizing XML data for physical storage. This means that DITA topics and maps are resources in the Web sense, and they are always XML documents as defined by the XML specification. One implication of this is that DITA maps and topics are objects in the generic sense, meaning they have identity and may be meaningfully processed in isolation.

DITA document   An *XML document* that conforms to the DITA specification and has as its root element map, topic, ditabase, val, or a specialization of one of those elements.

publication   A business object that represents a primary deliverable out of an authoring organization, such as a single technical manual, a single book, a magazine, a single website, etc. In DITA, publications are represented by maps that are the *root maps* for processing. Publication maps are usually distinguished by having publication-specific metadata in addition to topicrefs to the topics or *submaps* that make up the publication content.

While the DITA specification does not formally define the notion of "publication," in that there is no DITA-defined markup you can put in a map to indicate that it is or is not a root map, in practice you will have maps that represent publications and maps that do not.

The DITA bookmap and DITA for Publishers pubmap map types explicitly represent publications in the sense meant here. More generally a "publication" is the map you give to a processor to generate a complete deliverable.

root map   A root map is either a map that is not used by any other map or simply the map given to a processor as its initial input. In general, a root map is a map that may be usefully processed in isolation. Starting with DITA 1.2, key reference resolution requires knowing the root map that directly or indirectly contains the key definitions for the keys to be resolved.

Not all root maps are publications. For example, you might have a map that represents the set of topics for a specific information domain (for example, all tasks that support a set of related software components) but that is not itself intended for publishing. It is a root map in that there are no other maps that use it and it may be usefully processed (for example, to create a catalog of tasks for review purposes), but it is not a "publication" as defined here.

submap   A map that is referenced from another map when processed in the context of the referencing map. For example, a map that defines the structure of a chapter might be used as a submap by several different book maps.

document type shell   A file that implements the integration and configuration of a set of DITA vocabulary modules. DITA 1.2 defines rules for document type shells for DTD and XSD syntax.

content as authored   DITA documents as they are authored, that is, before any output processing is applied to them. This term is used to distinguish content as authored from "content as rendered" when talking about the data manipulation and processing that happens in the process of producing renditions from content as authored.

content as rendered   DITA content that has been processed to produce some sort of deliverable format, such as HTML, PDF, or new XML objects (DITA or otherwise) for delivery outside the scope of the authoring environment.

body of content   The set of resources a given authoring community works on. This may be product documentation, publications, a set of topics for a website, or something else. For a given authoring community the "body of content" is some known or knowable set of content to which the members of the community have access.

authoring tool   A software component designed primarily to enable the creation and modification of DITA documents. While DITA documents can be edited in any text editor or general-purpose XML editor, authoring is most effective in a DITA-aware tool such as XMetal or OxygenXML.

management environment   The overall system by which a body of content is managed for authoring within the context of a set of *business rules*. Normally, a management environment is built around a *component management system* or *version control system*. A complete management environment typically includes the configuration and integration of the authoring tools and processing system.

business rule   A rule or policy specific to a particular authoring community, body of content, and authoring environment. Business rules include editorial rules, security rules, naming practices, and so on. Some business rules can be enforced by software systems, some cannot. Most of the effort expended in configuring and customizing *management environments* is in implementing and enforcing local business rules.

component management system   A system designed to manage distributed access to interrelated document components (*resources*). In a DITA context this means a system that knows how to manage maps and topics as interrelated objects. Although often referred to as a "content management system," the community appears to be moving toward the term "component management system" to distinguish such systems from both HTML-specific management systems and more generic XML management systems. Component management requires *version management* and implies some degree of *link management* or *dependency management*.

version control system   A system that manages resources and changes in resources over time. A *component management system* must also be a version control system. Common version control systems include CVS, Subversion, GIT, and VCC. For many authoring communities a version control system may be sufficient to satisfy content management requirements, and one may be the only practical option when budgets are small or the community is not within a single enterprise (such as open-source projects).

addressing   The task of pointing to a resource using some syntax, e.g., a URI reference or, in DITA, a key reference. Address resolution and management is an important aspect of *link management* but addressing is not, by itself, linking.

link management   The management of knowledge about element-to-element or element-to-resource relationships within content as authored, with the primary purpose of answering these questions quickly:

- Where is a given element used within a given body of content? (E.g., "what points at me?")
- For a given map or topic, what components does it depend on? (E.g., "what do I point at?")
- For the purpose of link authoring, what potential link targets are available (E.g., "what can I point at?")

Link management is required for both authoring (creation and resolution of links during editing of content) and processing (quick resolution of links for delivery or viewing).

DITA link management is complicated by DITA's applicability features because a given link or address may only be applicable to specific conditions. For example, there may be multiple definitions for the same key name, where each definition has different applicability. In this case a system cannot simply say "this is the resource the key is bound to" but must say "this key is bound to these resources under these conditions."

dependency management   The management of knowledge of the resource-to-resource dependencies implied by links within a body of content.

For example, if Topic A has a cross-reference to Topic B.1 within Topic B, the cross-reference is an element-to-element link from the xref element in Topic A to the subordinate topic element in Topic B. However, the link implies that document Topic A depends on document Topic B. Dependency tracking serves the purpose of determining, for a given starting resource, all the other resources needed in order to resolve all the links. In DITA, the typical example is determining for a root map all the other maps, topics, and non-DITA objects used by that map. This set of resources is sometimes referred to as the *bounded object set* (*BOS*) for the map.

Dependency management is usually separated from link management because the number of dependencies is often a fraction of the number of links within a given body of content. If two topics have 100 links between themselves, that implies two dependencies: each topic depends on the other. When dependencies reflect link semantics (that is, the reason for a given link), then there may be multiple dependencies, one for each distinct type of link.

For example, of those 100 links between two topics, 80 might be content references (where content from one topic is pulled into another) and 20 cross-references (navigation links to other elements). That would imply four dependencies, one for each topic for the content references and one for each topic for the cross-references. That is, if the processing task is to determine the set of resources required to support some starting map or topic, you need to know that there is at least one link of a given type from one resource to another. The number of such links is not relevant for that processing task.

Dependency tracking supports the task of *packaging* resources to create self-contained sets, for example, as needed for export or interchange or as required by a given processing instance.

processing   Taking *content as authored* and applying some data processing to it (e.g., transformations) to produce a new data set.

rendering   *Processing* that produces a final-form deliverable from DITA content, such as HTML, PDF, EPUB, or whatever.

packaging   The task of gathering and organizing a set of resources for use as a single unit of storage or interchange. For example, creating a Zip file with all the maps, topics, and graphics used by a specific publication. Packaging often involves reorganizing resources into a specific folder or directory structure and, therefore, rewriting addresses to reflect the new structure.

export   Moving DITA resources from within a *management environment* to outside it, for example, to deliver data to an interchange partner or licensee. Export normally involves *packaging*.

import   Moving DITA resources from outside a *management environment* to inside it, for example to load a map and all its dependencies into a component management system.

XML catalog   A mapping from XML public or system identifiers (URIs) to files or resources within a specific storage system. Also called an *entity resolution catalog* because its primary purpose historically was to resolve references to external entities. OASIS Open defines two XML catalog formats, an older text-based format and a newer XML-based format. Most XML-aware tools support the XML-based format, including the DITA Open Toolkit. The Open Toolkit provides specific features for using plugins to manage catalogs for DITA vocabulary modules and document type shells.

When talking about documents, XML, and so forth, there are many terms that have both general meanings and specific technical meanings. In particular, the term "document" means any number of things.

Because a fundamental aspect of DITA is the ability to organize a single unit of delivery into multiple files, there is potential for confusion between the term "document" to mean "Something you publish for humans to read" and "document" in the XML sense (an atomic unit of XML storage rooted at a single element).

In this book I use the term "document" as a noun to mean "XML document," although I try to use the qualified term "XML document" consistently. I use the term "DITA document" to mean an XML document that conforms to the DITA specification (e.g., a map or topic document). I use the term "publication" to mean "a unit of information delivery to humans" (which is what we generally mean by "document" outside an XML context).

Thus, in the general authoring and management model used by this book, authors create XML documents that make up a body of content from which they may produce different publications.

.

Part I

End to End DITA Processing

This part focuses on the nuts and bolts of end-to-end DITA processing, that is, going from DITA content as authored, through component management to the production of various deliverable forms, such as PDF and compiled help, using typical tool sets.

The purpose of this part is to help you set up and use a realistic DITA system development environment. This system is then used as the basis for all the practical examples and tutorials in this book. The purpose of this part is also to enable you to do something useful with DITA as quickly as possible. If you have no experience with DITA and DITA technology, this is the best place to start.

If you are already familiar with common DITA tools and development practices you should still at least skim this part so that you understand how the development environment used by this book relates to your own environment.

While much of the common DITA tool set is open source, there are some components that are not. In particular, there is no open source XML and DITA development environment that integrates the DITA Open Toolkit. While the current Eclipse IDE comes close, it does not provide the depth of support and integration that commercial tools do, in particular the OxygenXML editor from SyncRO Soft. I specify the use of OxygenXML in this book because, while it is not a free tool, it is not that expensive and because its depth of features and completeness of support represents a tremendous value. It is an essential tool in my day-to-day toolbox, and it likely will be in yours as well. At the time of writing, OxygenXML is the only visual DITA-aware XML editor that supports DITA 1.2-specific features and runs on all platforms. (The Syntext Serna editor is a cross-platform, DITA-aware XML editor, but at the time of writing it supports DITA 1.1 out of the box and lacks support for some DITA 1.2 features, such as support for authoring key references.)

2

Setting Up Your Development Environment

There are many ways to set up a productive DITA development environment. This chapter describes a set of tools that works well for me, and which I use in describing the tutorials and how-to sections in this book.

The development and maintenance of DITA systems requires the following types of tools:

- An XML-aware editing environment for working with DITA documents, DTDs, XSDs, XSLT, XQuery, and other XML-specific artifacts. This book recommends the SyncRO Soft OxygenXML product for the simple reason that it offers the most functionality at the lowest price, reflects excellent engineering quality, excellent service, and the most complete DITA implementation of any authoring environment at the time of writing.
- A Java development environment for compiling and deploying Java code (optional). Many DITA systems never require the implementation of custom Java code but it can still be useful to be able to examine or modify the Java code that underlies the Open Toolkit. If you are integrating with a component management system you will likely need to write custom Java code. This book uses the Eclipse IDE, although similar systems, such as NetBeans, are comparable. Eclipse and similar tools can be useful simply as a way to run and manage Ant scripts even if you do not do any Java development.
- A Web browser.

- Output-specific viewers, including PDF readers, EPUB readers, Windows help viewers, etc.
- A source code control system, such as Subversion, GIT, or VCC, for managing your project's source components. A source code control system can manage DITA content quite effectively.

> **Note:** You should not use CVS with DITA content because it cannot handle Unicode documents properly (CVS is ASCII only).

General DITA development and the tutorials in this book require the following specific tools:

- A Java development kit (SDK), which is required by the DITA Open Toolkit and Java development. At the time of writing the latest Java version is Java 7, but Java 6 is the minimum version required by most of the tools you will be using. You should use Sun (Oracle) Java, as some tool components will not work with other Java distributions.
- The DITA Open Toolkit. Even if your system does not use the Toolkit itself, it is still useful for testing and validating DITA processing. The DITA Open Toolkit is the only free, open-source, and cross-platform general-purpose DITA implementation and serves as a reference implementation for the DITA standard (while it is not a product of OASIS or the DITA Technical Committee, the Open Toolkit developers coordinate with the Technical Committee so that new DITA features are implemented as quickly and correctly as possible upon final or near-final approval of new versions of the DITA specification). Many commercial DITA-related tools integrate the Open Toolkit. Even if the Toolkit will not be your primary processing environment, it is still useful for testing and managing access to document type shells and specialization vocabulary modules. You should expect to use the Toolkit for that purpose if for no other.
- Apache Ant. Ant is a general-purpose scripting system used to manage the building and deployment of software projects. It is used by the DITA Open Toolkit and is generally useful for lots of tasks. While Ant is included in the main Open Toolkit package, it is useful to have a separate standalone copy.

XML-Aware and DITA-Aware Editing Environment

At the time of writing, I use the OxygenXML editor as my primary XML development environment and heads-down authoring tool. As of the time of writing, OxygenXML provides unmatched support for DITA 1.2 features. It integrates with the DITA Open Toolkit and is as easy to configure for new DITA vocabulary modules as it is possible for a DITA-aware tool to be. For those reasons I strongly recommend OxygenXML as an XML and DITA development environment. While OxygenXML is a commercial product and is not free, it offers a tremendous value in terms of the features provided.

OxygenXML is provided as a standalone tool and as an Eclipse plugin. The two versions of OxygenXML are functionally equivalent and the same license will work for either. I personally use the standalone version of OxygenXML for largely historical reasons and also to avoid having to close down my

OxygenXML session when I have to close Eclipse, which happens fairly often with the type of development I typically do.

You can also use Eclipse alone for DITA-aware XML development using Eclipse's various XML-related support components and available plugins. Eclipse can be integrated with the Open Toolkit so that you can run the Toolkit from within Eclipse (see *Running the Open Toolkit from Eclipse* on page 142).

Other XML development environments, such as XML Spy, can of course be used to develop DITA-related components, but they do not, at the time of writing, offer the same degree of built-in DITA support or integration with the Open Toolkit as provided by OxygenXML.

Configuring OxygenXML For DITA Development

To make OxygenXML ready for DITA development you need only do one thing after installing the product: turn on use of external DTDs for determination of document type associations. You also have a choice in how you use the DITA Open Toolkit with OxygenXML.

OxygenXML can determine the document type associated with a given document and thereby determine the set of features to use for that document. OxygenXML has built-in DITA-specific features, and it will turn those on for any document that it recognizes as being a DITA document, regardless of the specific vocabulary the document uses. It does this by looking for the `@ditaarch:DITAArchVersion` attribute, which all conforming DITA documents must have and which serves to unambiguously identify a document as being a DITA document.

However, most DITA documents do not directly contain the `@ditaarch:DITAArchVersion` attribute because it is defaulted in the DTDs and schemas. Thus, in order to recognize a document as a DITA document the document must be parsed with respect to its DTD or schema.

OxygenXML can do this but it does not do it by default, because there is a performance cost in parsing documents to determine what type of document they are. So you must turn this feature on for Oxygen to automatically process your specialized DITA documents, or even documents that use local document type shells, as DITA documents.

To turn this feature on go to **Options** > **Preferences** > **Document Type Association** to bring up the Document Type Association panel. On that panel make sure that the "Enable DTD/XML Schema processing in document type detection" check box is checked and that the "Only for local DTDs/XML schemas" checkbox is checked. Save the new preference settings.

Once you have made this change, OxygenXML will automatically apply DITA-specific editor features to all DITA documents regardless of specialization.

OxygenXML includes a copy of the Open Toolkit, usually the latest released version current at the time the OxygenXML version is released. The OxygenXML-provided Toolkit includes some small patches to the Toolkit that improve its interaction with OxygenXML. These patches are not required to use the Toolkit with Oxygen.

OxygenXML uses, or can use, the master entity resolution catalog that is maintained by the Open Toolkit to resolve DITA DTDs and schemas. If you deploy your local shells and specialized vocabulary modules to Oxygen's built-in Toolkit, then your DITA documents that use those shells and modules will just work with no additional configuration actions required. Because OxygenXML is fully specialization aware it provides all its out-of-the-box DITA features to all DITA documents once it is able to parse them, which it can do if the DTDs and schemas are resolvable.

OxygenXML's built-in Open Toolkit is in `frameworks/dita/DITA-OT` below the OxygenXML installation directory.

To ensure that the master Toolkit catalog is being used, go to Preferences->Document Type Association and bring up the Document Type Association panel. Select the entry for "DITA" and select the "Edit" button to edit the document type association. Select the "Catalogs" tab to see the list of associated catalogs. You should see an entry for `${frameworks}/dita/catalog.xml`. The string `${frameworks}` is a reference to the OxygenXML-defined variable that resolves to the location of the OxygenXML `frameworks` directory. If you want Oxygen to use a Toolkit installed at a different location on your computer, you can change this setting to reflect the location of that Toolkit.

Depending on your Toolkit needs you have three choices for how to use OxygenXML with the DITA Open Toolkit:

1. You can use the OxygenXML-provided Toolkit and simply deploy new plugins to it as needed. This ensures that you get full advantage of OxygenXML's patches to the Toolkit. This limits you to the version of the Toolkit included with OxygenXML.
2. You can replace the OxygenXML-provided Toolkit with another Toolkit version in the same location on the file system. This loses the OxygenXML Toolkit patches but means all existing Toolkit-related transformation scenarios and catalog configurations will work without modification.
3. Use a Toolkit installed elsewhere on your computer and set the value of the dita.dir parameter used in OxygenXML transformation scenarios and update the catalog configuration for the DITA document type association. This preserves the OxygenXML-provided Toolkit but requires changes to any transformation scenarios you want to use with the non-Oxygen Toolkit.

I use option (2) most of the time because I find it easiest and most reliable to have my Toolkit be in an invariant location. I then configure that Toolkit instance with whatever I need at the moment. I do this primarily because my daily job involves working with many different Toolkit configurations and versions for clients. I find it easier to have a consistent process and supporting scripts (Ant scripts in my case) that swap into that one location the Toolkit versions and plugins I need for a specific project. This allows me to have exactly one Toolkit location that all my Toolkit-related activities use, removing the chance of accidentally doing things in the wrong location.

If you are working with just one Toolkit version or configuration most or all of the time, but you can't use the OxygenXML-provided version for whatever reason (for example, you need to use an older version or newer version of the Toolkit), then option (3) is probably the best practice since you only have to configure the DITA document type association and each transformation scenario once to reflect the Toolkit location. It does mean that you have to remember to change the default value for the dita.dir parameter whenever you create a new DITA transformation scenario.

3

Authoring, Managing, and Producing A DITA-Based Publication

This chapter walks you through the steps of authoring, revising, and producing a DITA-based publication using the out-of-the-box DITA document types. It also discusses managing DITA content, whether on a file system, in a source code control system, or in a component management system.

If you are already familiar with DITA markup, maps, topics, and the like, then you may skip this chapter. If you are not familiar with the DITA 1.2 keyref feature, you should at least read through the sections on creating key-based topicrefs, cross-references, and content references.

If you are completely new to DITA, this is the place to start.

This section assumes you are using the OxygenXML editor to author your documents and the DITA Open Toolkit to generate output. However, nothing in this section depends on the use of OxygenXML, and the detailed instructions on authoring DITA content should translate to other DITA-aware authoring tools fairly directly as all have similar facilities for working with DITA content.

If you are not already familiar with the DITA Open Toolkit, please review the introductory sections in *Running, Configuring, and Customizing the Open Toolkit* on page 129. This tutorial describes running the

Toolkit from within OxygenXML, but you can perform the same operations from the command line if you prefer.

The term *publication* has no formally-defined meaning in the DITA specification (at least through DITA 1.2). However, most uses of DITA do, in fact, revolve around the creation and management of one or more publications. By "publication" I mean a well-defined unit of delivery, such as a book, a website, a help package, etc.

A publication is (almost) always represented by a single root DITA map. See *Essential Terminology* on page 10 for more about the concept of "publication" as I use it here. And a publication must have one or more topics (because only topics can contain content).

Thus, creation of a publication normally involves creating one or more DITA maps that define the publication structure and metadata and creating one or more topics that contain the content of the publication.

The business process you use to create a publication and its topics depends entirely on the nature of the content. In the most "pure" DITA process for technical documentation, each topic focuses on one well-defined task, concept, or reference item and can be developed in isolation. Topics are then assembled into any number of publication packages by people whose job it is to define the publications.

This capability is one of the distinguishing features of DITA. However, it is fairly rare for DITA-based content to be developed this way. Human authors usually have a specific publication or set of publications in mind when they author content, and they will naturally want to have at least some of the publication structure defined as a guide to development.

For publications that are not task-centric technical documentation, there is often exactly one publication involved, at least initially. This is certainly the case for documents, such as books and magazines, where the primary business goal is the development of a specific publication and where any subsequent reuse of topics is a secondary concern that has little or no effect on authoring.

There is no one "right way" to develop DITA publications. There are many different useful ways, depending on the nature of your business.

The roles of "topic author" and "map author" are conceptually distinct roles that may be played by different people. It is often useful to have one or more map-authoring specialists who understand the details of map markup and the business and editorial rules that govern a particular set of publications. This is especially useful when you need to author topics without regard to the potential publications they might be used in.

In an ideal DITA environment, topic authors need have no knowledge of or concern for where their topics will be used (and therefore no concern for what other specific topics might be included in those different use contexts), and map authors must have absolute knowledge. In practice, map authors will have absolute knowledge (because they must have at least read-only access to all the topics they use in the maps they're creating), but topic authors will also have at least some knowledge of known or likely use contexts, and they will have some knowledge of the other topics used in those contexts so they can create dependencies on them.

A primary challenge of DITA authoring support systems is providing appropriate contextual information about where topics are used and helping map and topic authors maintain working dependencies (that is, links) among maps and topics as the content is revised over its service lifetime.

In the case of publishing workflows where content comes from external authors or is captured from pre-existing publications, you often only need a map specialist to prepare publication-level metadata or publication-specific details that define what type of publication you want. In many publishing business processes the topics themselves are never directly authored in their XML form because all of the editorial work is done in a non-XML format such as Microsoft Word or Adobe InCopy and converted to XML late in the process.

Overview of Maps and Topics

In DITA, topics contain the prose content of a document, and maps organize the topics into an appropriate structure. The map is always a separate document from the topics it organizes. Maps may point to other maps.

Topics normally reflect a specific *information type*, which is indicated by the tagname of the topic element, e.g., the concept, task, or reference types used in task-driven technical documentation. The information type associated with a topic may be very specific ("hardware installation task") or very general ("narrative content"), depending on your needs. DITA comes out of formal technical documentation writing practice, so it provides facilities for creating arbitrarily-precise topic types, but you don't have to determine a specific information type for every topic at first. It is perfectly OK to start with topics of type `<topic>` and apply more formal information typing later. Likewise, topic types may be more reflective of structural roles rather than abstract information types, e.g., the "chapter" and "article" topic types defined by the DITA for Publishers project. Some topics will be, by their nature, very general, and some will be very specific, even within the same publication or content set.

Maps normally reflect a specific publication type or packaging use. For the same content you might have a map that represents the book view of the content (e.g., DITA's built-in bookmap map type), a Web view of the content, and an authoring view of the content.

This map and topics model provides a separation of concerns[2] between the authoring of content (topics) and the authoring of publications (maps). It also provides a separation of semantic concerns between

---

[2]   The phrase *separation of concerns* is simply the practice of keeping different areas of responsibility separate. In software engineering it means having each code component focus on one thing so the implementation is clean and modular. In human endeavour it means keeping job roles distinct and not requiring, for example, technical authors whose primary or only job role is to create tasks to

information types (topics) and publication structures (maps). For example, the distinction between concept, task, and reference information is an information type concern and is reflected in the topic types defined in the base DITA vocabulary. The distinction between part, chapter, and appendix is a publication structure concern and is reflected in the specialized topic references defined by the Bookmap map type, for example. A topic of any information type may act as the root of a chapter or appendix in a given publication—the use of the topic doesn't change its fundamental information type.

The map and topics model does add some complexity. You don't normally write a complete DITA publication as a single file in the way that many authors are used to doing when using non-XML tools like Word or FrameMaker or other XML applications like DocBook. You can create a complete publication as one giant topic, but that would be a very rare DITA practice. This complexity means that convenient and effective authoring in DITA requires tools that help with map creation and management. Fortunately, all the major XML editors are DITA aware, and all provide good features for authoring maps and topics. But the map and topics model may require a change in how authors think about the overall writing practice and authoring habits.

Maps are essentially trees of hyperlinks—topic references (`<topicref>`)—where the links are to topics. In addition to topicrefs, maps may have a title and metadata that applies to the publication as a whole. Maps can also include sets of extended links that relate topics in non-hierarchical ways (relationship tables, `<reltable>`). A map "uses" topics by linking to them with `<topicref>` elements. The same topic may be used by any number of maps. This ability for topics to be used by different maps is one of the two forms of reuse built into DITA (the other being the content reference facility).

Topics are the containers of your content, where a topic has a required title (`<title>`) and additional optional content and metadata. In addition to its title, a topic may have any of the following, in this order:

- A short description (`<shortdesc>`) or abstract (`<abstract>`)
- A prolog containing metadata for the topic as a whole (`<prolog>`)
- A body (`<body>`), containing the direct content of the topic (paragraphs, lists, figures, and tables)
- Child topics.[3]

---

also be map experts. Ultimately, *separation of concerns* is about being clear to all involved what skills and responsibilities go with which roles. Even if a person plays the role of both topic author and map author, it should be clear to everyone that these are two different concerns that could be addressed by two different people.

[3] The tagnames shown here and throughout the document indicate base element types. Because of DITA's specialization feature, the specific elements allowed in a given context are a function of each document's specific document type. What's shown here is the *pattern* for topics that all valid DITA topics must follow, regardless of what specific element types they might use. For example, the built-in `<concept>` topic type uses the element type `<conbody>` rather than `<body>` because it needs to impose additional constraints on what can go in the body of concept topics (`<conbody>` is a specialization of `<body>`). It uses the other element types: `<title>`, `<shortdesc>`, `<abstract>`,

A typical topic has a title, a short description, and a body. The short description is intended to hold the "topic sentence" of the topic and is usually rendered as the first paragraph of the topic. Short descriptions are often also used in navigation views or in tool tips to provide more information about the topic.

Topics are the primary unit of titled information within DITA content. While other elements may have titles (`<fig>`, `<table>`, and `<section>` chief among them), topics are the only titled elements that may nest without restriction. Thus, topics are the only way to create hierarchies of titles, for example, to define the structure of a book with chapters, subsections, subsubsections, and so on. Maps may have titles, but only the titles of root maps are relevant—the titles of subordinate maps are essentially ignored.

A small digression in order to avoid a source of common confusion and pain in DITA, the `<section>` element: Topic bodies may contain `<section>` elements. However, `<section>` elements, while allowing (but not requiring) titles, do not contribute to the navigation hierarchy of the topics that contain them. The `<section>` element is to be used with care. Do not make the mistake of thinking that the general notion of "section" used in typical publishing practice—a titled subdivision within a hierarchy of titled divisions—maps to the DITA `<section>` element. It does not.

The `<section>` element is intended for very specific purposes, primarily for use within reference topics to create repeating and consistent labels for the components of the reference entry, for example, "Usage," "Syntax," "Examples," and so on. It is intended primarily as a base for specialization and not as an element type to be used directly. While there are legitimate uses for `<section>` in non-reference content, the use of `<section>` outside of reference information tends to lead to confusion or frustration when authors realize that it cannot nest. In almost all cases, any potential use of `<section>` is better done through the use of nested topics. It is also worth repeating that no aspect of DITA requires that all topics be separate files—it is perfectly sensible to nest topics within a single XML document, especially when the document represents a single unit of authoring or reuse.

In normal technical writing practice a topic should be an atomic unit of information, for example, a single concept, a single reference item, or a single task. However, this approach to topics is a matter of practice and is not required or enforceable by the DITA architecture. Sometimes it's useful or required to have large topics, such as topics that represent complete chapters. Sometimes it's useful to have very small topics that contain small pieces of information that are not meaningful outside the context of some containing or associated topic. But for most authors using DITA, a topic is intended to be a neat module of information that can be more or less blindly combined with other topics to form complete publications.

See *Maps and Topics* on page 197 for a more complete discussion of maps and topics.

---

and `<prolog>`, directly. But it must, and does, reflect the pattern shown here. For example, it would be invalid for `<content>` to allow `<conbody>` to occur before `<prolog>` or `<shortdesc>` to occur after `<prolog>`, because all topics must reflect the base pattern established by the base `<topic>` element type.

Authoring a Publication's Maps and Topics

This section walks you through the process of creating a non-trivial publication consisting of a map tree and several topics.

For this tutorial you will create a small publication consisting of several topics organized by a map with submaps. The goal is to give you some experience with all the major features of DITA markup.

This tutorial is written for the OxygenXML editor, but you should be able to do it using any current DITA-1.2-aware editor, such as XMetal, Arbortext Editor, or FrameMaker.

For simplicity, in this tutorial you will create maps and topics using the DITA TC-provided document type shells. However, for production use of DITA you should *always* create local shells even if you have no immediate need to do any configuration or specialization.

With DITA you can write the topics and then link them into a map, or you can create the topicrefs in the map to work out the organizational structure and then add references to the topics. In OxygenXML, if you create a topicref with a reference to a file that doesn't exist and then try to open that file, Oxygen will ask you if want to create the file and will give you the usual **File** > **New** dialog. Most editors that provide DITA map editing make it easy to add references to topics you have open in the editor, so a common strategy is to write the topics and then add them to the map as you go.

Why You Should *Always* Create Local Shell Document Types

Document type shells *integrate* vocabulary and constraint modules into a working DTD or XSD document that can be used to validate documents that should conform to the document type.

Often the only thing you need to do to configure your DITA environment is to create document type shells, at least initially. For example, your writers probably do not need all the domains defined by the DITA standard and included in the OASIS-provided document type shells. You may also want to allow the nesting of different topic types or similar configurations that do not, themselves, require new specialization or constraint modules.

In a production DITA environment (meaning one where you will be doing real work as opposed to simply evaluating DITA technology) you should *always* create local shells even if you have no immediate need to impose constraints, adjust domain usage, or do specialization.

The reason for this recommendation is that as soon as you *do* need to do any of these things (and you will, sooner rather than later), you *must* have local document type shells. If you have not created local shells in advance, then you will have to create new shells, then modify all existing documents to point to the new shells. That could be a very disruptive change depending on how your documents are managed and which tools you are using to manage and author them.

It is much better to set up local shells first and get the configuration and deployment details worked out. Then, when the inevitable change is required, you won't have to worry about modifying existing documents. You can just change your local shells.

For more about DITA document types and document type shells, see *Vocabulary Composition and Specialization* on page 183. The document type shell creation tutorial is available at *http://www.xiruss.org/tutorials/dita-specialization/* and will be in Volume 2 of *DITA for Practitioners*.

Authoring Step 1: Set up the publication

The first step is to set up your publication by creating a directory to contain the publication's files. There are no hard and fast rules here, but I find the following organizational scheme works well:

- A directory whose name is the same as the name of the publication's root map file, e.g., `myprod-installation-guide`.
- Within that directory, a DITA map whose name matches the name of the directory, e.g., `myprod-installation-guide.ditamap`. If I have several maps for the same publication, I sometimes use a suffix on the base name to distinguish them, e.g., `myprod-installation-guide-bookmap.ditamap`. Note that by convention the extension for DITA maps is `.ditamap`. Most DITA-aware tools expect this convention and some may enforce it.
- One or more directories under the publication's directory to hold topics, non-DITA resources, and submaps. A common convention is `topics` but there's no particular magic here, it's mostly about neatness. If you have multiple publications, it's good to have a consistent naming scheme or organizational pattern.
- If you will have topics that are shared across publications, have separate directory at the same level as the publication directories named something like `common`.

There were issues in the past with the Open Toolkit and certain output types (e.g., Windows help) when you had topics that were not below the root map on the file system. However, that issue has been addressed and should no longer be a problem. There is a Toolkit parameter (generate.copy.outer) that will automatically ensure that generated files are handled correctly when there are files that are not under the root map on the file system. However, if you are managing things on the file system, try to keep things relatively close together to avoid the system having to create a lot of ancestor directories to keep output in the correct relative location.

There have also been, and may still be, issues handling spaces in filenames. It *shouldn't* be a problem to have spaces in filenames, but sometimes it is. For that reason, I try to avoid spaces in filenames, especially in directory names. This avoids potential issues, especially when processing files on different operating systems.

I like the publication's directory and root map to have the same name so that it's obvious which map is the root. Having the root map within a directory makes it easy to package the directory and have everything you need right there. It can make automation easier because you can use the directory name as a parameter to scripts, which can then automatically find the root map. This makes it easier to support new publications without having to necessarily update scripts.

To keep things really obvious, have exactly one map in the main publication directory and all submaps in subdirectories. With a complex publication, where the major components of the publication are managed through submaps, it can make sense to have a subdirectory for each part or chapter. Each subdirectory would then have one map and topics would be in a subdirectory below that. Having a consistent pattern of nested directories can make working with large numbers of files easier.

For example, for the book you are reading I have a subdirectory for each major region of the publication: frontmatter, backmatter, and body, and then within the body subdirectory, a subdirectory for each part.

For this exercise, do the following:[4]

1. Create the directory `intro-to-aikido` in your workspace.

    This will be the root directory for a publication about the Japanese martial art Aikido.

2. Create the directory `topics` under `intro-to-aikido`.
3. Create the file `intro-to-aikido.ditamap` within the directory `intro-to-aikido` as a generic DITA map (`<map>`).

    In OxygenXML, you can create a new map using the built-in DITA templates:

    1. Click the New button in the toolbar or do **File** > **New**.

        You should see the "New" dialog.

    2. Type "Map" in the **Search** field.

---

[4] The sample publication you are about to create provides information about the Japanese martial art *Aikido*. Aikido is distinguished by being an entirely defensive martial art in which the highest goal is to resolve conflict non-violently or, if violence is unavoidable, with the least injury to the attacker. I have chosen Aikido as the subject for this tutorial because I couldn't face yet another artificial technical documentation example, and because Aikido is something I'm studying. Aikido as a philosophy of interaction with the world is about fostering cooperation and harmony, and that seems to have resonance with DITA as a standard designed to foster interchange and interoperation. The word *aikido* translates literally as "harmonious spirit path" or "the path of peace." The practice of Aikido is about connection, cooperation, and harmony. So it should be with DITA. The sample document created in this tutorial has been useful for my training partners, and it has real value as a document in its own right. The nature of Aikido as a technical subject benefits from all of the features that make DITA so useful for technical documentation generally.

The list of templates should be narrowed to several that include "Map" in their name.

3. Select the one named just "Map," which is probably under **Framework templates** > **DITA Map** > **Map**.

   This should create a new map document in the Oxygen DITA Maps Manager view.

   If you don't see the Map Manager, go to **Window** > **Show View** and select "DITA Maps Manager" from the list of views.

4. Save the new map as `intro-to-aikido.ditamap` in the `intro-to-aikido` directory.

   The OxygenXML window should look something like this:

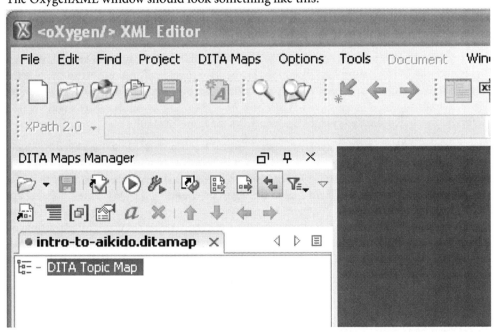

5. Edit the map in the main editor by clicking on the **Open Map in Editor** button (⊡) in the Maps Manager tool bar and then selecting the **Text** view at the bottom of the editor window. It should look something like this:

```
<?xml version="1.0" encoding="UTF-8"?>
<!DOCTYPE map PUBLIC "-//OASIS//DTD DITA Map//EN" "map.dtd">
<map>
  <title>DITA Topic Map</title>
</map>
```

6. Change the text "Main book title" to "Introduction to Aikido" and save the file:

```
<?xml version="1.0" encoding="UTF-8"?>
<!DOCTYPE map PUBLIC "-//OASIS//DTD DITA Map//EN" "map.dtd">
<map>
   <title>Introduction to Aikido</title>
</map>
```

Having saved the file from the main editor window, when you click in the Maps Manager view, it should automatically update to reflect the new title.

At this point you have the publication's directories and root map set up. You are now ready to start creating topics and adding them to the publication.

This step creates a completely generic map. The base DITA vocabulary includes several map types, including Bookmap and Learning Map. Bookmap is intended specifically for representing more traditional books with parts and chapters, as opposed to pure online help or websites. For this exercise you're starting with a generic map to keep things simple. Once you have the publication structure defined and some topics written, you will create a separate Bookmap for the same content.

Part of the point of DITA, and for XML in general, is to make it possible to generated different rendered forms of the same source ("single sourcing"). From this map you can generate HTML, PDF, and other formats using the out-of-the-box DITA Open Toolkit, and you can generate even more formats using 3rd-party plugins, such as the EPUB and Kindle plugins provided by the DITA for Publishers project (the EPUB plugin is included with OxygenXML starting with version 12.2 and in the XMetal editor starting with version 7). You don't have to use Bookmap in order to get printable output from your maps, but the base Toolkit's PDF transform has been optimized for Bookmap and provides additional functionality for Bookmap maps that it doesn't or can't provide for generic maps. You'll see more about Bookmaps at the end of this tutorial.

Authoring Step 2: Create some topics

For this exercise you will create a few topics and add them to the map.

To create the topics, perform these steps:

1. Open the New dialog and type "Topic" in the search field.

The list should be narrowed to those templates that are within a directory named "topic" or that have topic in their name. You should see the base DITA topic types of "topic," "concept," "task," "reference," "glossentry," and probably a few others.

2. Select the Concept topic template to create a new concept.

The first topic will be for the introductory chapter, which is certainly conceptual in nature, so "concept" is an appropriate choice.

The raw markup should look something like:

```
<?xml version="1.0" encoding="UTF-8"?>
<!DOCTYPE concept PUBLIC "-//OASIS//DTD DITA Concept//EN" "concept.dtd">
<concept id="conceptId">
 <title>Concept title</title>
 <shortdesc></shortdesc>
 <conbody>
  <p>Concept definition.</p>
 </conbody>
</concept>
```

Note that the `@id` attribute value may be set dynamically to some generated value. For this tutorial the only requirement is that the `@id` attribute have a value, as all topics must specify the `@id` attribute, but the value only needs to be unique within the XML document that contains the topic.

3. Save the file as `intro-to-aikido/topics/chapter-intro.xml` or `intro-to-aikido/topics/chapter-intro.dita`.

    Many people prefer to use the extension `.dita` for topic documents, but `.xml` is fine too. DITA-aware tools should not require `.dita`, and XML-aware tools may not recognize `.dita` as being XML, so I tend to prefer `.xml`, but it shouldn't really matter.

    In OxygenXML, the extension on the template document determines what extension it uses by default when you save a newly-created file and the built-in templates use `.dita`. You can change them to use `.xml` if you care by simply renaming the files in the `frameworks/dita/templates` directory within the OxygenXML installation directory. For production use, you will be creating new document type shells and, presumably, new template documents that use those shells, so as part of that setup activity you can use `.xml` or `.dita` as you choose or as your tools dictate.

    By "template documents" I simply mean documents that serve as templates for creating new documents. There's nothing special about template documents other than that you intend them to be templates. Different editors have different facilities for managing the templates available through the typical **File** > **New** action, and they may also have conventions for templates like naming conventions or facilities that let you control how a document is created from a template. For example, in Arbortext Editor you can indicate where the input cursor should be positioned when the document opens.

    In OxygenXML you can set any number of directories as "template" directories, and OxygenXML will automatically list any XML documents within those directories in the **New** dialog. Therefore, I always create a directory named `templates` as part of setting up a new DITA project and put templates for each distinct topic and map type in that directory.

4. Edit the topic to change the title to "Aikido, The Gentle Martial Art" and save the file:

```
<?xml version="1.0" encoding="UTF-8"?>
<!DOCTYPE concept PUBLIC "-//OASIS//DTD DITA Concept//EN" "concept.dtd">
<concept id="conceptId">
 <title>Aikido, The Gentle Martial Art</title>
 <shortdesc></shortdesc>
 <conbody>
  <p>Concept definition.</p>
 </conbody>
</concept>
```

👉 **Note:** I'm showing the raw markup here so you know exactly what you should have, but you will probably prefer to edit in OxygenXML's Author mode, which can hide the tags and provides a more WYSIWYG-style view. In OxygenXML, you can toggle between the Text and Author views at will. Other editors have similar "tags off" views and various ways of seeing the raw markup.

5. Now add the topic to the map:

a. Go to the DITA Map Manager view (usually in the upper-left pane of the main OxygenXML window) and right click on the root node in the tree view (which should be the only node) and select **Append child > Reference to the currently-edited file**.

You will get the **Insert Reference [Topic Reference]** dialog. There's a lot you can do on this dialog, but in this case you can take all the defaults and just click **Insert and close** to create the topicref and close the dialog.

You should now have a single child node under "Introduction to Aikido" with the title "Aikido, the Gentle Martial Art. "

6. Test the link by double-clicking on the node in the map tree.

It should make the main editor tab for `chapter-intro.dita` active (you should see the insertion cursor in the window).

7. Save the change to the map by clicking on the **File > Save** button (💾) in the Map Manager toolbar.

Note that the Map Manager has its own save button separate from the main save button. I find it easy to forget to save changes I make to the map, which is why I broke it out as a separate step here.

The map markup should now look like this:

```
<?xml version="1.0" encoding="UTF-8"?>
<!DOCTYPE map PUBLIC "-//OASIS//DTD DITA Map//EN" "map.dtd">
<map>
  <title>Introduction to Aikido</title>
  <topicref href="topics/chapter-intro.dita"/>
</map>
```

The @href attribute contains a URI reference to the topic, in this case, the relative URL topics/chapter-intro.dita. Most map-editing tools should create relative URLs whenever possible.

Note also that the URL refers to the topic document, not to the topic's ID. By the rules of DITA, a reference to a topic document is implicitly a reference to the root or first topic in that document.

Another detail is that OxygenXML did not set the @navtitle attribute on the <topicref> element or include a nested <navtitle> element. Topic references can impose navigation titles onto the topics they reference, but in general you should not specify a navigation title unless you really intend to impose a title. Otherwise, when the topic is edited to change its title, any navigation view of the publication will reflect the imposed title, not the title as specified in the topic itself.

The map shown here is about the simplest possible useful map. There are a lot of things you can do, but many maps can be this simple.

The next step is to put some more realistic content into the topic.

Check Your Work: Generate HTML for the publication

Test the new publication by generating HTML from it using the Open Toolkit.

In OxygenXML you can do this as follows:

1. Select the map in the DITA Map Manager view.
2. Click the **Configure transformation scenario** button (&) in the Map Manager tool bar (don't confuse the **configure transformation scenario** button with the **Validate and Check for Completeness** button (&).

This brings up the **Configure Transformation Scenario** dialog.

3. Select the "DITA Map XHTML" transform type and click **Duplicate**. Set the name to whatever you want, e.g., remove the "Duplicate" that OxygenXML adds (the name can be the same as one of the locked transformation types).

    Click **OK** to save the new scenario.

    You can run the locked scenario directly, but it's handy to create a duplicate so you can easily modify the transformation parameters.

4. Click the **Transform now** button to run the transform.

    Assuming you haven't done anything to OxygenXML's built-in Toolkit, the transform should run, and after a couple of seconds you should get a new browser window in the table of contents view consisting of a single link to the one topic:

    If you click on the link it should open the page for the topic:

Aikido, The Gentle Martial Art

Concept definition.

    I usually use the XHTML transform to test my maps because it's fast and forgiving, but it gives you good feedback if something's not right in your map.

    You should also be able to generate PDF from this map using the built-in DITA PDF transformation type. The Open Toolkit comes with the FOP XSL-FO engine out of the box, which is certainly good enough to test PDF output.

If you only get a browser window for the topic, and not the map, it means you applied the transform with the topic selected in the main editor window, not the map selected in the Maps Manager. It's easy to lose track of which tab you have selected, so if you don't get the result you expect, always double check your selection first.

Just to be 100% sure your map is good, use OxygenXML's "validate map" function to validate the entire publication:

1. Select the map in the DITA Map Manager view.

2. Click the **Validate and Check for Completeness** button (⛊) in the Map Manager toolbar.

   This will bring up the **DITA Map Completeness Check** dialog.

3. Take the defaults and click the **Check** button to run the validation.

   If the validation is successful you should see a green "Validation successful" message at the bottom of the screen. If errors or warnings are detected, they will be reported in a new tab in the messages area at the bottom of the OxygenXML window. For this map, the validation should succeed.

   If you see "Document is valid," rather than "Validation successful," it means you validated the topic document, not the map.

   Other map-aware editors have similar map validation features.

If you want to run the HTML generation process from the command line, you can do this:

1. Open a command window and navigate to the Open Toolkit's root directory.

   For OxygenXML, this will be `frameworks/dita/DITA-OT` under the OxygenXML installation directory, otherwise it's wherever you installed the toolkit (see *Installing the DITA Open Toolkit* on page 133).

2. Run the command `startcmd.bat` (Windows) or `startcmd.sh` (non-Windows).

   This creates a Toolkit-specific command window with the Java class path set correctly.

3. Run the command:

```
java -jar lib/dost.jar /transtype:xhtml
    /i:c:\workspace\intro-to-aikido\intro-to-aikido.ditamap
    /outdir:c:\workspace\intro-to-aikido\output\html
```

   Assuming that the `java` command is in your PATH, this should run and generate the HTML output in the directory `c:\workspace\intro-to-aikido\output\html`.

Authoring Step 3: Add realistic topic content

Primary topics should have short descriptions or abstracts. In addition, the topic needs some more body content so you have reason to explore additional DITA features.

Modify the `chapter-intro.dita` topic as follows:

1. Edit the `<shortdesc>` element to add the text

> Aikido is a purely defensive martial art in which you train cooperatively with a partner with the goal of achieving harmony between attacker and defender.

```xml
<?xml version="1.0" encoding="UTF-8"?>
<!DOCTYPE concept PUBLIC "-//OASIS//DTD DITA Concept//EN" "concept.dtd">
<concept id="conceptId">
 <title>Aikido, The Gentle Martial Art</title>
 <shortdesc>Aikido is a purely defensive martial art in which
 you train cooperatively with a partner with the goal of achieving
 harmony between attacker and defender.</shortdesc>
 <conbody>
  <p>Concept definition.</p>
 </conbody>
</concept>
```

2. Modify the body paragraph to have this content

> The practice of Aikido is based on a set of principles taken from the movements of traditional Japanese sword fighting.

```xml
<?xml version="1.0" encoding="UTF-8"?>
<!DOCTYPE concept PUBLIC "-//OASIS//DTD DITA Concept//EN" "concept.dtd">
<concept id="conceptId">
 <title>Aikido, The Gentle Martial Art</title>
 <shortdesc>Aikido is a purely defensive martial art in which
 you train cooperatively with a partner with the goal of achieving
 harmony between attacker and defender.</shortdesc>
 <conbody>
   <p>The practice of Aikido is based on a set of principles
taken from the movements of traditional Japanese sword fighting.</p>
 </conbody>
</concept>
```

3. Following the paragraph within `<conbody>`, add this content:

```
<p>Beginners typically start with learning just the
first two or three principles:
<ul>
  <li><term>ikkyo</term>, First Principle</li>
  <li><term>nikyo</term>, Second Principle</li>
  <li><term>sankyo</term>, Third Principle</li>
</ul></p>
```

4. Save the topic file and re-generate HTML from the map.

The rendered topic should look like this:

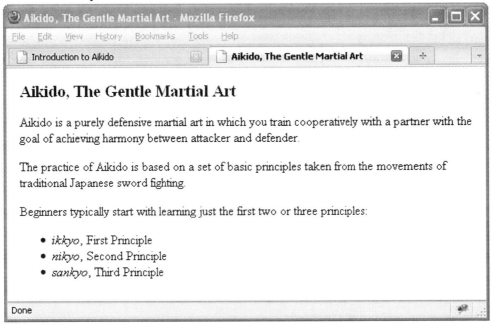

Observe that the short description is rendered as the first paragraph of the topic. Observe also that the `<term>` elements have been rendered in italics. These represent the default styling for those element types. These rendition behaviors are suggested by the DITA standard but are not required.

Authoring Step 4: Create a second topic

You need another topic to see the implications of creating a hierarchy through the map. In this step you will create a new topic and add it to the map as a subordinate topic to the first topic.

1. Create a new concept topic as file `rokyu-requirements.dita` and give it this content:

```xml
<?xml version="1.0" encoding="UTF-8"?>
<!DOCTYPE concept PUBLIC "-//OASIS//DTD DITA Concept//EN" "concept.dtd">
<concept id="conceptId">
 <title>Rokyu (6th Kyu) Requirements</title>
 <shortdesc>6th Kyu is the first level of white belt earned by Aikido
           beginners.</shortdesc>
 <conbody>
  <p>For 6th Kyu you must demonstrate the following techniques:
  <ul>
   <li><term>Tenkan</term> </li>
   <li><term>Shomenuchi</term> <term>ikkyo</term> and
       <term>iriminage</term> </li>
   <li><term>Munetsuki</term> <term>kotegaeshi</term> </li>
   <li><term>Katate</term> <term>dori</term> <term>shihonage</term></li>
   <li><term>Yokomenuchi</term> <term>shihonage</term> </li>
   <li><term>Kokyu</term> <term>tanden</term> <term>ho</term></li>
  </ul></p>
 </conbody>
</concept>
```

2. Go to the map in DITA Map Manager view and select the node: "Aikido, The Gentle Martial Art."

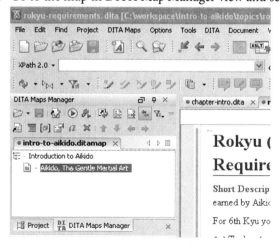

3. Right click and select **Append Child > Reference to the currently edited file**. Click **Insert and close** to create the topicref.

4. Save the map and open it in the editor. The markup should look like this:

```
<?xml version="1.0" encoding="UTF-8"?>
<!DOCTYPE map PUBLIC "-//OASIS//DTD DITA Map//EN" "map.dtd">
<map>
  <title>Introduction to Aikido</title>
  <topicref
    href="topics/chapter-intro.dita">
    <topicref
      href="topics/rokyu-requirements.dita"/>
  </topicref>
</map>
```

5. Generate HTML from the map.

   The contents page should now show the same structure as the map view, with " Rokyu (6th Kyu) Requirements" subordinate to "Aikido, The Gentle Martial Art."

6. Click on the link to "Aikido, The Gentle Martial Art." The HTML page should look like this:

Observe that there is now a link to the new subordinate topic and that that topic's short description is included after the link.

This automatically-generated link is an example of a "related link," in this case reflecting the parent/child relationship between the two topics created by the nested `<topicref>` elements.

This demonstrates one way that short descriptions can be used to aid in navigation. In this case, unless you were already familiar with Aikido terminology you would have no idea what "Rokyu requirements" might be. By including the short description, the significance of the linked topic is clearer.

At this point it's starting to feel like a real document, but you need a few more topics to have enough content to demonstrate more features of DITA maps and topics.

Authoring Step 5: Create some reference topics

You need a few more topics so that you have some topics to apply a relationship table to. For this exercise you will create reference topics for some of the Aikido techniques required on the 6th Kyu examination.

Reference topics are more formally structured than concept topics. They are intended to be used to create consistently-structured entries within a reference, such as Unix man pages, API references, and so on. If I was really creating a reference manual for Aikido techniques I would design a specialization of `<reference>` that reflects the specific things an Aikido technique description requires. For this exercise you will use generic `<reference>` topics.

The general pattern for a reference topic is that it consists of some optional initial paragraphs or other body-level elements, followed by one or more `<section>` elements, each `<section>` representing one of the aspects of the reference entry. While `<section>` allows `<title>` as a subelement, it also takes the attribute `@spectitle`, which can be used to set the title in DTDs when specializing `<section>` in a `<reference>` specialization.

You can also specify `@spectitle` directly. For example, you might set up a template document for a specific kind of reference entry with the different `<section>` elements created with the appropriate `@spectitle` values. This gives you much of the value of a specialization without having to implement the specialization immediately. If you subsequently implement a specialization that matches the template, migrating unspecialized documents to use the specialized markup is fairly easy. Because rendering tools should use the `@spectitle` value as the rendered titles of the sections, the rendered result for the specialized and unspecialized topics should be the same.

Create the reference topics by creating the files `shomenuchi-ikkyo.dita`, `shomenunchi-shihonage.dita`, and `munetsuki-kotegaeshi.dita` in the `topics` directory, with the following content respectively, using the "Reference" template in OxygenXML.

☞ **Note:** The topics include references to graphics that you of course don't have yet. The graphics are available in the worked version of this tutorial. Note that each `<image>` element contains an `<alt>` element. The contents of the `<alt>` element will be used when the graphic can't be shown. It is good practice to always have an `<alt>` element for images.

`shomenuchi-ikkyo.dita`:

```
<?xml version="1.0" encoding="UTF-8"?>
<!DOCTYPE reference PUBLIC "-//OASIS//DTD DITA Reference//EN" "reference.dtd">
<reference id="referenceId">
  <title>Shomenuchi ikkyo</title>
  <shortdesc>First principle (<term>ikkyo</term>) for <term>Shomenuchi</term>
 attack.</shortdesc>
  <refbody>
    <section spectitle="Description">
      <p>As <term>uke</term> strikes to the top of <term>nage's</term> head,

nage slides in and catches <term>uke's</term> arm with both hands,
catching the arm at wrist and above the elbow.
<term>Nage</term> sweeps <term>nage's</term> arm down and around in
normal <term>ikkyo</term> fashion. The technique may be completed
<term>omote</term> or <term>ura</term>. </p>
    </section>
    <section
      spectitle="Diagram">
      <fig>
        <image
          href="graphics/shomenuchi-ikkyo-01.jpg">
        <alt>Shomenuchi ikkyo showing initial response to the attack.</alt>

        </image>
      </fig>
    </section>
    <section spectitle="Video">
      <p>No video available.</p>
    </section>
  </refbody>
</reference>
```

`shomenunchi-iriminage.dita`:

```
<?xml version="1.0" encoding="UTF-8"?>
<!DOCTYPE reference PUBLIC "-//OASIS//DTD DITA Reference//EN" "reference.dtd">
<reference id="referenceId">
  <title>Shomenuchi iriminage</title>
  <shortdesc>Entering throw (<term>iriminage</term>) for
<term>Shomenuchi</term> attack.</shortdesc>
```

```
  <refbody>
    <section spectitle="Description">
<p>As <term>uke</term> strikes to the top of <term>nage's</term> head,
nage slides in and lightly blocks uke's arm, at the same time placing his
other hand on uke's rear shoulder. Nage extends his blocking hand and
performs a <term>tenkan</term>, pulling slightly on uke's shoulder to
take his balance. As uke's rotational momentum carries him around,
nage performs a <term>tenkai</term>, pulls uke's shoulder in closer
to maintain connection, and raises his blocking hand up and over uke's
head, leading his thumb down uke's spine, throwing uke into a backward roll.
  </p>
    </section>
    <section
      spectitle="Diagram">
      <fig>
        <image
          href="graphics/shomenuchi-iriminage-01.jpg">
          <alt>Shomenuchi iriminage showing nage sweeping uke's arm as nage
 begins his tenkan.</alt>
        </image>
      </fig>
    </section>
    <section spectitle="Video">
      <p>No video available.</p>
    </section>
  </refbody>
</reference>
```

munetsuki-kotegaeshi.dita:

```
<?xml version="1.0" encoding="UTF-8"?>
<!DOCTYPE reference PUBLIC "-//OASIS//DTD DITA Reference//EN" "reference.dtd">
<reference id="referenceId">
  <title>Munetsuki kotegaeshi</title>
  <shortdesc>Wrist out turn (<term>kotegaeshi</term>) for strike to the
abdomen (<term>munetsuki</term>) attack.</shortdesc>
  <refbody>
    <section spectitle="Description">
<p>As Uke throws a punch toward Nage's abdomen, Nage steps off
  the line of attack, performs a <term>tenkan</term>, and
  blocks the punch by pushing the punching arm sideways.
  Nage slides his blocking hand down the punching arm and
  establishes a <term>gotegaeshi</term> grip on Uke's hand.
  Nage waits for Uke to either turn towards him to punch with
  his free hand or pull back with his punching hand. In either
  case, Nage performs a <term>tenkai</term> to face Uke, turning
  Uke's wrist outward, causing Uke to fall backwards. Nage pins
  Uke by walking the held hand around Uke's head and pinning the
  out turned wrist against his knee. Nage leans slightly into the
```

```
 wrist to immobilize Uke. </p>
   </section>
   <section
     spectitle="Diagram">
     <fig>
       <image
         href="graphics/munetsuki-kotegaeshi-01.jpg">
         <alt>Munetsuki strike</alt>
       </image>
     </fig>
   </section>
   <section spectitle="Video">
     <p>No video available.</p>
   </section>
 </refbody>
</reference>
```

Observe that all three reference topics follow exactly the same markup pattern. Each topic uses the same pattern of `<section>` elements with consistent `@spectitle` attributes.

The next step is to add these topics to the map.

Authoring Step 6: Add reference topics to map

This step demonstrates the use of topic heads within maps to create navigation hierarchy without having a topic.

A "topic head" is simply a topic reference that has a navigation title but does not link to a topic. It establishes a titled grouping within the map's navigation hierarchy.

The base DITA vocabulary provides a specialization of `<topicref>`, `<topichead>`, that simply disallows the `@href` and `<keyref>` attributes, which means it can only be a topic head. However, any topic reference element acts as a topic head if it has a navigation title but no reference to a topic. Because the base tagname for topic heads is `<topichead>`, DITA uses the shorthand term *topichead* to mean "any topic reference with a navigation title but no topic reference."

Conceptually, a topichead is equivalent to a topic reference to a title-only topic, so you can think of it as a convenience that spares you having to create title-only topics. You can even force processors to generate actual title-only topics for topicheads by specifying the `@chunk` attribute[5] on the topichead.

---

[5] The `@chunk` attribute controls how topic references translate into physical content files when processed. For example, you can use `chunk="to-content"` to indicate that a tree of nested topicrefs should be processed as though they were in a single source XML document, which for multi-file outputs like HTML results in a corresponding single HTML result file.

A title-only topic is simply a topic that has only a `<title>` element as its content, e.g.:

```
<topic id="topicid">
  <title>This is A Title Only Topic</title>
</topic>
```

This is a perfectly-valid topic, but in theory it shouldn't be needed because a topic head should produce the same effect as a topic reference to a title-only topic. But some tools require explicit topics for every level in the publication hierarchy. If you use such a tool, you will need to create title-only topics.

For the introduction to the Aikido publication, you want to group the technique reference entries under their own heading, but you don't need to create a topic to do that. Instead, you will create a `<topichead>` and put the topic references to the reference topics inside the `<topichead>`.

To add the reference topics to the map, perform the following steps:

1. Go to the map in the DITA Map Manager and select the "Aikido, The Gentle Martial Art" node.
2. Right click and select **Append Child** > **Topic heading....**

   The **Insert topic heading** dialog will open.

3. Set the navigation title to "Aikido Techniques" and click **OK** to create the topic heading.
4. Save the map and open it in the main editor. It should look like this:

```
<?xml version="1.0" encoding="UTF-8"?>
<!DOCTYPE map PUBLIC "-//OASIS//DTD DITA Map//EN" "map.dtd">
<map>
  <title>Introduction to Aikido</title>
  <topicref  href="topics/chapter-intro.dita">
    <topicref  href="topics/rokyu-requirements.dita"/>
    <topichead  navtitle="Aikido Techniques"/>
  </topicref>
</map>
```

Note that OxygenXML has put the navigation title into a `@navtitle` attribute. The `@navtitle` attribute is deprecated as of DITA 1.2, which instead favors using the `<navtitle>` element within `<topicmeta>`, because attributes cannot contain markup and because translation support tools often lock attribute values and only allow element content to be modified.

5. Change the `@navtitle` attribute into a `<navtitle>` element, editing the map in Text mode:

   a. Select the text "Aikido Techniques" from the `@navtitle` value and copy it to the clipboard.
   b. Delete the `@navtitle` attribute.
   c. Delete the "/" in the `<topichead>` tag. In OxygenXML this automatically adds the close tag.
   d. Type a "<," which brings up the list of allowed elements.

e. Select `<topicmeta>` and press enter (you can type the first few characters of the tagname to scroll the list down to `<topicmeta>`).

f. Move the cursor inside the newly-created `<topicmeta>` element and type "<."

g. Select `<navtitle>` from the list (type "n" to select `<navtitle>`).

h. Move the cursor inside `<navtitle>` and paste the text you copied from the `@navtitle` attribute.

i. Press the **Format and indent** button (≣) to neaten up the markup. The map should look like this:

```
<?xml version="1.0" encoding="UTF-8"?>
<!DOCTYPE map PUBLIC "-//OASIS//DTD DITA Map//EN" "map.dtd">
<map>
  <title>Introduction to Aikido</title>
  <topicref  href="topics/chapter-intro.dita">
    <topicref href="topics/rokyu-requirements.dita"/>
    <topichead>
      <topicmeta>
        <navtitle>Aikido Techniques</navtitle>
      </topicmeta>
    </topichead>
  </topicref>
</map>
```

j. Save the map.

k. Click on the Map Manager to refresh the map. It should look just like it did before (it may update automatically, requiring you to re-expand the map).

6. Add the reference topics to the topic head by selecting the topic head in the map tree, right clicking, and selecting **Append child > Reference**. This brings up the **Insert Reference [Topic Reference]** dialog.

7. Use the file chooser to navigate to the directory containing the reference topics and then find the three reference topics. You can use **ctrl+click** to select multiple files, or you can select the files individual and then click the **Insert** button to insert references to them without closing the dialog. Save the map from the DITA Maps Manager.

After you have inserted a reference for each topic, the map should look like this:

```
<?xml version="1.0" encoding="UTF-8"?>
<!DOCTYPE map PUBLIC "-//OASIS//DTD DITA Map//EN" "map.dtd">
<map>
    <title>Introduction to Aikido</title>
    <topicref href="topics/chapter-intro.dita">
        <topicref href="topics/rokyu-requirements.dita"/>
        <topichead>
            <topicmeta>
                <navtitle>Aikido Techniques</navtitle>
```

```
          </topicmeta>
          <topicref href="topics/munetsuki-kotegaeshi.dita"/>
          <topicref href="topics/shomenuchi-ikkyo.dita"/>
          <topicref href="topics/shomenuchi-iriminage.dita"/>
        </topichead>
    </topicref>
</map>
```

The DITA Map Manager should look like this:

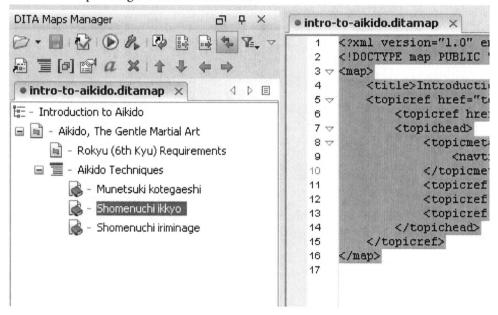

8. Generate HTML from the map.

Observe that the TOC page has an entry for the topic heading, but it's not a link because there's nothing to link to.

Click on a link for one of the reference targets. Note that the reference entry uses the values of the @spectitle attribute as headings for each section.

Note also that there are no related links from the reference topics to their parent topic as there are for the Rokyu Requirements topic. That's because these topics have no direct parent topic (because of the topichead). This is an example of a behavioral difference between topic headings and title-only topics that you should be aware of.

You can change these default behaviors by adding additional attributes to the various topic references.

Authoring Step 7: Refine topicref details

Using attributes of `<topicref>` elements, you can do the following:

- Control whether or not a given topic should be reflected in tables of contents (`@toc`)
- Indicate that a given topicref contains an ordered sequence of items or an unordered collection of related items ((`@collection-type`)
- Specify the effective topic filename for the topic as used by the topicref or for a topichead (`@copy-to`).
- Indicate that a hierarchy of topics should be treated as a single effective file, that a file containing multiple topics should be treated as a set of separate topic files , or that a topichead should be treated as though it was a reference to a title-only topic (`@chunk`).
- Indicate that the resource referenced by a topicref is part of the map's publication ("local"), is part of a closely-related publication ("peer"), or is completely separate ("external") (`@scope`).
- Indicate that the resource is part of the navigation tree ("normal") or should be processed as part of the map but is not part of the navigation tree ("resource-only") (`@processing-role`).
- Indicate the data type of the resource referenced (`@format`).

For the Aikido map, you need to force the topic head to behave as though it was a reference to a title-only topic and indicate that it represents a related set of topics. Make these refinements as follows:

1. In the Map Manager, select the node for "Aikido Techniques," right click, and select **Edit attributes**. This brings up the Edit Attributes dialogs.

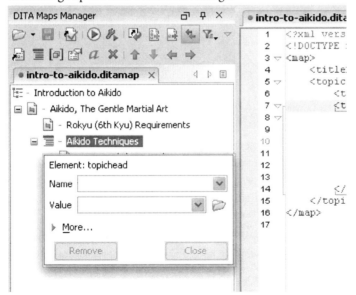

2. In the **Name** field type "copy-to."
3. In the **Value** field type "aikido-techniques.dita."
4. Click **Close** to save the attribute.
5. Open the **Edit Attributes** dialog again and set the @chunk attribute to the value "to-content." This signals the processor to treat the topichead as a virtual reference to a title-only topic.
6. Save the map and re-generate the HTML. You should see a link to the "Aikido Techniques" topic.
7. Open the **Edit Attributes** dialog and set the @collection-type attribute to the value "sequence."
8. Save the map. The map markup should now look like this:

```
<?xml version="1.0" encoding="UTF-8"?>
<!DOCTYPE map PUBLIC "-//OASIS//DTD DITA Map//EN" "map.dtd">
<map>
    <title>Introduction to Aikido</title>
    <topicref href="topics/chapter-intro.dita">
        <topicref href="topics/rokyu-requirements.dita"/>
        <topichead
            copy-to="aikido-techniques.dita"
            chunk="to-content"
            collection-type="sequence">
            <topicmeta>
                <navtitle>Aikido Techniques</navtitle>
            </topicmeta>
            <topicref
                href="topics/munetsuki-kotegaeshi.dita"/>
            <topicref
                href="topics/shomenuchi-ikkyo.dita"/>
            <topicref
                href="topics/shomenuchi-iriminage.dita"/>
        </topichead>
    </topicref>
</map>
```

9. Re-generate the HTML. Go to the Shomenuchi Ikkyo topic in the HTML. You should see "Next topic" and "Previous topic" links connecting it to the previous and next topic.
10. Change @collection-type to "family" and regenerate the HTML. Go to one of the reference topics. You should see a link to each of the other two reference topics from each reference topic.
11. Remove the @collection-type attribute from the topic head. While this example only has three reference entries, in a real document, where you might have scores or hundreds of reference topics, it would not be useful to have each topic link to all of the other topics.

You now have feel for how you can control features of at least the HTML rendition by modifying details in the map without making any changes to the topics themselves. This is an important feature of DITA.

The next step is to add a relationship table to relate topics to each other in non-hierarchical ways.

Authoring Step 8: Add a relationship table

Because a given topic may be used in any number of maps, it is not possible for the topic's author to know all the other topics which might be related to that topic. While DITA does provide for embedded cross-references and links within topics, true modular writing must avoid their use except when the topics involved have a very tight dependency on each other and must always be used together. This appears to present a conflict between re-usability and completeness of links.

DITA's solution is "relationship tables" (`<reltable>`), a form of "extended linking" (in the XLink sense) whereby you can establish links among topics from within maps. Relationship tables, or "reltables," let you describe relationships among the topics in a map without having to modify the topics themselves.

In a reltable, each row represents a link among two or more sets of topics. Each cell of the row represents one "end" or role of the link and contains one or more topicref elements pointing to the topics (or non-DITA resources) that play that role for the link instance. Where a single reltable cell contains multiple topic references, all the topics together represent the link end collectively, in that they all play the same role in the link.

The rendered result of relationship table links can take many forms, but a typical presentation is that provided by the Open Toolkit's HTML transform where each reltable link results in the generation of individual HTML links in the "related links" section of each topic involved in the reltable link. A single reltable link may result in many HTML links, one for each pair of topics across each pair of cells in the reltable row. For example, if each cell of a two-column relationship table has two topics, then each topic will have two generate HTML links, one for each of the two topics in the other column of the relationship table. In a three-column relationship table, with two topics in each cell, each topic would have four HTML links, because the three columns represent four unique topic-to-topic pairs for each topic.

Relationship tables are discussed in more detail in *Relationship Tables* on page 263.

For this exercise you want to relate the 6th Kyu examination requirements topic to the reference entries for the techniques required by the test. While you could do it with embedded cross-references in the 6th Kyu topic, that would create a hard dependency between that topic and the technique topics. That would be a problem if you wanted to create a separate publication that was just the examination requirements for the different Aikido belt levels. You could make the cross-references conditional, but that would require you to know, while you are authoring, the conditions under which the cross-references should or shouldn't be applicable. This can quickly become very complex, requiring you to update topics any time you want a new publication to use them.

Relationship tables avoid these problems at the cost of reduced control over where the links will be presented in different outputs. In particular, there's no obvious practical way to indicate something like the following in a topic: "if a reltable link is applied to this topic, make it look like it is an embedded cross-reference at this point in the body content." So the typical approach is to collect the reltable-imposed links at the start or end of the topic or create some equivalent link traversal user interface.

Relationship tables always go at the end of the map, after any `<topicref>` elements.

To create the relationship table, perform these steps:

1. Open the Intro to Aikido map in the main editor and select the Author mode. If they are not already on, turn on full tags using the tag view setting button ( ) in the toolbar.

2. Position the cursor between the end tag for the root topicref and the end tag for the map:

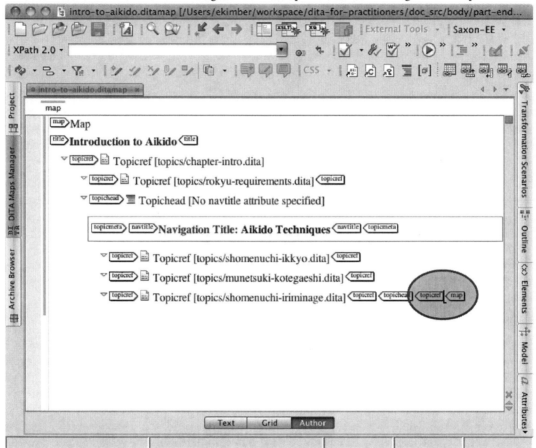

3. Click the **Insert a DITA Reltable** button ( ) in the tool bar. This brings up the **Insert Relationship Table** dialog.

4. Set the title to "Exam requirements to techniques" and the number of rows to 1. Click **OK** to create the table.

The Author view presents the relationship table as a graphical table. The markup looks like this:

```
  . . .
  </topicref>
  <reltable title="Exam requirements to techniques">
    <relheader>
      <relcolspec type="topic"/>
      <relcolspec type="topic"/>
    </relheader>
    <relrow>
      <relcell/>
      <relcell/>
    </relrow>
  </reltable>
</map>
```

The reltable title is just documentation—it is not presented anywhere by default and the DITA specification doesn't say anything about it.

The `<relheader>` contains `<relcolspec>` elements, which define the details of each column of the table and may also set default attribute values for the topicrefs that occur in that column.

The `<relrow>` element establishes a link from each of the topics referenced in one cell to each of the topics referenced in each of the other cells. A reltable may have more than two columns.

As created by OxygenXML, the `<relcolspec>` specifies a `@type` attribute with the value of "topic." The `@type` attribute specifies the base topic type that topicrefs are allowed to point to, in this case "topic," meaning any topic, specialized or not. If you wanted to limit the first column to say concept topics and the second to reference topics, you would set the first `<relcolspec>`'s `@type` attribute to "concept" and the second to "reference." Some DITA processors will validate the references and at least warn you when the wrong kind of topic is referenced. DITA-aware editors may also use the type value to limit the set of topics listed when creating topicrefs.

You are not required to set the `@type` attribute, but it is useful to do so when you want the topic type to be used as the semantic role of that column. For example, if you are relating tasks to supporting concepts, the role of the column linking to tasks would be "task" and the role of the column linking to concepts would be "concept." Specifying the `@type` values "task" and "concept" makes it clear to authors and tools that all the links from the task column should be to task topics and all the links from the concept column should be to concepts. However, it is not always the case that the roles of the columns correspond directly to topic types.

For this exercise, the topic type of the topics to be linked is neither important nor predictable, so you can leave the `@type` value as "topic" or remove the attribute, the effect will be the same.

5. Put your cursor in the `<relcell>` of the first (and only) `<relrow>` element.

6. Click the **Insert DITA Topic Reference** button (⬚) on the toolbar. This brings up the **Insert Reference [Topic Reference]** dialog.

7. Find the `rokyu-requirements.dita` topic and insert a reference to it.

8. Put your cursor in the second `<relcell>` in the `<relrow>` element and insert references to the topics `munetsuki-kotegaeshi.dita`, `shomenuchi-ikkyo.dita`, and `shomenuchi-iriminage.dita`. Close the insert reference dialog.

   The reltable markup should now look like this:

```
<reltable title="Exam requirements to techniques">
  <relheader>
    <relcolspec type="topic"/>
    <relcolspec type="topic"/>
  </relheader>
  <relrow>
    <relcell>
      <topicref href="topics/rokyu-requirements.dita"/>
    </relcell>
    <relcell>
      <topicref href="topics/munetsuki-kotegaeshi.dita"/>
      <topicref href="topics/shomenuchi-ikkyo.dita"/>
      <topicref href="topics/shomenuchi-iriminage.dita"/>
    </relcell>
  </relrow>
</reltable>
```

9. Generate HTML from the map and go to the Rokyu Requirements topic. It should look like this:

The heading "Related information" is the default heading for links generated from relationship tables. You can change the heading in a number of ways, but the most direct is to specify a title for each column of the relationship table.

10. Set the labels for the columns of the relationship table as follows:

    a. Put your cursor in the first `<relcolspec>` element in the table.

    b. Press **Enter** to bring up the **insert element** list and select "topichead"

    c. Press **Enter** again, select "topicmeta" and press **Enter** again and select "navtitle."

    d. Type the text "Belt Examination Requirements."

    e. Put your cursor in the second `<relcolspec>` element and create another `<topichead>` with a `<navtitle>` element.

    f. Type the text "Technique Descriptions."

The `<relheader>` markup should now look like this:

```
<reltable title="Exam requirements to techniques">
  <relheader>
    <relcolspec type="topic">
      <topichead>
        <topicmeta>
          <navtitle>Belt Examination Requirements</navtitle>
        </topicmeta>
      </topichead>
    </relcolspec>
    <relcolspec type="topic">
      <topichead>
        <topicmeta>
          <navtitle>Technique Descriptions</navtitle>
        </topicmeta>
      </topichead>
    </relcolspec>
  </relheader>
  . . .
```

11. Regenerate the HTML and check the topics for the 6th Kyu examination and the techniques. The related links should now be labeled with the titles from the `<relcolspec>` elements:

If you look at the pages for the technique descriptions you'll of course find a link from each one back to the Rokyu requirements topic, confirming that the relationship table has been correctly processed and that it really does represent bi-directional links between the topics.

Note that I had you put three topics in the technique descriptions cell, rather than creating a separate row for each exam/technique pair. You could have done that, and the linking effect would be the same. However, by grouping the techniques together you create a more compact table that is easier to read and understand. Grouping the topic references also makes it possible to group links together in the link-traversal user interface.

For example, rather than generating a flat list of links with a heading, the HTML could make the heading the initial link, which then presents a list of the topics grouped in the reltable cell. This could allow, for example, meaningful groupings of items within what could be a very long list.

In the context of Aikido techniques, the more advanced belt examinations involve dozens of techniques. It could be helpful to group the techniques by the attack involved or by basic principle applied, for example.

Relationship tables present numerous opportunities to do quite sophisticated things with linking. As users become more familiar with HTML5-type presentations with more sophisticated navigation interactions, there will be more demand for applying relationship tables in more sophisticated ways, and the supporting tools will follow.

This example is a very small data set, but if it was realistically large—for example, if each of the belt level exams and all of the techniques were included—each technique would have links to all the exams it applied to. And if the links were labeled meaningfully, the resulting HTML page could answer questions like, "will I need to know this technique for my next belt exam?"

Relationship table links are pretty cool, but they are not the only way to make links between topics manageable when there is reuse. DITA's key reference facility (`<keydef>`, `@keyref`, `@conkeyref`) also offers a lot of power. So the next step is to create some direct topic-to-topic dependencies to better understand what keys can do.

Authoring Step 9: Create a cross-reference

Even in highly modular writing you sometimes need to unconditionally link one topic to another. For example, a task may have a mandatory prerequisite task that it needs to link to. That type of link represents a requirement that essentially says, "regardless of where this topic is used, this other topic must exist in the same use context." Authors use the DITA cross-reference (`<xref>`) element to establish this type of direct topic-to-topic dependency.

The problem, of course, is that this sort of hard dependency creates a management challenge. Either the author or a component management system has to know about the dependency and ensure that both topics involved are managed in concert.

To really understand the issue you have to create a second use context, meaning a separate publication map, but first you need to create the cross-references and establish the dependency so you can then break it and then fix it again through the magic of keys.

To create the cross-references, perform the following steps:

1. Create a new `<glossentry>` topic in the `topics` directory with the name `gloss-tenkan.dita` with this content:[6]

```
<?xml version="1.0" encoding="utf-8"?>
<!DOCTYPE glossentry PUBLIC "-//OASIS//DTD DITA Glossary//EN"
"glossary.dtd">
<glossentry
id="ddl">
<glossterm>tenkan</glossterm>
<glossdef>180 degree turn</glossdef>
</glossentry>
```

---

[6] Glossary terms are taken from Stefan Stenudd's Aikido glossary, available here: *http://www.stenudd.com/aikido/aikido-glossary.htm*. Glossary used by permission.

2. Create a second `<glossentry>` topic with the name `gloss-tenkai.dita` with this content:

```
<?xml version="1.0" encoding="utf-8"?>
<!DOCTYPE glossentry PUBLIC "-//OASIS//DTD DITA Glossary//EN"
"glossary.dtd">
<glossentry
id="ddl">
<glossterm>tenkai</glossterm>
<glossdef>About face.</glossdef>
</glossentry>
```

3. In the map, insert a new topic head after the "Aikido Techniques" topichead and give it the title "Glossary of Aikido Terms."

4. Within the glossary `<topichead>`, create another topic head titled "T."

A topic head creates a titled level in the table of contents and may also result in a title in the main content presentation (for example, in PDF). In HTML, by default a topic head shows up in the table of contents but does not generate a separate HTML file.

In OxygenXML, if you select the glossary `<topichead>` and then click the **Insert Topic Heading** button (▤), it will create the `<topichead>` after the one you selected. You can use drag and drop to move the newly-created topichead under the glossary topichead.

5. Create references to the two glossary entry topics.

The map should now look like this up to the `<reltable>` element:

```
<map>
  <title>Introduction to Aikido</title>
  <topicref href="topics/chapter-intro.dita">
    <topicref href="topics/rokyu-requirements.dita"/>
    <topichead
      chunk="to-content"
      copy-to="aikido-techniques.dita"
      collection-type="sequence">
      <topicmeta>
        <navtitle>Aikido
          Techniques</navtitle>
      </topicmeta>
      <topicref href="topics/shomenuchi-ikkyo.dita"/>
      <topicref href="topics/munetsuki-kotegaeshi.dita"/>
      <topicref href="topics/shomenuchi-iriminage.dita"/>
    </topichead>
    <topichead
      navtitle="Glossary of Aikido Terms">
      <topichead
        navtitle="T">
```

```
            <topicref href="topics/gloss-tenkai.dita"/>
            <topicref href="topics/gloss-tenkan.dita"/>
        </topichead>
      </topichead>
    </topicref>
    ...
```

6. Regenerate the HTML to see your new glossary.

7. Open the Rokyu requirements topic in Author mode (you can double click on the reference to it in the Map Manager view to open it in the editor).

8. Find the `<term>` element with the text "tenkan" and select the entire element.

   An easy way to select an element is to use OxygenXML's Outline view and simply click on the element you want to select.

9. Click on the **Link** button in the Toolbar (ⓐ) and select **Cross Reference**. This opens the **Insert Reference** dialog.

10. Use the file chooser to navigate to the file `gloss-tenkan.dita` and select it. The dialog will list all the potential cross-reference targets in the selected file.

   In this case there is only one possible target, the topic itself.

11. Select the topic and click **OK** to create the cross-reference. The cross-reference markup should look something like this:

```
    ...
    <p>For 6th Kyu you must demonstrate
      the following techniques:<ul>
      <li><xref
        href="gloss-tenkan.dita#ddl"
        format="dita"><term>Tenkan</term></xref> </li>
      ...
```

The value of the `@href` attribute is the URL of the target topic. The fragment identifier (the part after the "#" is ID of the target topic.

The `@format` attribute indicates the format of the target resource. The value "dita" simply indicates that the target is a DITA topic, which is the default value. For cross-references to non-topic elements the `@format` attribute indicates the expected type of element, for example, "fig," "table," etc. The value may be a tagname or a module/name value as used in `@class` attributes. For references to DITA elements the `@format` attribute is somewhat redundant as the type of the referenced resource can be determined from the resource itself, assuming the reference can be resolved, so you should be able to omit `@format` for references to DITA elements if you want.

12. Regenerate the HTML and go to the Rokyu requirements topic. The term "tenkan" should now be a link to the glossary entry for *tenkan*:

You've now established a hard dependency between the Rokyu requirements topic and the glossary entry, but you've made the information more useful by providing a direct link to the definition of a jargon term.

Now it's time to break the hyperlink through reuse.

Authoring Step 10: Reuse a topic in a new publication

Link and dependency management doesn't really get interesting until you have to start doing reuse, which means having a system of two or more publications that have one or more topics in common.

To create a new publication, perform the following steps:

1. In your workspace create a new directory named `aikido-belt-requirements` as a sibling of the `intro-to-aikido` directory. Create the subdirectory `topics` under the new directory.
2. Create a new generic `<map>` document named `aikido-belt-requirements.ditamap`. Give it the title "Aikido Belt Examination Requirements."[7]

---

[7] The requirements used in this example reflect the rules of the Aikido Schools of Ueshiba, which is one of several Aikido organizations sanctioned by the international Aikido governing body. Other Aikido organizations have different rank requirements.

3. Create a new concept topic in the `aikido-belt-requirements/topics` directory with this content:

```
<?xml version="1.0" encoding="UTF-8"?>
<!DOCTYPE concept PUBLIC "-//OASIS//DTD DITA Concept//EN" "concept.dtd">
<concept id="conceptId">
<title>Aikido Belt Examination
Requirements</title>
<conbody>
<p>Aikido students are either white
belts or black belts. There are
six levels of white belt, from 6th
Kyu to 1st Kyu. Black belts start
with 1st degree black belt
(<term>shodan</term>) and progress
through higher degrees, with 6th
degree being the highest degree it
is realistically possible to
earn.</p>
</conbody>
</concept>
```

4. Create a reference to this topic from the examination requirements map.

5. Select the reference to the root topic and add a child reference to the topic `rokyu-requirements.dita` from the introduction to Aikido publication.

   The new map should look like this:

```
<?xml version="1.0" encoding="UTF-8"?>
<!DOCTYPE map PUBLIC "-//OASIS//DTD DITA Map//EN" "map.dtd">
<map>
  <title>Aikido Belt Examination
    Requirements</title>
  <topicref
    href="topics/aikido-belt-requirements.dita">
    <topicref
      href="../intro-to-aikido/topics/rokyu-requirements.dita"/>
  </topicref>
</map>
```

6. In the DITA Map Manager view, select the belt requirements map and click the **Validate and Check for Completeness** button (🗹). The **DITA Map Completeness Check** dialog should open. Make sure that the **Report links to topics not in the DITA map** check box is checked.

7. Click **OK** to do the validation. You should get a message like this:

```
/Users/ekimber/workspace/dita-for-practitioners/doc_src/body/
   part-end-to-end/samples/intro-to-aikido/topics/rokyu-requirements.dita

  W [REF] Topic referenced in other topics but not in DITA Map
    :"file:/Users/ekimber/workspace/dita-for-practitioners/doc_src/body/

       part-end-to-end/samples/intro-to-aikido/topics/gloss-tenkan.dita"
  13:11
```

OxygenXML correctly reports that you have a cross-reference to a topic that is not included explicitly in the map.

8. Generate HTML from the belt requirements map.

   You should get messages about the Rokyu requirements document being outside the scope of the root map.

9. Attempt to navigate to the Rokyu requirements topic. The link should fail with a "file not found" message.

   The link fails because the Rokyu requirements topic is not below the root map. By default, the Open Toolkit's XHTML transform only generates output for topics that are below the map. You can change the behavior with the generate.copy.outer so that it generates output for all the topics by creating any necessary ancestor directories in the output to ensure the relative locations of all the generated HTML files are correct.[8]

10. Change the generate.copy.outer and "only topics in map" settings as follows:

    a. In the Map Manager view, select the belt requirements map and then click the **Configure Transformation Scenario** button (✖). This brings up the **Configuration Transformation Scenario** dialog.

---

[8] This is totally 100% bogus because the output structure of the HTML files should not in any way be dependent on the organization of the original source files, and the DITA for Publishers HTML2 transformation type fixes that problem. The Toolkit's behavior reflects a simplifying assumption made long ago when DITA was still an IBM internal technology and reflects the fact that some delivery systems, such as Windows help, require that all the files be below a single root directory that contains the main entry point. It also reflects the fact that with XSLT 1.0 it was difficult, if not impossible, to generate multiple output files from a single XSLT transform, so all the output file location determination had to be done as part of a preprocess before generating the HTML. But with XSLT 2 that is no longer a problem. The HTML2 transform uses XSLT 2 to generate all the output HTML files in a single transform, which means you can have complete control over the output structure of the HTML without regard to how the source content is structured.

b. Select the DITA Map XHTML scenario you created earlier and click the **Edit** button. This brings up the **Edit DITA Scenario** dialog.

c. Scroll down through the list of parameters to the onlytopic.in.map parameter. Set the value to "true."

By default the Open Toolkit will process topics that are referenced from other topics but not referenced by the map itself. However, you can turn this behavior off, which I recommend. It is a good simplifying constraint to require that all dependencies on a given publication be defined in the map. This means that you can process just the map in order to reliably know what you need in order to package or process or otherwise act on the publication as a whole. If you don't impose this rule then you have no choice but to process every topic in the publication in order to see if it has a cross-reference or a content reference to something else. Don't do that.

d. Find the property generate.copy.outer and set its value to "2."

11. Regenerate the HTML from the belt requirements map.

You should get a message about the gloss-tenkan.xml file not being available to resolve a link.

Now you should get the Rokyu requirements topic but the link to the *tenkan* glossary entry should fail. If you look in the Open Toolkit log at the messages in the section starting `topicpull:` you should see messages like:

```
     [xslt] [DOTX056W][WARN]: The file
file:///Users/ekimber/workspace/dita-for-practitioners/doc_src/body/
part-end-to-end/samples/aikido-belt-requirements/temp/
intro-to-aikido/topics/gloss-tenkan.xml is not available to resolve
link information. Possible causes are: the file could not be found;
a DITAVAL file was used to remove the file's contents; the file is
located outside of the input directory. Be aware that the path
information above may not match the link in your topic. Check to make
sure the file exists and that a DITAVAL file isn't used to remove the
contents of the file. Also, ensure the file exists within the input
directory, or else turn off the ant parameter "onlytopic.in.map".
The location of this problem was at (File = /Users/ekimber/workspace/
dita-for-practitioners/doc_src/body/part-end-to-end/samples/intro-to-aikido/
topics/rokyu-requirements.dita, Element = xref:1)
```

If you are using OxygenXML to run the Toolkit, the Toolkit log is captured in the message area at the bottom of the OxygenXML window. If you are running it from the command line, the log is simply the console output unless you have done something explicit to capture it to a file, either by directing the output to a file or specifying the /logdir command line parameter or args.logdir Ant parameter.

What to do? The author innocently created a topic-to-topic cross-reference and it was only later that somebody else said "hey, that topic looks useful, I think I'll use it in my map," only to discover it used something they didn't want in their map.

There are several possible ways to solve this problem:

1. Go ahead and use the dependent topic in the second map. This is of course a reasonable solution in many cases, but for the purposes of this exercise we definitely do not want the glossary terms in the belt exam document, so this solution will not work.

2. Copy the original topic and rewrite it to remove the cross-reference. Not a sustainable solution and runs counter to one of the primary reasons for using DITA in the first place.

3. Remove the cross-reference from the original and replace it with a reltable link. Doable, of course, but the original document should really have a direct link from the mention of the term to its definition.

4. Remove the cross-reference and implement some custom processing that automatically creates links from `<term>` elements to glossary entries for those terms. This can work for more-constrained data, such as programming APIs or XML element types, but in the general case it is not possible to reliably map arbitrary `<term>` content to glossary entries. This approach to linking is called "implicit linking" by the DITA architects, and there is work under way to enable it formally in a future version of DITA. Something to think about, but not a solution for this exercise.

5. Use DITA's key reference facility to create an *indirect* linkage between the term and its definition. Because keys are defined in maps, the same key can have different bindings in different map contexts, removing the need for authors to know or care about where a topic will be used. This is the solution you want for the `<term>` linkage.

Putting keys in place takes a little extra work, but if you plan for their use from the start, they're easy enough to use and manage, and using them gives you more options than you would have otherwise.

So the next step is to replace the use of the direct reference from the `<xref>` element with a reference to a key that then takes you to the appropriate resource in the context of each map.

Authoring Step 11: Replace `@href` with `@keyref` on `<xref>`

DITA's key reference facility provides a *late-bound* indirect addressing facility. "Late bound" means that the binding from keys to resources is determined as late as possible during processing, rather than being statically defined during authoring. Indirect addressing means that there is at least one level of indirection between the reference to a key and the ultimate resource the key is bound to.

Indirection is important because it lets you have many references to a keyname but a single definition of what a given key points to. This minimizes the work required when the location of something changes, because you only have to change the key definition, and you don't have to change each reference to the key. For something like a glossary term, there could be tens or hundreds of references to the term, but if you go through a key reference, there is only one key definition. If the location of the glossary entry topic changes you only have to update the one key definition, not each of the hundreds of references to the key.

It is the late binding that lets you have different bindings for the same key in different maps, because the effective binding is determined dynamically when a root map is processed. In particular, a new map can override the base definition for a key defined in a subordinate map.

See *Pointing to Things: Linking and Addressing in DITA* on page 227 for a complete discussion of DITA's linking and addressing features.

For this exercise, we will define a key for the glossary entry for *tenkan* and then use that key, rather than a direct URL reference, to link the reference to the term *tenkan* to the glossary entry in the context of the Intro to Aikido map and to nothing in the context of the belt requirements map.

Keys are defined on the `<topicref>` element using the `@keys` attribute. Any `<topicref>` can have keys, but typical practice is to define the keys using one set of topicrefs outside the navigation tree and then use those keys to put the topics in the tree. The topicref specialization `<keydef>` is a convenience element configured to define keys. It sets `@processing-role` to "resource-only, "which indicates that the linked resource is part of the map but not bound to the navigation tree by that topicref.

The easiest thing to do with the Intro to Aikido map would be to add a `@keys` attribute to the topicref to the *tenkan* glossary entry. However, if you are going to define keys for all the glossary entries it makes sense to create a separate set of key definitions specifically for the glossary. This set of key definitions can then act as a catalog of all the available glossary entries. Having a separate map for the glossary keys makes it easier to re-use the glossary entries.

Finally, if you're working from an existing body of data, it is usually pretty easy to write a script or XSLT transform that takes your glossary entries and generates a map with appropriate key definitions and navigation topicrefs. Having the key definitions in a separate file makes it easier to generate and manage the key definitions automatically.

To set up the key definitions for the glossary, perform these steps:

1. Create a new map document named `aikido-master-glossary-keydefs.ditamap` in the `intro-to-aikido/topics` directory.

2. Set the title to "Aikido Master Glossary Keydefs." This title won't be used for anything when the map is included in other maps, but it serves as documentation and provides a title if the map is processed as a root map.

3. Create a `<topicgroup>` element as the root `<topicref>` in the map:

```
<?xml version="1.0" encoding="UTF-8"?>
<!DOCTYPE map PUBLIC "-//OASIS//DTD DITA Map//EN" "map.dtd">
<map>
   <title>Aikido Master Glossary Keydefs</title>
   <topicgroup>

   </topicgroup>
</map>
```

This `<topicgroup>` isn't strictly necessary, but it serves to provide a single parent element for all the key definitions, which is useful and reflects a general "neatness" policy that I try to follow and encourage. For example, when viewing the map in any sort of tree view, having the single parent lets you collapse the view in the tree rather than always being faced with a potentially very long list of items.

You could, of course, use nested topic groups to further organize the key definitions in some useful way, such as by letter group for a glossary. A `<topicgroup>` element has no functional effect if it has no attributes, it just serves as a neutral container. If it has attributes, then any attributes that can propagate (cascade) to descendant topicrefs will be propagated, which can be handy in some situations. If a `<topicgroup>` element has a navigation title, the element is still treated as a topic group and not a topic head and the title will be treated as if it were not there. This lets you have labels on your topic groups that make the data easier to understand or navigate, but that don't affect the navigation hierarchy generated by the map.

4. Within the `<topicgroup>` create a `<keydef>` element with the @keys value "gloss-tenkan" and an @href value of "gloss-tenkan.dita":

```
<?xml version="1.0" encoding="UTF-8"?>
<!DOCTYPE map PUBLIC "-//OASIS//DTD DITA Map//EN" "map.dtd">
<map>
   <title>Aikido Master Glossary Keydefs</title>
   <topicgroup>
    <keydef
      href="gloss-tenkan.dita"
      keys="gloss-tenkan"/>
   </topicgroup>
</map>
```

This key definition binds the key name "gloss-tenkan" to the topic `gloss-tenkan.dita`. Because the `<keydef>` element sets @processing-role to "resource-only" by default, this `<topicref>` will not, by itself, cause the topic to be included in any map's navigation tree.

5. Open the `intro-to-aikido.ditamap` in the DITA Map Manager and select the root node in the map tree (the one labeled "Introduction to Aikido").

6. Click **Insert Reference**, select `topics/aikido-master-glossary-keydefs.ditamap`, set the topicref type to "mapref," and insert the reference. OxygenXML will insert the reference at the end of the map.

`<mapref>` is a convenience specialization of `<topicref>` that sets @format to "ditamap," which indicates that the referenced resource is a map, not a topic. You can, of course, use `<topicref>` and simply set @format to "ditamap" yourself. But the `<mapref>` tagname makes your intention clear.

7. Move the `<mapref>` to the top of the map as the first child of the map. The Intro to Aikido map should look like this at the start:

```
<?xml version="1.0" encoding="UTF-8"?>
<!DOCTYPE map PUBLIC "-//OASIS//DTD DITA Map//EN" "map.dtd">
<map>
  <title>Introduction to Aikido</title>
  <mapref href="topics/aikido-master-glossary-keydefs.ditamap"
          format="ditamap"/>
  <topicref href="topics/chapter-intro.dita">
  ...
```

The general practice is to put all key definitions and references to key-defining maps at the start of the map so that it's easy to see what resources the map includes.

8. Validate the map just to make sure you haven't made any typing mistakes.

The next task is to rework the Rokyu requirements topic to make the cross-reference use the key rather than the URI reference. To do this, perform these steps:

1. Open the Rokyu requirements topic in the editor in Author mode.
2. Close the Intro to Aikido and Aikido Master Glossary Key Definitions maps in the DITA Map Manager view if they are open there.
3. Put your cursor just after the `<xref>` end tag. This is easiest to do if you turn on full tags or partial tags in OxygenXML's Author view.
4. Press **Delete** to delete the `<xref>` element.
5. Click the **Link** button ( ) in the tool bar, and select **Key Reference**. This brings up the **Insert Key Reference** dialog. The dialog should be empty.

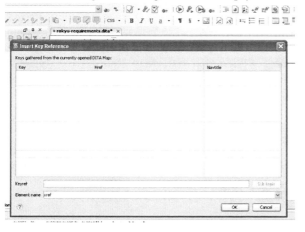

The list is empty because OxygenXML uses the selected map in the Map Manager to determine the set of available keys, and you don't have any maps open (at least none with key definitions).

6. Open the Intro to Aikido map in the DITA Map Manager.

7. In the Rokyo requirements topic, try to insert a key reference again.

You should now see an entry for the key "gloss-tenkan." Note that OxygenXML has looked at the selected map and its submaps and has determined, correctly, that the key "gloss-tenkan" is defined within the *map tree* rooted at the Intro to Aikido map.

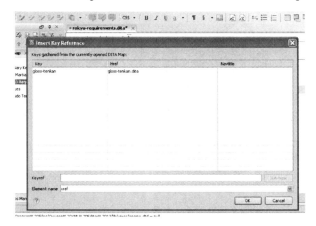

The *map tree* is the tree of maps descending from a root map as defined by the map-to-map references like the `<mapref>` you created here.

8. Select the gloss-tenkan key in the list, make sure the **Element Type** field is set to "xref," and click **OK** to insert the `<xref>`.

You can test the reference in OxygenXML by double clicking on the key reference, which should be underlined and have next to it a little link icon (🖉). OxygenXML should open the *tenkan* glossary entry topic in the editor. If you close the Intro to Aikido map in the Map Manager and try again, the link should not be resolvable. That demonstrates clearly that the keys are specific to the map and that without the map you have no way of resolving the key reference to a resource.

9. Move the `<term>` element inside the `<xref>` element. An easy way to do this is in OxygenXML's Outline view, where you can simply drag the `<term>` element into the `<xref>` element.

The reworked cross-reference should look like this:

```
<li><xref keyref="gloss-tenkan"><term>Tenkan</term></xref> </li>
```

10. Regenerate the HTML for the Intro to Aikido map. Go to the Rokyu requirements topic and verify that the link to the glossary entry is working.

Note that I used the prefix "gloss-" for the key name. This sort of naming convention makes it easier to know what a particular key is for and to group related keys together in an alphabetized list of keys, such as OxygenXML's **Insert Key Reference** dialog. Once you have thousands of keys, naming conventions will be very important. Note also that the key name matches the filename of the topic. That's another useful convention that makes it easier to correlate keys to the topics they relate to. This is useful for debugging and helps to ensure consistency in your data.

The next step is to create a different definition of the key "gloss-tenkan" in the belt requirements topic so that the cross-reference goes somewhere sensible.

Authoring Step 12: Replace `@href` with `@keyref` on `<image>`

The reference topics have references to graphics. As originally authored, the `<image>` elements use `@href` to point directly to the graphic files. These references have the same issues as the direct topic-to-topic references. You can replace the direct URI reference with a key reference to the graphic files.

By now you should be able to predict how this is going to go: create a new submap to hold the key definitions for the graphics, include that in the root map, then update the reference topics to use the keys.

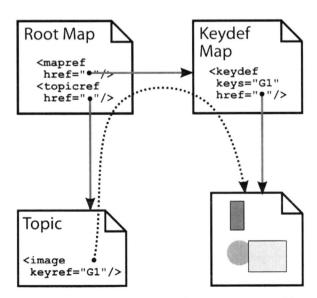

Figure 1: Topic with a key reference to a graphic

If you have a large set of graphics to make keys for, you would probably want to generate the map from a list of files. That type of scripting is outside the scope of this book, but a brute force approach is to simply capture a directory listing to a text file and then use regular expression search and replace to make the markup. And of course you can always script it in your favorite scripting language.

To replace the @href attributes with @keyref on <image>, perform these steps:

1. Create a new map file aikido-graphics-keydefs.ditamap in the directory intro-to-aikido/topics/graphics. Set its title to "Aikido Graphics Key Definitions":

```
<?xml version="1.0" encoding="UTF-8"?>
<!DOCTYPE map PUBLIC "-//OASIS//DTD DITA Map//EN" "map.dtd">
<map>
  <title>Aikido Graphics Key Definitions</title>
</map>
```

2. In the map, add key definitions for each of the graphics:

```
<?xml version="1.0" encoding="UTF-8"?>
<!DOCTYPE map PUBLIC "-//OASIS//DTD DITA Map//EN" "map.dtd">
<map>
  <title>Aikido Graphics Key Definitions</title>

  <keydef keys="munetsuki-kotegaeshi-01"
          href="munetsuki-kotegaeshi-01.jpg"
          format="jpg"/>
  <keydef keys="shomenuchi-ikkyo-01"
          href="shomenuchi-ikkyo-01.jpg"
          format="jpg"/>
  <keydef keys="shomenuchi-iriminage-01"
          href="shomenuchi-iriminage-01.jpg"
          format="jpg"/>
</map>
```

3. Edit the intro-to-aikido.ditamap and add a reference to the aikido-graphics-keydefs.ditamap:

```
<map>
  <title>Introduction to Aikido</title>
  <mapref href="topics/aikido-master-glossary-keydefs.ditamap"
          format="ditamap"/>
  <mapref href="topics/graphics/aikido-graphics-keydefs.ditamap"
          format="ditamap"/>
  ...
</map>
```

Validate the map in OxygenXML to verify that the new maps are correct.

If you haven't put the graphics in the graphics directory, the validation will tell you it can't find the graphics.

4. Edit each of the reference topics and change the `@href` attributes on the `<image>` elements to `@keyref`, deleting the parts of the URL that are not the key name, producing references like this:

```
...
<fig>
  <image
    keyref="munetsuki-kotegaeshi-01">
    <alt>Munetsuki strike</alt>
  </image>
</fig>
...
```

This type of change is easiest to make in Text mode.

Because in this case the key names are the same as the file names without the extension, you could use a global regular expression search and replace to make this update, e.g., find `href="graphics/(.+)\.jpg"` and replace it with `keyref="$1"`. Because the URLs include `"graphics/"` and the extension, this should be a safe global change to make.

5. To see the change in Author mode, close the reference topic, make sure the `intro-to-aikido.ditamap` is *not* selected in the Map Manager, and reopen the reference topic in Author mode. OxygenXML should report that it cannot resolve the reference to the graphic, confirming that you have a key reference.

6. Open or select the `intro-to-aikido.ditamap` in the Map Manager and close and reopen the reference topic in Author mode. OxygenXML should show the graphic inline.

7. Generate PDF or HTML from the map. You should see the graphic in the output.

Using keys for graphics has a number of benefits, but one benefit specific to graphics is that you can have different key definitions for different formats of the same logical graphic. For example, you can have a set of key definitions for PNG graphics for the Web and EPS or SVG graphics for print, and then use conditional processing to select the appropriate set of key definitions. The base DITA vocabulary does not provide a built-in selection attribute specifically for output format, but the DITA for Publishers vocabulary includes the "rendition target" attribute domain (d4p_renditionTargetAttDomain) that you can add to your map and topic types.

Another value of having key definitions for graphics is that you can use the key definitions to capture metadata about the graphics. While you can embed metadata into most graphics formats using various technologies, such as EXIF metadata used by most digital cameras or Adobe's XMP embedded markup, that metadata is not easily accessible to XML-aware tools. By adding metadata to the key definition topicrefs for the graphics, you can search on the maps to find graphics based on their metadata. For example, the Aikido graphics might contain metadata that captures the technique details the graphic reflects, something like this:

```
...
<keydef keys="munetsuki-kotegaeshi-01"
  href="munetsuki-kotegaeshi-01.jpg"
  format="jpg"
>
  <topicmeta>
    <keywords>
      <keyword>munetsuki</keyword>
      <keyword>kotegaeshi</keyword>
      <keyword>strike</keyword>
      <keyword>pin</keyword>
    </keywords>
  </topicmeta>
</keydef>
...
```

You'll see more about conditional processing and metadata in upcoming steps.

Authoring Step 13: Redefine key in second map

For the belt requirements map you want the cross-reference to the term *tenkan* to go somewhere other than the glossary entry topic. That might be nowhere or somewhere else, where somewhere else could include:

- A paragraph saying where to go to find the term defined.
- A link to an external resource where the term could be found.
- A different topic that also defines the term but is specific to the publication.

Going nowhere is a little harder, but DITA does offer a potential solution, which is to put the definition text in the key definition itself or define a key definition that isn't associated with any resource at all, effectively a "null" key definition. That might work (or it might not). This step explores the process of "null" keys. This is important because you may need to have existing key references resolve to "nothing" in particular map contexts. It's not immediately obvious from the DITA specification how to do that and different processors may provide different results for specific techniques.

A third option is to replace the cross-reference entirely so that if the key isn't defined the key reference is simply ignored. More about this option later.

The first task is to define the key "gloss-tenkan" in the belt requirements map. Given that definition, you can then experiment with different options for what to bind the key to.

To create the new key definition perform the following steps:

1. Edit the `aikido-belt-requirements.ditamap` in the DITA Map Manager.

2. Select the root node in the map tree (the node labeled "Aikido Belt Examination Requirements"), right click, and select **Append Child** > **Key Definition**. This brings up the **Insert Reference [Key Definition]** dialog.

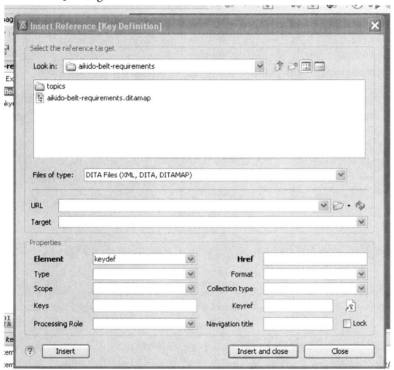

3. In the **keys** field, enter "gloss-tenkan" and select **Insert and Close** to create the key definition.

   The map should now look something like this:

```xml
<?xml version="1.0" encoding="UTF-8"?>
<!DOCTYPE map PUBLIC "-//OASIS//DTD DITA Map//EN" "map.dtd">
<map>
  <title>Aikido Belt Examination
    Requirements</title>
  <topicref href="topics/aikido-belt-requirements.dita">
    <topicref href="../intro-to-aikido/topics/rokyu-requirements.dita"/>
  </topicref>
  <keydef keys="gloss-tenkan"/>
</map>
```

4. Generate HTML from the map and navigate to the Rokyu requirements topic.

You should see that there is still a link from the *tenkan* term. However, that link will either be unresolved or it will link to the root map.

This specific case is not really handled in the DITA 1.2 specification, but it's definitely an edge case and an argument can be made that not specifying @href is equivalent to specifying an empty @href ("").

The next thing to try is creating a key definition that specifies empty link text. A key definition can define link text for the target in addition to, or instead of, pointing to separate resource. An empty link text might be interpreted as meaning that there is nothing to link to (or it might not).

5. Edit the map in the main editor and add a <topicmeta> element inside the <keydef> element. Inside the <topicmeta> create an empty <linktext> element:

```
<keydef
  keys="gloss-tenkan">
  <topicmeta>
    <linktext/>
  </topicmeta>
</keydef>
```

6. Regenerate the HTML and again check the link from the *tenkan* term. You should get the same behavior.

In fact, there is no way to simply disable the cross-reference by creating a "null" key definition or empty link text, at least using the Open Toolkit. So that leaves either pointing to a topic within the current map or an external resource.

As it happens, the glossary used in this sample document is, at the time of writing, available as a Web page, so you could bind the key to that. To do that, add an @href attribute with the value "http://www.stenudd.com/aikido/aikido-glossary.htm":

```
<keydef
  keys="gloss-tenkan"
  href="http://www.stenudd.com/aikido/aikido-glossary.htm"
  />
```

When you save the map, you should see an entry for the Web page in the Map Manager view with an exclamation point on it. Validate the map in Oxygen. You should see several messages about invalid

@class attribute values and this message (or some other message—there are many ways the processing of an HTML page can go wrong):

```
E [Xerces]
Problem parsing "http://www.stenudd.com/aikido/aikido-glossary.htm"
as DITA content. Cause:The entity "ouml" was not declared, but was
referenced in the attribute "CONTENT" of the element "META".
```

The problem is that you didn't tell the processor that this HTML page is a local resource. You also didn't say it was an HTML-format resource.

This is an easy mistake to make, especially when creating topicrefs and cross-references manually, rather than through a link-creation dialog such as OxygenXML provides. It can lead to mysterious failures and general frustration.

As a rule, if you refer to a Web page or any non-DITA resource that is not a graphic used by topics within the map, then you must specify @scope to indicate that the resource is an external (not local) resource and @format to indicate what its format is (HTML or whatever).

Add scope="external" and format="html" to the key definition:

```
<keydef
   keys="gloss-tenkan"
   href="http://www.stenudd.com/aikido/aikido-glossary.htm"
   scope="external"
   format="html"
   />
```

When you save the changes to the map, the Map Manager view should now show the Web page with a little Web page icon.

Regenerate the HTML. The link around the <term> element should now take you to the Aikido glossary page.[9]

This is a reasonable solution and may be appropriate in some situations, but for this exercise the goal is for there to be no link at all. The solution is to remove the cross-reference entirely and put the key reference on the <term> element itself.

---

[9]   At the time of writing there was a bug in the 1.5.3 version of the Open Toolkit whereby the HTML usually did not reflect the link, but PDF did. So if the HTML doesn't show the link, try generating PDF. If neither shows the link but OxygenXML lets you navigate from the link to the target, then you know that the markup is correct and the problem is with the Toolkit. The link should work correctly in the 1.5.4 version of the Toolkit.

Many of the DITA inline elements, including `<ph>`, `<keyword>`, and `<term>`, can specify @keyref and thereby do one or both of the following:

- Become a link to the remote resource bound to the key (that is, the topic or non-DITA resource bound to the key).
- Reflect the link text defined in the key definition if the referencing element does not have any content and the key definition includes link text as a descendant element.

If the key is not resolvable then the element does not act as a link.

This is just what you want for the `<term>` elements.

The change to the Rokyu requirements topic is simple: move the @keyref attribute from the `<xref>` element to the `<term>` element and delete the `<xref>` element:

```
...
<li><term
   keyref="gloss-tenkan">Tenkan</term></li>
...
```

Regenerate the HTML for both the Intro to Aikido and the belt requirements maps. The link should work in both cases but take you to different targets. In the Introduction to Aikido it should take you to the glossary entry for *tenkan* and in the belt requirements it should take you to the Web page.

Finally, remove the key definition from the belt requirements map and regenerate the HTML. There should be no link from the *tenkan* `<term>` element. There may be a message in the Toolkit log to the effect that it could not find a definition for the key "gloss-tenkan."

At this point you should have a general understanding of how keys work and how they allow you to have the same link within a topic produce different results in different maps. There's more to be done with keys but this is enough for now. There's also more to say about the general approach to managing things like large glossaries, but that will be covered in the section on managing DITA content.

You should also have a general understanding of using topics from maps and what it can mean to reuse a topic in two or more maps.

The next step is to add content references to the mix, taking reuse from topics to elements within topics.

Authoring Step 14: Add content references

DITA content references (conref) allow you to use elements from one topic or map within other topics or maps by reference. (For a complete discussion of the content reference feature, see *Reuse at the Element Level: The Content Reference Facility* on page 269.) Typical examples are notes, cautions, and warnings (admonitions) and steps that occur in many tasks. You can have one topic that contains the admonitions to be reused and then link to those admonitions using content reference links from other topics that need to include them. Conref can also be used for "variables," such as product names, that should be set once and used many places. I put the term "variables" in quotes because they are not really variables as most people use the term. Rather, they are fairly static and, if using keys, invariant for a given root map.

With conref, any element, with just a few exceptions (`<title>` chief among them), can link to another element of the same or more specialized type and use the referenced element at the location of the referencing element. DITA's conref is similar to XInclude, but has some important differences.

Like cross-references, conrefs create topic-to-topic dependencies and therefore pose the same management challenges. A conref link can use either a direct URL reference (`@conref`) or a key reference (`@conkeyref`). Direct URL references create the same problem as direct cross-references: if the referencing topic is used in a new map, then the referenced topic must also be used by the map, either as a resource-only topic or as part of the navigation tree. Using key references for conref provides the same value as it does for cross-references: you can bind the same key to different resources in different maps. You also get the value of indirection, where references to an referenced element are not affected if the location of the element changes, only the key definition is affected.

As in the glossary example, you can use a set of key definitions to act as a catalog for a set of topics that contain reusable elements. However, because the point of maps is to organize topics, topicrefs can only point to topics and not to elements within topics. This means that you cannot use keys to create a catalog of individual elements within topics to be reused. To create a catalog of elements DITA would need some form of indirect addressing for elements within topics and it does not have that facility. Through DITA 1.2 (and probably through DITA 1.3), the DITA Technical Committee has decided that providing that level of addressing indirection would add too much complexity to DITA for too little value.

You can use keys to point to elements within topics, but you do it by using a key reference to point to the topic that contains the element and then the element's ID to point to the element. The `@keyref` and `@conkeyref` syntax is *keyname/elementID*, e.g. `<xref keyref="gloss-tenkan/p-01"/>`, where `gloss-tenkan` is the key name and `p-01` is the ID on an element. This form of key reference is equivalent to the DITA-specific URL of *topicFilePath*#*topicid/elementID*. You're simply replacing the topic file path and topic ID with a key reference. The element ID component is the same. Or said another way, in DITA you always address a element within a topic by first addressing the topic that contains the element. This is different from typical XML practice where you address elements by ID within the XML document that contains those elements.

The main limitation with this approach to key-based addressing of elements is that, even if you bind the key to a different topic, the element ID must be the same. This is bad in theory but in practice it's manageable because you usually have to manage your content pretty closely to do element-level linking anyway, so coordinating IDs ends up being not that big a deal, and it's usually easier than it would be to manage another level of indirection and addressing. So it's an appropriate compromise between functional completeness and practical usability.

As a matter of practice, you should *always* use keys for content references—it makes your data much less sensitive to the details of how it's stored and managed and avoids many potential problems. If you know that re-used topics will be making content references then you really must use keys, but even if you don't initially have a topic re-use requirement, it is still to your advantage to use keys.

For the Introduction to Aikido you will use content references to reuse common components of technique descriptions. As in most martial arts, Aikido techniques are built up from combinations of fundamental components. Because Aikido is based on cooperative practice between an attacker, *Uke,* and a defender, *Nage,* there is always an attack as part of the technique. This means the discussion of Aikido techniques naturally breaks down into a set of re-usable components that are combined into specific technique descriptions.

For the Rokyu belt exam there are two techniques that start with the same attack and two techniques that apply the same defence to two different attacks. This means you can factor out the common components as re-usable resources and then reconstruct the descriptions of those techniques using conrefs. The same will often be true in technical documentation where different products are really just different configurations of the same basic building blocks of features, plugins, or what have you.

While you can create a conref to any element that has an ID, general practice is to collect reusable components into "resource" topics that are not, themselves, part of any navigation tree, and then use those components from topics that are in the navigation tree. (Of course, having said that, it might still be useful to have a separate map that serves to collect all the resource topics into a single structure so you can publish a catalog of reusable components as a tool for authors or for review purposes or whatever.)

For this exercise you will create a new resource topic that collects the reusable parts of the technique descriptions and reworks the existing reference topics to use those bits.

To create the resource topic, perform these steps:

1. Create the directory common/techniques under your workspace directory.

   The "common" directory makes it clear that the stuff within it is intended for reuse across publications. The techniques directory points toward a topical organization scheme, anticipating other types of things, such as graphics, glossary entries, and so on. Because this type of common repository of content can get quite large, it's important to keep it organized and logical.

2. Create a new <map> document with the name aikido-technique-resources.ditamap in the common/techniques directory. Set the map's title to "Common Aikido Technique Resources":

```
<?xml version="1.0" encoding="UTF-8"?>
<!DOCTYPE map PUBLIC "-//OASIS//DTD DITA Map//EN" "map.dtd">
<map>
  <title>Common Aikido Technique Resources</title>
</map>
```

This map will define the keys for the resource topics and non-DITA resources related to techniques, such as graphics and videos.

3. Create the directory `topics` under `common/techniques` and create a new `<topic>` document with the name `aikido-technique-components.dita` in the new directory. Give it the title "Aikido Technique Components" and set the content of the body paragraph to "Contains reusable parts of Aikido technique descriptions."

    The title and initial paragraph simply serve to document the purpose of the topic.

4. In the DITA Map Manager, create a key definition linked to the Aikido technique components topic with the key "res-technique-comps."

    The prefix "res-" indicates that the key is for a resource topic. You want the key to be short but not cryptic, like file names and similar identifiers that will be used directly by humans.

    The map should look like this:

```
<?xml version="1.0" encoding="UTF-8"?>
<!DOCTYPE map PUBLIC "-//OASIS//DTD DITA Map//EN" "map.dtd">
<map>
  <title>Common Aikido Technique
    Resources</title>
  <keydef
    href="topics/aikido-technique-descriptions.dita"
    keys="res-technique-comps"/>
</map>
```

5. Edit the `aikido-technique-description.dita` topic and add the following markup after the existing paragraph:

```
<section> <title>Attacks</title>
  <p><ph
  id="shomenuchi"/></p> </section>
<section><title>Throws</title>
  <p><ph
  id="shihonage"/></p> </section>
```

Because you will be building up paragraphs from re-used components, the elements to be referenced must have a parent element of `<p>`. The element type `<ph>` is a generic element intended in part to allow re-use of text within paragraphs and similar contexts. To be used by reference the `<ph>` elements must have IDs. The IDs only need to be unique within the containing parent topic.

I've used the `<section>` elements to simply group the different phrases into logical categories. Here I'm using `<section>` with literal titles, rather than `@spectitle`, because the sections are just for convenience and documentation.

6. Open the topic for *shomenuchi ikkyo* (`shomenuchi-ikkyo.dita`). Select the text "Uke strikes to the top of Nage's head" and paste it into the "shomenuchi" `<ph>` element in the resource topic.

7. Open the topic for *katatedori shihonage* (`katatedori-shihonage.dita`) and select everything in the description paragraph except the starting text "*Omote*: Uke grabs Nage's opposite hand.." Paste it into the "shihonage" `<ph>` element in the resource topic. Save the changes to the resource topic.

8. Open the Intro to Aikido map (`intro-to-aikido.ditamap`) in the DITA Map Manager. Insert a map reference to the `aikido-technique-resources.ditamap` map document:

```
<?xml version="1.0" encoding="UTF-8"?>
<!DOCTYPE map PUBLIC "-//OASIS//DTD DITA Map//EN" "map.dtd">
<map>
   <title>Introduction to Aikido</title>
   <topicref
      format="ditamap"
      href="topics/aikido-master-glossary-keydefs.ditamap"/>
   <mapref
      href="topics/graphics/aikido-graphics-keydefs.ditamap"
      format="ditamap"/>
   <mapref
      href="../common/techniques/aikido-technique-resources.ditamap"
      format="ditamap"/>
   ...
</map>
```

9. With the Intro to Aikido map selected in the Map Manager, edit the topic for *shomenuchi ikkyo* (`shomenuchi-ikkyo.dita`). Delete the text "Uke strikes to the top of Nage's head."

10. Without moving the cursor, click the **Insert a DITA Content Key Reference** button (⬚) in the tool bar. This opens the **Insert Content Key Reference** dialog. The dialog show two keys, one for the glossary entry for *tenkan* and one for the technique components topic.

11. Select the "res-technique-comps" key and click the **Subtopic** button to bring up the **Reference** dialog. You should see three entries, one for the topic and one for each of the `<ph>` elements.

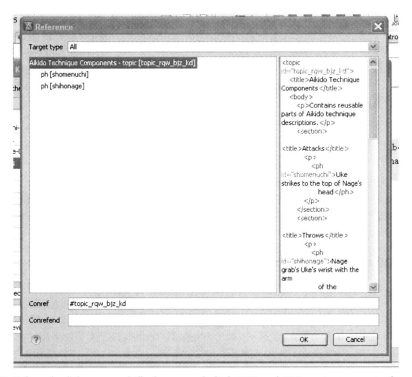

12. Select the "shomenuchi" phrase and click **OK** and **OK** again to create the content reference.

In OxygenXML's Author mode, you should see the text of the referenced <ph> element reflected in the editor view, confirming that you created the content reference correctly. The markup should look like this:

```
...
<p>As <ph
  conkeyref="res-technique-comps/shomenuchi"/>,
  Nage slides in and catches Uke's
...
```

13. Generate HTML or PDF from the Intro to Aikido map. You should see the *shomenuchi* text where you expect it in the *shomenuchi ikkyo* topic.

If you want to prove that the conref is really working, change the content in the resource topic and regenerate the HTML or PDF and verify that you get the new content.

14. Edit the topic for *shomenuchi iriminage* (`shomenuchi-iriminage.dita`) and make the same change as in the other topic. You can simply copy and paste the conref from the *shomenuchi ikkyo* topic into the *iriminage* topic.

15. Generate HTML or PDF again and verify that the conref worked in the *shomenuchi iriminage* topic. If you had modified the text of the phrase to verify the conrefs, change it back, regenerate, and verify that the corrected text is reflected in both uses.

If you want to make the example complete, you can add similar conrefs for the *shomenuchi* technique. The materials on the DITA for Practitioners website contains a complete example of factoring out all the common text into reusable phrases.

Observe that the value of the `@conkeyref` attribute is a key name/element ID pair. It is not a path. Note also that I chose the element IDs to be meaningful. They could be arbitrary identifiers but it's much more useful to have meaningful values whenever possible. In this case, each attack, throw, pin, or footwork movement has a specific name, usually one or two words, which serves as a natural ID that will be clear to the subject matter experts authoring the content. In addition, these terms are unlikely to change since the practice of Aikido has been well established for almost 100 years.

However, if your terminology is not stable but evolving, it would be inappropriate to use the names as IDs because after a while the current names wouldn't match the IDs, and people would get confused. In that case, a simple numbering scheme, or even just random generated IDs, would be better. Authors would then need to depend on the actual text to know what to select. However, DITA-aware editors can help by providing text or other aspects of potential target elements as part of their conref creation user interfaces, just as OxygenXML does.

For fun, generate HTML from the `aikido-technique-resources.ditamap` map. What happened?

You should have gotten an empty Web page. This is because all the topics are included with a `@processing-role` of "resource-only," meaning they are not part of the navigation tree. Thus, there is no navigation tree. Doh!

If you want to be able to render the resource topics you must create a separate map that includes the technique resources map and uses a normal topicref to each topic's key, e.g.:

```
<?xml version="1.0" encoding="UTF-8"?>
<!DOCTYPE map PUBLIC "-//OASIS//DTD DITA Map//EN" "map.dtd">
<map>
  <title>Aikido Common Resources</title>
  <mapref href="techniques/aikido-technique-resources.ditamap"
          format="ditamap"/>
  <topichead navtitle="Technique Resources">
    <topicref keyref="res-technique-comps"/>
  </topichead>
</map>
```

If you render this map you'll see that the reusable phrases are there, but they're not really distinguished in any way. If you expect to create this sort of component catalog rendition it would probably be useful to include labels or other distinguishing information along with the reusable bits. For example, you could put the paragraphs with the phrase into definition lists, where the definition terms are the phrase IDs or the natural names for the components, or whatever. E.g.:

```
<topic
  id="topic_rqw_bjz_kd">
  <title>Aikido Technique
    Components</title>
  <body>
    <p>Contains reusable parts of Aikido
      technique descriptions.</p>
    <section> <title>Attacks</title>
      <dl>
        <dlentry>
          <dt>shomenuchi</dt>
          <dd>
            <p><ph
              id="shomenuchi">Uke
              strikes to the top of
              Nage's head</ph></p>
          </dd>
        </dlentry>
      </dl> </section>
    <section><title>Throws</title>
      <dl>
        <dlentry>
          <dt>shihonage</dt>
          <dd>
            . . .
```

This also makes for a more usable presentation in a tags-off view like OxygenXML's Author mode. As long as the parent of the re-usable element is appropriate, it doesn't matter what other elements contain the parent elements.

It should be clear at this point how you could apply the conref pattern you've established to all the content in the Introduction to Aikido publication to eliminate pretty much all redundant text and make it fairly easy to build new technique descriptions.

Applying what you learned from the cross-reference exercise, it should also be clear what you might need to do if you reuse the technique descriptions in another map: include the same resource map or bind the keys to new resources.

One wrinkle in the reuse scenario is the implication for element IDs. Because the `@conkeyref` value is a key/id pair, every topic to which the key is bound must use the same ID values for the target elements it contains. There is no mechanism in DITA 1.2 for redirecting a reference to one element ID to another element ID. The DITA Technical Committee (TC) recognizes that this is a functional gap in DITA's addressing facilities, but has chosen to date to accept the gap in order to avoid the complexity inherent in yet another indirect addressing facility. The TC's analysis as of DITA 1.2 is that in practice the problem is manageable because content references and resources intended for reuse tend to be very carefully managed, and thus managing correspondence of IDs in different topics bound to the same key in different maps is not a serious imposition.

You now have a pretty sophisticated set of DITA publications. You have topics reused in two distinctly different publications. You have relationship tables to impose useful links. You have manageable references between topics. And you have used content reference to minimize redundancy in your content.

About the only major feature left to explore is conditional processing.

Authoring Step 15: Conditional processing

Conditional processing is a general feature of most technical documentation authoring systems and standards, and DITA is no exception. You can add attributes to elements to indicate the conditions to which they apply and then set the active conditions at runtime to include or exclude elements based on the active conditions. This is referred to as "filtering" in DITA. DITA's filtering facility is sometimes called profiling or effectivity, although "applicability" is the more correct term in my opinion.

You can also flag elements that apply to a given set of conditions with, for example, distinguishing graphic icons or text. DITA's flagging facility is comparable to "effectivity statements" used in some technical manuals (flagging is demonstrated in *Authoring Step 17: Configure DITAVAL for flagging* on page 94).

See *Conditional Processing: Filtering and Flagging* on page 291 for an in-depth discussion of DITA's conditional processing features.

Using conditional processing, or "applicability," requires two things:

1. Setting attributes on elements to indicate the conditions to which they apply.
2. Configuring your processing tool to reflect a particular set of conditions for a given processing instance.

For item (1) you can use one of the selection attributes defined in the base DITA vocabulary or specialized selection attributes you or someone else defines. The base selection attributes are described in the section titled "select-atts attribute group" in the DITA 1.2 specification. Specialized selection attributes are defined in "attribute domain" vocabulary modules. Attribute domains are the easiest specialization to define, and it is likely that you will need custom selection attributes if your local business processes or subject matter require conditional processing.

Item (2) is necessarily tool-specific. However, the DITA standard defines a standard way to configure conditional processing at runtime, the DITAVAL document type. The Open Toolkit uses DITAVAL documents to configure how it handles conditional elements, and other tools support DITAVAL as well, including the OxygenXML editor.

The base selection attributes are:

- `@platform`
- `@product`
- `@audience`
- `@importance`
- `@rev`
- `@status`
- `@otherprops`

In addition, the `@props` attribute can be used for arbitrary conditions and as a basis for specialization to create custom selection attributes. The `@rev` attribute is a selection attribute, but it is intended only for flagging (for example, revision bars), not filtering.

The `@otherprops` attribute is obsolete and deprecated in favor of `@props` (although `@otherprops` may be rehabilitated in DITA 1.3 by allowing it to have the same syntax as `@props` and thus be usable for arbitrary conditions).

The values of the selection attributes are space-delimited tokens, where each token represents a distinct condition value. For example the value "dan" for `@audience` would indicate information specific to black belts ("dan"-level belts in Aikido), while a value of "dan kyu" would be for both black and white belts.

At processing time you can specify for each value of any condition whether that value is to be treated as "include" or "exclude."

When a processor evaluates the selection attributes on a given element, it compares the attribute values with the condition values specified at runtime. If a selection attribute value matches a condition value that has been set as "include" at runtime, then the condition is "true." If the value matches a condition value that has been set as "exclude" at runtime, then the condition is "false." If a condition has not been specified at all at runtime, then the selection attribute is ignored for the purposes of conditional processing.

When an element has multiple selection attributes, all the conditions must resolve to "true" (or be ignored) for the element to be applicable to the current condition set. When a single attribute has multiple tokens, it is true if any token evaluates to "include," even if other tokens evaluate to "exclude."

For example, if you use the built-in `@platform` attribute as the "Aikido school" condition (stretching the concept of platform here), then you might have an element like:

```
<p platform="asu"
   audience="kyu">Your first belt level is 6th kyu</p>
<p platform="aikikai usaf"
   audience="kyu">Your first belt level is 5th kyu</p>
```

When you process this content, if the active value for condition @platform is "asu" and the value for condition @audience is "kyu" then the first paragraph will be applicable but the second paragraph will not be. If the active value of @platform is either "aikikai" or "usaf" then the second paragraph will be applicable and the first will not be. If the active value for @audience is not "kyu," then neither paragraph will be applicable regardless of the value for the condition @platform.

Note that you can use any values you want for the built-in conditions. The DITA vocabulary does not define any particular values. You can use constraint modules to impose specific value lists (*Constraints and Vocabulary Module Integration* on page 186), or you can use subject scheme maps to define value lists (*Value Lists, Taxonomies, and Ontologies: SubjectScheme Maps* on page 305). However, not all DITA-aware editors support subject scheme for value lists at this time (although OxygenXML version 13 does).

For this exercise, you will have different versions of the technique descriptions for beginning students and advanced students. You will use the values "beginner" and "experienced" for the @audience attribute.

To add conditional content, perform the following steps:

1. Select the intro-to-aikido.ditamap map in the Map Manager and open the *Yokomenuchi shihonage* topic (yokomenuchi-shihonage.dita) in the editor.

2. In the description paragraph, delete all the text after "*Omote*: Uke strikes toward the near side of Nage's head." and replace it with a content key reference to the phrase "shihonage" from the Aikido technique components topic, resulting in this markup:

```
<p><term>Omote</term>: Uke strikes
  toward the near side of Nage's
  head. <ph
  conkeyref="res-technique-comps/shihonage"/></p>
```

3. In the editor, click on the conref you just created to bring up the component's resource topic (aikido-technique-descriptions.dita).

4. Put your cursor inside the *shihonage* <ph> element and either open the attribute editor (**alt-Enter**) or select the **Attributes** view.

5. Edit the @audience attribute and set the value to "beginner":

```
  ...
  <section><title>Throws</title>
   <p><ph
     id="shihonage"
     audience="beginner">Nage grab's Uke's wrist...
```

6. Copy and paste the paragraph containing the *shihonage* phrase.

If you do this copy in OxygenXML in Author mode, Oxygen will probably remove the `@id` attribute from the copied `<ph>` element because otherwise it would be a duplicate ID. But if you do the copy in Text mode, the `@id` attribute is not removed.

If you do the copy in text mode, copying the `@id` attribute, you will create duplicate ID within the topic. However, normal DTD validation will not report this because in DITA `@id` attributes on non-topic elements are not declared as type ID. However, it is still a DITA error for two elements within a given parent topic to have the same ID. Jarno Elovirta, a contributor to the DITA Open Toolkit and developer of DITA-related tools in general, has developed a set of DITA Schematrons[10] that check for this. OxygenXML, starting with version 12, includes these Schematrons and uses them for interactive validation. Oxygen should report that you now have a duplicate ID value.

7. Set or change the ID of the copied `@ph` element to "shihonage-expert."
8. Set the `@audience` value to "expert" on the shihonage-expert phrase.
9. Edit the expert phrase to change the 2nd and 3rd sentences to "Nage slides deeply across Uke's front. As he slides he grab's Uke's arm with his other hand just above the wrist, holding the arm much as he would hold a sword, twisting the arm slightly toward Nage's body and raising Uke's arm above Nage's head.":

```
<p><ph id="shihonage-expert"
  audience="expert">Nage grab's Uke's wrist with the arm of the grabbed
hand. Nage slides deeply across Uke's front. As he slides he grab's
Uke's arm with his other hand just above the wrist, holding the arm
much as he would hold a sword, twisting the arm slightly toward Nage's
body and raising Uke's arm above Nage's head. Nage lowers his hips to
. . .
```

10. Save the resource topic (`aikido-technique-descriptions.dita`) and return to the yokomenuchi shihonage topic (`yomenuchi-shihonage.dita`).
11. Place your cursor just inside the end tag for the paragraph containing the conref to the *shihonage* phrase and insert a content key reference to the shihonage-expert phrase:

```
<p><term>Omote</term>: Uke strikes toward the near side of Nage's head.
  <ph conkeyref="res-technique-comps/shihonage"/>
  <ph conkeyref="res-technique-comps/shihonage-expert"/></p>
```

---

[10] Schematron is an ISO/IEC standard for validating XML documents using XPath-based rules that can check aspects of documents that DTDs and XSDs cannot validate. An instance of a Schematron validation configuration is itself called a *Schematron*, analogous to "a DTD" or "an XSD." See *http://standards.iso.org/ittf/PubliclyAvailableStandards/index.html*) and *http://www.schematron.com/* for more information.

You should now see both versions of the technique description in the Author mode view.

12. Generate HTML for the Intro to Aikido map.

You should see both versions of the description in the *yokomenuchi shihonage* topic. If you don't specify any active conditions then by default all conditions are true.

The next step is to configure the Toolkit to use your conditions to either filter things out that don't apply or to flag things based on those conditions.

Authoring Step 16: Configure DITAVAL file for filtering

In OxygenXML you can set up filtering based on DITA selection attributes. You define one or more "Profiling Condition Sets," and then you can select different condition sets to selectively hide or show conditional text in the editor. OxygenXML will also use your condition sets to configure the Open Toolkit.

To set up condition sets for the @author property with values of "beginner" and "expert," perform these steps:

1. Select the **Profiling/Conditional Text** button ($\mathbb{Y}$.) in the main toolbar (there's also one in the Map Manager tool bar) and select **Configure Profiling Condition Sets....** This opens the **Preferences** dialog to **Editor** > **Edit Modes** > **Author** > **Profiling/Conditional Text** settings.
2. In the **Profiling Attributes** area find the entry for "DITA* | audience" and click **Edit**.
3. Use the **New** button to add the values "beginner" and "expert" and click **OK** to close the dialog.
4. In the **Profiling Condition Sets** area click the **New** button to create a new condition set.
5. Set the condition set name to "Audience Beginner" and check "beginner" under Audience in the list of available properties and values. Click **OK** to save the condition set.
6. Create another condition set named "Audience Expert" and select "expert" rather than "beginner."
7. Click **OK** in the **Preferences** dialog to close it.

You can now use the **Profiling** pulldown to select an active condition set. Test this by editing either the *Yokomenuchi shihonage* topic or the technique descriptions resource topic and selecting either of the new condition sets from the **Profiling/Conditional Text** button. OxygenXML should highlight the applicable phrase and obscure (but not hide) the inapplicable phrase.

You can turn off the use of a condition by right clicking on the item in the condition set list. You can also turn on display of selection attributes without having a condition set active. This feature of OxygenXML verifies that you have set up the conditions and attributes correctly.

The next step is to create a DITAVAL file to control the Open Toolkit. While OxygenXML will generate a DITAVAL from its condition sets under the covers, OxygenXML condition sets don't reflect the full range of options you can specify in a DITAVAL file. In particular, OxygenXML doesn't provide any way to set up flagging or invert the selection logic for a specific property.

For filtering you need one DITAVAL file for each different set of conditions you want to filter on, which for this exercise means two DITAVALs, one for audience of "beginner" and one for "expert." For flagging you usually just need one DITAVAL file for each different combination of flags you want to be able to apply, which is usually just one combination for a given document or set of documents using the same conditions.

For the first DITAVAL you want to exclude everything that specifies an audience other than "expert." To set up this DITAVAL, perform these steps:

1. Create the directory `ditavals` in your workspace and then create a new DITAVAL document with the name `audience-expert.ditaval` in the `ditavals` directory. There should be a DITAVAL template available from the OxygenXML **New File** dialog.

   The starting DITAVAL file should look something like this:

   ```xml
   <?xml version="1.0" encoding="UTF-8"?>
   <val>
     <prop
       action="exclude"
       att="audience"
       val="novice"/>
     <prop
       action="flag"
       att="audience"
       val="general"/>
   </val>
   ```

2. From the first `<prop>` element remove the `@val` attribute.

   By specifying an action of "exclude," but no `@val` attribute, you are saying that any value for the `@audience` attribute should be excluded unless the value is explicitly included. This effectively inverts the normal logic for the `@audience` attribute. It removes the need for you to explicitly exclude every value you don't want.

3. On the second `<prop>` element, change the `@action` value to "include" and the `@val` value to "expert."

   This explicitly includes the value "expert."

   The DITAVAL file should now look like this:

   ```xml
   <?xml version="1.0" encoding="UTF-8"?>
   <val>
     <prop
       action="exclude"
       att="audience"/>
     <prop
   ```

```
      action="include"
      att="audience"
      val="expert"/>
</val>
```

4. Select the Intro to Aikido map in the Map Manager and click the **Configure Transformation Scenario** button (🔧).
5. Select the DITA Map XHTML scenario and click **Edit**.
6. Click on the **Filters** tab and then select the **Use DITAVAL File** radio button.
7. Use the file chooser to navigate to the `audience-expert.ditaval` DITAVAL file. Click **OK** to close the dialog.
8. click **Transform Now** to run the transform.

    The *Yokomenuchi shihonage* topic should reflect only the expert phrase.

9. Save the `audience-expert.ditaval` file as `audience-beginner.ditaval`.
10. Change "expert" to "beginner" in the second `<prop>` element and save the file.
11. Change the transformation scenario to use the beginner DITAVAL file and regenerate the HTML. You should see the beginner version of the technique.

You are now set up to produce either an expert or beginner version of the technique descriptions. But what if you want to produce a version for both experts and beginners?

Authoring Step 17: Configure DITAVAL for flagging

To produce a publication that reflects multiple conditions you need to use flagging rather than filtering. There are many ways that flagging can be implemented. The Open Toolkit lets you do any of the following:

*   Put a graphic before or after the flagged element.
*   Set the foreground or background color of the flagged element.
*   Generate text before or after the flagged element.

For example, you might have nice icons indicating expert and beginner items.

For this exercise you will use generated text to label the descriptions as beginner or advanced. To set up the flagging, perform the following steps:

1. Create a new DITAVAL file or save the one you were just editing as `audience-flag.ditaval`.
2. Delete the first `<prop>` element.

3. On the remaining `<prop>` element, change the `@action` value from "filter" to "flag":

```
<?xml version="1.0" encoding="UTF-8"?>
<val>
  <prop
    action="flag"
    att="audience"
    val="beginner"/>
</val>
```

4. Within the `<prop>` element insert a new `<startflag>` element:

```
<?xml version="1.0" encoding="UTF-8"?>
<val>
  <prop
    action="flag"
    att="audience"
    val="beginner">
    <startflag></startflag>
  </prop>
</val>
```

5. Within the `<startflag>` insert an `<alt-text>` element set its content to "Beginner form: ":

```
<?xml version="1.0" encoding="UTF-8"?>
<val>
  <prop
    action="flag"
    att="audience"
    val="beginner">
    <startflag>
      <alt-text>Beginner form: </alt-text>
    </startflag>
  </prop>
</val>
```

6. Duplicate the `<prop>` element and change `@val` to "expert" and the `<alt-text>` to "Expert form: "

7. In the Map Manager, select the Intro to Aikido map, click the **Configure Transform Scenario**, select the DITA Map XHTML scenario, and click **Edit** to edit it.

8. Select the **Filters** tab and set the DITAVAL file to the `audience-flag.ditaval` file.

9. Generate the HTML and verify that the flagging has been applied.

   If you don't see the flagging, one trick is to set the `@color` attribute on each `<prop>` element. My experiments with Open Toolkit version 1.5.4M2 suggest there is a bug with the textual flagging of

<ph> elements in HTML but that the color is always applied. Using color also makes it easier to visually verify that the flagging is being applied. Once you're satisfied that your DITAVAL configuration is correct, you can remove the color settings.

About the only thing to add to the flagging is the use of graphical icons. For the Intro to Aikido document I have these two graphics:

Figure 2: Beginner and expert icons for flagging

To use these for flagging, you put them in a directory relative to your DITAVAL file, for example, ditavals/icons. You reference the graphics from the DITAVAL file using relative URLs on the <startflag> or <endflag> elements:

```
<prop
  action="flag"
  att="audience"
  val="beginner">
  <startflag imageref="icons/beginner-icon-01.gif">
    <alt-text> Beginner form: </alt-text>
  </startflag>
</prop>
```

The PDF result looks like this:

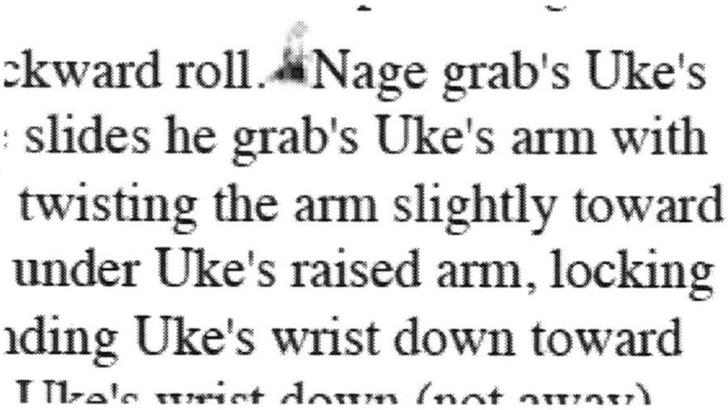

ckward roll. Nage grab's Uke's
slides he grab's Uke's arm with
twisting the arm slightly toward
under Uke's raised arm, locking
ding Uke's wrist down toward
Uke's wrist down (not away)

Figure 3: PDF showing flagging icon

The graphic design of the content is pretty weak in this example, but it demonstrates the behavior.

Having gotten this far, I am seeing that having the description structured as a single paragraph is probably not the most effective presentation and that I need to rethink how I structure the description content. But that sort of refinement of approach is part of the process you should expect if you are trying to apply DITA to a specific body of content. Until you implement use of specific features it will be hard to know how the presentation does or doesn't work. If I was really writing a book about Aikido I would probably start working with a graphic designer to develop a more effective presentation approach and then work out how best to realize that presentation using DITA markup and the processing tools at hand.

Authoring Step 18: Adding metadata to the data

In DITA, metadata is primarily intended to classify content in order to aid in searching. There's more to metadata than classification, of course, but classification is the primary focus of metadata. For a more complete discussion of DITA metadata, see *Data and Metadata in DITA* on page 219.

DITA provides three primary ways to classify content:

- keywords (`<keyword>`) in topic prologs.
- Index entries (`<indexterm>`) in topic prologs or in topic content.
- Arbitrary metadata items (`<data>`) in topic prologs or topic content.

These metadata items can then be used to optimize search in different delivery or management environments. For example, when you generate HTML using the Open Toolkit, keywords and index entries in topics are output as HTML `<meta>` elements, for example:

```
<meta
  name="DC.subject"
  content="development environment,
  setting up, OxygenXML, configuring, Eclipse,
  configuring Ant, configuring for Open Toolkit,
  Ant, within Eclipse"/>
<meta
  name="keywords"
  content="development environment, setting up,
  OxygenXML, configuring, Eclipse,
  configuring Ant, configuring for Open Toolkit,
  Ant, within Eclipse"/>
```

Index entries within topic prologs also contribute to back-of-the-book indexes.

Arbitrary metadata modeled with `<data>` is often the first or second form of specialization that enterprises implement, because every business and subject area has unique aspects to which metadata should refer. Implementing custom `<data>` domains is an easy specialization to do, and you should plan on doing it fairly early if you are applying DITA to documents managed within a non-trivial business process or for non-trivial or specialized products.

In the context of the Introduction to Aikido publication, useful aspects for classification include:

- The specific attack used for a technique, for example, *shomenuchi* (strike to the head) vs. *katate dori* (opposite hand grab).
- Type of attack: strike or grab.
- Instrument of attack: hand, foot, or weapon.
- Type of weapon: hand, foot, knife, stick, or sword.
- Type of response: pin or throw.
- The basic principle applied: *ikkyo* (first principle), *nikkyo* (second principle), etc.
- Whether the technique is an entering technique (*irrimi*) or an avoiding technique (*tenkan*).
- Whether the technique is performed to the inside (*omote*) or outside (*ura*).
- Whether the technique is the formal version expected on exams (*kihon waza*) or an informal version (not *kihon waza*).
- Whether the technique is performed with both parties standing, one standing and one kneeling, or both kneeling.
- The type of *ukemi* (attacker's response) resulting from application of the technique: forward roll, backward roll, break fall, etc.

Looking at these aspects, it should be clear that there is a taxonomy by which all Aikido techniques can be classified. Given a catalog of Aikido techniques you could provide a faceted search or similar search facility to find specific techniques, for example, "find all responses to *shihonage* involving *ikkyo*" or "find all responses to attack with a knife."

To implement this type of search, each technique must be precisely classified in terms of this taxonomy. This requires you to define specialized metadata elements that reflect the taxonomy subjects (type of attack, attack name, instrument of attack, etc.) and specify values taken from controlled lists (to ensure consistency and correctness).

On the other hand, if you just want to generate useful back-of-the-book indexes, you can just add index entries that reflect the terminology and the classifications. However, being simply textual, these aren't quite as precise as using a formal taxonomy.

If you just want to enable reasonably reliable search on specific terms, then you can just use `<keyword>` in topic prologs. In the case of a subject like Aikido, where the terminology is distinctive and there are few ambiguous terms, a simple keyword-based approach will work pretty well.

For other subject areas, where the terminology is not so distinctive and there are lots of ambiguous terms, a taxonomy-based approach will be required. This is typical in scientific and medical publishing, for example.

For this exercise, the goal is to add keywords and index entries to the topics to enable some searching and indexing.

To add classifications, perform these steps

1. Open the Intro to Aikido map in the DITA Map Manager.
2. Open the Rokyu requirements topic (`rokyu-requirements.dita`) in the editor in Author mode.
3. Position the insertion point between the `<shortdesc>` and `<conbody>` elements. Press **Enter** and insert a `<prolog>` element.
4. Press **Enter** and insert a `<metadata>` element. Press **Enter** again and insert a `<keywords>` element.

   `<keywords>` is the container for both `<keyword>` and `<indexterm>` elements within `<prolog>`.

5. Press **Enter** and insert a `<keyword>` element. Set the text to "rokyu."

   The markup should look like this:

```
...
<shortdesc>6th Kyu is the first level
   of white belt earned by Aikido
   beginners.</shortdesc>
<prolog>
   <metadata>
     <keywords>
        <keyword>rokyu</keyword>
     </keywords>
   </metadata>
</prolog>
<conbody>
...
```

6. Move the insertion point outside the `<keyword>` you just created. Press **Enter**, insert an `<indexterm>` element, and set the content to "belt exams."
7. Without moving the insertion point, press **Enter**, insert another `<indexterm>` element, and set the content to "Rokyu."

   The markup should look like this:

```
<prolog>
   <metadata>
     <keywords>
        <keyword>rokyu</keyword>
        <indexterm>belt
          exams<indexterm>Rokyu</indexterm></indexterm>
     </keywords>
   </metadata>
</prolog>
```

8. Generate HTML from the Intro to Aikido map and edit the HTML file
`rokyu-requirements.html`. You should see these two `<meta>` elements:

```
<meta name="DC.subject" content="rokyu, belt exams, Rokyu"/>
<meta name="keywords" content="rokyu, belt exams, Rokyu"/>
```

You can also generate PDF, but you won't see a back-of-the-book index unless you are using an FO engine other than FOP, as FOP does not support index generation. You can get an evaluation license of either Antenna House XSL Formatter or RenderX XEP. When you render to PDF with either of those engines, you should see an index like this:

9. To be more complete, add these index entries as children of `<keywords>`:

```
<prolog>
  <metadata>
    <keywords>
      ...
      <indexterm>belt exams
        <indexterm>Rokyu</indexterm>
        </indexterm>
      <indexterm>belt exams
        <indexterm>6th Kyu</indexterm>
        </indexterm>
      <indexterm>Kyu exams
        <indexterm>6th Kyu</indexterm>
        </indexterm>
    </keywords>
  </metadata>
</prolog>
```

Note the repeat of the top-level index term "belt exams" for the 2nd-level entry "6th Kyu." In theory it should not be necessary to have two separate top-level entries. You should be able to have a single top-level entry with two 2nd-level entries, for example:

```
<indexterm>belt exams
  <indexterm>Rokyu</indexterm>
  <indexterm>6th  dKyu</indexterm>
  </indexterm>
```

However, index processing in the various common DITA tools has historically been flaky at best and not all tools correctly handle this case, including the Open Toolkit, so it's safer to have a new top-level entry for each different 2nd-level or 3rd-level entry you want to create.

10. Edit the *Shomenuchi ikkyo* topic and add a prolog with `<metadata>` and `<keywords>` to it.

11. Add `<keyword>` elements for "shomenuchi," "ikkyo," "strike," and "pin":

```
...
<prolog>
  <metadata>
    <keywords>
      <keyword>shomenuchi</keyword>
      <keyword>ikkyo</keyword>
      <keyword>strike</keyword>
      <keyword>pin</keyword>
    </keywords>
  </metadata>
</prolog>
...
```

This is a cheap form of classification in terms of the informal taxonomy outlined above.

12. Add the following index entries to the `<keywords>` element:

```
      ...
      <indexterm>strikes
          <indexterm>shomenuchi</indexterm></indexterm>
      <indexterm>shomenuchi<indexterm>to
          ikkyo response</indexterm></indexterm>
    </keywords>
  </metdata>
</prolog>
```

13. Edit the *Shomenuchi iriminage* topic, then copy and paste the `<prolog>` from the *Shomenuchi ikkyo* topic into the topic.

14. Change "ikkyo" to "iriminageq" and "pin" to "throw."

15. Add a new keyword for "backward roll."

The markup should look like:

```
...
<prolog>
  <metadata>
    <keywords>
      <keyword>shomenuchi</keyword>
```

```
        <keyword>iriminage</keyword>
        <keyword>strike</keyword>
        <keyword>throw</keyword>
        <keyword>backward roll</keyword>
      </keywords>
    </metadata>
  </prolog>
  . . .
```

You have now added some useful classification and a few index entries to the content. If you generated HTML from the map and published it to a public website, indexing services would index the pages on the specific keywords, so a Google search on "iriminage" would find the *Shomenuchi iriminage* topic and probably rank it a bit higher because of the `<meta>` element.

You can simulate how an XML-aware system might take advantage of the keywords by using OxygenXML's search-over-maps facility to find specific terms only within `<keyword>` elements:

1. Select the Intro to Aikido map in the Map Manager.
2. Right click on one of the nodes in the map and select **Find/Replace in Files....** This opens the **Find/Replace in Files** dialog.
3. The **Scope** should be set to "Current DITA map hierarchy" but if it's not, select that. This will restrict the search to just those files used from the map.
4. Set the **Text to find** field to "strike."
5. Set the **Restrict to XPath** field to "//keyword"
6. Set the **Include Files** field to "*.xml, *.dita."
7. Perform the search. You should get a hit for the two *shomenuchi* topics.
8. Change the text to search on to "pin" and search again. You should only get a hit for the *shomenuchi ikkyo* topic.

This type of XML-aware search is what you would expect tools like XML-aware component management systems to do. In a fully-DITA-aware management system, you would expect to find built-in search features specifically for DITA-defined metadata, as DITA makes a clear distinction between data and metadata.

For delivery using a system like the MarkLogic XML database, you could configure specific indexes for `<keyword>` elements, for example, to enable searching on only those values that occur in the content (in MarkLogic this is a "range index").

It should also be clear from this exercise that just using `<keyword>` to hold the classification values, while it works, is really not sufficiently precise to ensure either authoring consistency or precise retrieval. A complete solution for the Aikido content would require both formally defining the classifying taxonomy and specializing either `<keyword>` or `<data>` to reflect the different aspects and allow for constraining the allowed values. But that is an exercise for later.

It should also be clear how the indexing would go if you were to fully index each topic. This is another place where having specialized classification markup could help. The index entries you created above are, to a large degree, redundant with what you could express with more specialized markup.

The two index entries "strikes, shomenuchi" and "shomenuchi, response to ikkyo" would be derivable from specialized markup like this:

```
<strike>shomenuchi</strike>
<response>ikkyo</response>
```

From these two classifications in the context of the *shomenuchi ikkyo* technique description, you could generate all of these index entries:

- strikes, shomenuchi
- shomenuchi, to ikkyo response
- attacks, strikes, shomenuchi
- responses, to strikes, shomenuchi
- ikkyo, response to shomenuchi
- responses, ikkyo

And others I'm sure I haven't thought of. Multiply that by the number of techniques, and the savings for authors by having the more-precise classification markup is pretty dramatic. Defining the markup as a specialization would not be hard, but implementing generation of the index entries would take a bit more implementation effort, but not a huge amount if you had a general index generation framework that you could extend to contribute synthesized entries.

The final thing to say about metadata is that the markup is pretty straightforward, but the analysis can be quite challenging. Some organizations have well-defined classification taxonomies, but most do not. Taxonomy analysis and design is a specialized skill that most people do not possess. If you need a taxonomy defined, I strongly recommend hiring a taxonomy specialist to help you develop it. Once you have a well-defined taxonomy, working out how to apply it through markup is relatively easy.

Authoring Epilogue: Making a Bookmap

The Bookmap map type is part of the standard DITA vocabulary. It is intended to represent print-primary publications and provides both specialized publication metadata and specialized topicref types that let you explicitly represent things like parts, chapters, and appendixes in the map. The Bookmap design has some flaws (see *Bookmap: An Unfortunate Design* on page 323), but it's still useful for a lot of applications, especially traditional technical documents.

Bookmap is also interesting because the Open Toolkit's PDF transformation type has built-in support for Bookmap that provides more book-like formatting for your map than you get with a generic map. So, if you want a more complete book-style rendering in PDF and you can live within the constraints of the Bookmap markup design, Bookmap can be quite handy.

The Introduction to Aikido publication could certainly benefit from being recast as a bookmap. This is not a hard change to make.

Depending on your publishing requirements you may have different maps for different renditions of the same publication. For example, you might have one map specifically for non-print outputs (online help, websites, etc.) and another for print. In the case of the Aikido information set, you can easily imagine having a single website that includes the content of the Introduction to Aikido and the belt requirements publications as a single unified website with no redundancy, while maintaining the separate print publications for those who want them.

Following that approach, let us create a separate publication structure for the print version of the Introduction to Aikido manual, using the existing topics from their current location.

To create the new Bookmap-based publication, perform these steps:

1. Create the new directory `aikido-introduction-book` under your workspace directory.

    Note that I'm following my earlier recommendation to begin publication file names with "aikido-".

2. Copy the file `intro-to-aikido/intro-to-aikido.ditamap` into the `aikido-introduction-book` directory as file `aikido-introduction-book.ditamap`.

3. Edit the `aikido-introduction-book.ditamap` file in OxygenXML in text mode.

4. In the DOCTYPE declaration change "DITA Map//" to "DITA BookMap//" and "map.dtd" to "bookmap.dtd."

    Note the uppercase "M" in BookMap.

    You don't actually have to change "map.dtd" to "bookmap.dtd" because you should always be resolving the public ID, not the system ID, for the DTD. But people will get confused if you don't change it.

    The markup should now look like this:

    ```
    <!DOCTYPE map PUBLIC "-//OASIS//DTD DITA BookMap//EN" "bookmap.dtd">
    <map>
      <title>Introduction to Aikido</title>
      ...
    ```

5. Change "DOCTYPE map " to "DOCTYPE bookmap " and "map" to "bookmap" in the `<map>` start tag. Note that OxygenXML automatically changes the `<map>` end tag to match the changes you make to the start tag.

The new markup should look like this:

```
<?xml version="1.0" encoding="UTF-8"?>
<!DOCTYPE bookmap PUBLIC "-//OASIS//DTD DITA BookMap//EN" "bookmap.dtd">
<bookmap>
  <title>Introduction to Aikido</title>
  <mapref
    href="topics/aikido-master-glossary-keydefs.ditamap"
    format="ditamap"/>
  ...
  </reltable>
</bookmap>
```

As soon as you make the change, you should see an error message like:

```
Unexpected element "mapref". The content of the parent element type must
match
"((title|booktitle)?,bookmeta?,frontmatter?,chapter*,part*,
(appendices?|appendix*),backmatter?,reltable*)".
```

This is telling you that `<bookmap>` doesn't allow `<mapref>` as a direct child of `<bookmap>` and also shows you what the content model for `<bookmap>` is. Clearly there is a bit more work to do to make the map correct.

6. Select the two `<mapref>` elements and press **ctrl+e** to get the **Tag** dialog. Select `<frontmatter>` and press **Enter** to wrap it around the `<mapref>` elements, resulting in this markup:

```
  ...
  <frontmatter>
    <mapref
href="../intro-to-aikido/topics/aikido-master-glossary-keydefs.ditamap"
      format="ditamap"/>
    <mapref
      href="../common/techniques/aikido-technique-resources.ditamap"
      format="ditamap"/>
  </frontmatter>
  ...
```

The message about the `<mapref>` elements should go away, to be replaced by one for the topicref elements.

7. Look at the message or open the **Model** view and put your cursor just inside the `<bookmap>` start tag. You can see that `<bookmap>` requires the main topicrefs to be either `<part>` or `<chapter>`. That suggests the `<topicref>` should become a `<chapter>` element.

You can, of course, just replace "topicref" with "chapter" in the start tag, but it's useful to explore OxygenXML's XML refactoring features. These let you change markup in bulk reasonably safely.

For example, you can't just do a global change of "topicref" to "chapter" because that would change descendant topicrefs, which you don't want to do.

8. Put your cursor inside the `<topicref>` start tag, right click, and select **Refactoring > Rename Element...**.

This brings up the **Rename** dialog.

9. Make sure that **Rename Element** is selected and select "chapter" from the pulldown list of element types. The list should reflect only those elements that are valid in the current location.

10. Press enter to make the change.

The error message should go away and OxygenXML should report the document as valid. The new markup should look like this:

```
<?xml version="1.0" encoding="UTF-8"?>
<!DOCTYPE bookmap PUBLIC "-//OASIS//DTD DITA BookMap//EN" "bookmap.dtd">
<bookmap>
  <title>Introduction to Aikido</title>
  <frontmatter><mapref
    href="topics/aikido-master-glossary-keydefs.ditamap"
    format="ditamap"/>
  <mapref
    href="../common/techniques/aikido-technique-resources.ditamap"
    format="ditamap"/></frontmatter>
  <chapter
    href="topics/chapter-intro.dita">
    <topicref
      href="topics/rokyu-requirements.dita"/>
  ...
```

11. Save the file and open it in the DITA Map Manager if it's not already open there.

The map manager should show all the references as unresolvable (in the Map Manager you should see red icons with an exclamation point for each unresolvable reference), because you just copied the file from the original directory but haven't updated the @href values to point to the new location.

You could just do a global change on the @href values to fix the references to the topics within the intro-to-aikido directory. Another trick is to save the map into the intro-to-aikido directory, then use OxygenXML to do a save-as into the aikido-intro-book directory. OxygenXML should ask you if you want to update all the topicrefs to reflect the new location.

12. Since you've already made the copy, just do a global change. Return to the main editor window in Text mode and change `href="topics/"` to `href="../intro-to-aikido/topics/"`. Save the file.

13. Return the Map Manager. OxygenXML should automatically update the map and all the topicrefs should resolve correctly. If they don't, check the XML source to make sure you didn't make a mistake in your global change.

You can also use OxygenXML's map validator to check for errors.

14. Generate PDF from the bookmap.

It should work. Open the PDF and see what you got. The chapter topic should be formatted like this:

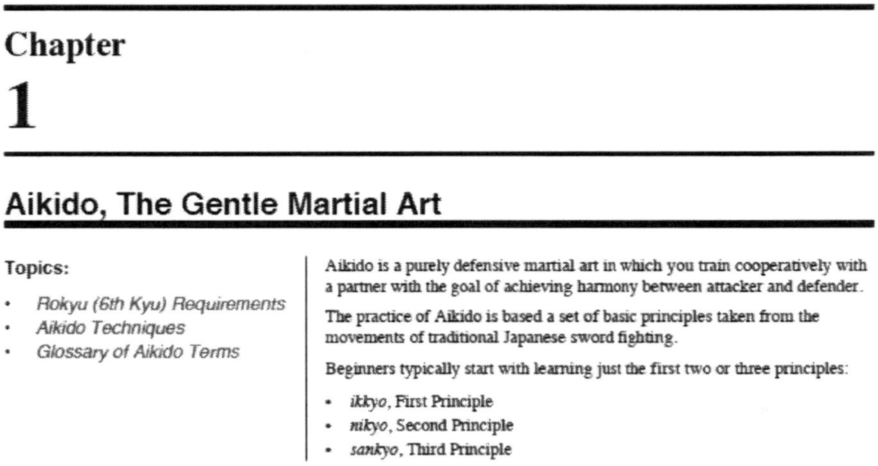

Chapter

1

Aikido, The Gentle Martial Art

Topics:

- *Rokyu (6th Kyu) Requirements*
- *Aikido Techniques*
- *Glossary of Aikido Terms*

Aikido is a purely defensive martial art in which you train cooperatively with a partner with the goal of achieving harmony between attacker and defender.

The practice of Aikido is based a set of basic principles taken from the movements of traditional Japanese sword fighting.

Beginners typically start with learning just the first two or three principles:

- *ikkyo*, First Principle
- *nikyo*, Second Principle
- *sankyo*, Third Principle

Figure 4: PDF rendering of first chapter using Bookmap

You get this chapter treatment because the PDF transform implements special processing for "chapter" topics and it has built-in rules that map topics referenced by `<chapter>` topicrefs to the topic type "chapter."

The PDF should look reasonably nice. The page design is just the default and you can customize it however you need to using the techniques described in this book and in *Customizing the DITA Open Toolkit for Print* by Leigh White.

If you look through the PDF you'll notice that the running heads include the text "OpenTopic." "OpenTopic" is a placeholder for the "product name," where "Open Topic" is the product for which the PDF transformation type was originally implemented by Idiom Inc. (now part of SDL). The presumption of the original Open-Topic-produced PDF transformation was that a given bookmap reflected a specific product being documented and that you'd want to reflect the product name in the running heading.

You can set the product name in several ways, but an easy way to do it is to use the `<prodinfo>` element in the Bookmap's metadata. For example, to set the "product name" to just "Aikido," you would add this markup to the bookmap:

```
<bookmap>
  <title>Introduction to Aikido</title>
  <bookmeta>
    <prodinfo>
      <prodname>Aikido</prodname>
      <vrmlist>
        <vrm version="1"
          release="0"
        />
      </vrmlist>
    </prodinfo>
  </bookmeta>
  <frontmatter>
  ...
```

The `<vrmlist>` element is required by `<prodinfo>` so it has to be there, even if it's not meaningful for your publication. If you regenerate the PDF you should now see "Aikido" where "OpenTopic" was. Not the best running head string, but changing it more would require some customization work.

You should also notice that there is a PDF bookmark tree, but no Contents page in the publication. To get the contents page you must add a `<toc>` element within a `<booklists>` element within `<frontmatter>`:

```
  ...
  <frontmatter>
    <mapref
      href="../intro-to-aikido/topics/aikido-master-glossary-keydefs.ditamap"

      format="ditamap"/>
    <mapref
      href="../common/techniques/aikido-technique-resources.ditamap"
      format="ditamap"/>
    <booklists>
      <toc/>
    </booklists>
  </frontmatter>
  ...
```

Regenerate the PDF, and you should now have a Contents page.

There is of course more you can do with Bookmap, but this gets you a publication with an appropriate publication-specific running head, nice chapter openers, and a Table of Contents page.

Observe how all the formatting changes were the result of using a different map, one that uses specific topicref types to impose different semantics onto topics, namely being a chapter or an appendix. The PDF processing then uses those imposed types to do the right thing in the output. This is a powerful bit of leverage that distinguishes DITA from other XML applications, where the content and its structural role within a publication are inextricably bound together.

Authoring: Wrap Up

You have now done pretty much everything there is to do with DITA documents. You should have a feeling for how authoring works, for the general practice and implications for reuse, and for what it means to classify and index DITA content. You should also be more comfortable with applying the DITA Open Toolkit to content, at least through OxygenXML's user interface.

Note that I didn't show you how to run the Toolkit from the command line because, with tools like OxygenXML, there's simply no reason to use the command line, except in rare cases. I almost never do. I do have project-specific Ant scripts that will run the Toolkit, but I normally run them from Eclipse and not from the command line. It's good to know how to run transforms from the command line, but I will leave that as an exercise for the reader.

You may have also noticed that the organization of the files for this exercise is not necessarily ideal. The subject of file organization and naming is covered in the next section.

Managing a Publication's Maps and Topics

The term *management* can mean a number of different things, but in this context I primarily mean the task of storing and organizing the maps, topics, and non-DITA resources (graphics, videos, etc.) that make up the information set you are responsible for.

For the purposes of this section, I will use the term *repository* to mean "the body of information components you or your system is directly responsible for." This use of the term *repository* does not imply the use of a literal repository in the sense of a source code control system or a component management system. It just means "all the stuff you've got that you might organize with maps and publish in a DITA-ey way."

Managing DITA content usually involves the following:

- Managing the names of files, IDs used on elements, and key names for key references.
- Managing the document source files using some form of versioning system, such as a source code control system, component management system, or document management system.
- Managing different configurations of content maintained concurrently, such as multiple versions of a product for which distinct versions of the documentation are required.
- Managing knowledge of the dependencies among topics and among maps.

- Managing the working vocabulary modules and shell document types used by the DITA documents.
- Managing the data processing systems that act on the DITA content during ingestion, export, or output generation.

Larger authoring system management tasks include managing the integration of the data management systems with authoring tools, with other information systems, and so on. Specific content or component management tools will have their own attendant configuration, customization, and management tasks. Those are beyond the scope of this book.

The DITA architecture was designed to support management of large volumes of data acted on by large teams using minimal tools. DITA relies very little on the kind of "magic" that requires a dedicated content management system to manage, such as resolving abstract identifiers into specific resources dynamically. However, the DITA 1.2 key reference facility does approach that sort of magic, and it does allow you to use whatever degree of indirection and abstraction is required for connecting things together. It's a powerful feature of DITA, but it's optional and, therefore, not a cost of entry.

Many groups, even large groups, using DITA have been quite successful using off-the-shelf editors with open-source code control repositories like SVN or GIT and the Open Toolkit to produce the output they need. By the same token, many groups have failed by trying to implement too quickly a component management system that was too ambitious. It is usually easier to add to a system that is underpowered than to take away from a system that is over featured.

At the end of the day, good DITA management is fundamentally about good organization, clear conventions, especially naming conventions, and simplicity. Your focus should primarily be on getting the data and content right and not on the specific features of a given tool. Tools will come and go, but your data is, ideally, timeless.

When looking at requirements, I ask the question, "can this work on the file system with brute force or does it require some complex management system to work at all?" I try to think of content and component management systems as nothing more than very large optimization strategies for things you can do just as well, if not as quickly, from the command line using normal tools. I find that to be a very good test of requirements.

You have to look at component management requirements critically. In particular, requirements that demand lots of fine-grained reuse or lots of fine-grained linking are always suspect because people tend to over value these features, and they usually require a huge effort to support and implement.

DITA does a nice job of making re-use at the topic level (coarse-grained reuse) about as easy as it can be. Fine-grained reuse at the element level (conref) is also easy, but it is more difficult to manage because of the tight dependencies created, both the topic-to-topic dependencies and the rhetorical dependency of a topic on the information correctness, not just addressability, of the re-used content. When you are doing reuse and have multiple versions in time or parallel variants of the same topic, the configuration management and quality control challenges can be daunting indeed. Quite often they erase any potential savings from the reuse itself.

On the other hand, where reuse is a hard requirement, for example, in safety-critical applications where it is essential to avoid error by removing duplication of critical values like part numbers or tolerances, DITA gives you tools to author and manage the reuse.

Before I get too much farther into this section, I need to make a few disclaimers. At the time of writing I work for a company, RSI Content Solutions, that builds and sells DITA-aware component management systems. I have spent a good part of my career as a practitioner implementing SGML- and XML- and DITA-aware component management systems. I have integrated or customized almost every SGML- and XML-aware content management tool there is or was.

And I can tell you with some authority that you can get a huge amount of mileage out of Subversion or its equivalent, any of the top-tier commercial DITA-aware editors (Arbortext Editor, OxygenXML, XMetal), and the Open Toolkit if you have a technical resource to put on the task. That is, somebody, maybe you, who can hook up the pieces, do the configuration and customization required, and train users.

If you don't have that technical resource, there are relatively low-cost turnkey systems, such as EasyDITA and DocZone, that can get you up and running with a minimal investment.

If you have complex business processes to automate, complex editorial processes to support with capabilities like automated review tools, large volumes of data to search quickly and effectively, or requirements that go beyond simply authoring DITA content and producing HTML, PDF, and EPUB, then you will want to look at more complete and involved component management solutions.

But, based on my experience, unless you have a good understanding of your requirements going in, you will be best served by starting small and only moving toward larger systems after you understand your requirements and can really justify the investment.

And of course, the DITA technology landscape is constantly improving, with new tools coming out and old tools constantly improving their game. A cool thing about XML, and DITA in particular, is that you should be able to move your content from one management environment to another with a relatively modest effort, especially if you've kept the focus on your data and avoided depending any more than you absolutely have to on proprietary features of specific products.

A War Story: I fail by succeeding completely

By way of illustration, a war story.

In the late 90's I was part of a team hired by Woodward Governor Company to design and do the initial implementation of an SGML-based system for managing the assembly, repair, test, and disassembly manuals for Woodward's jet engine fuel controls. This particular division of Woodward built (and still builds) fuel controls for jet engines. These are, of course, a safety-critical device, and the accuracy of the manuals is of paramount importance. The content is constantly being updated as the engineers refine the devices.

For this project, we had the following primary requirements:

1. Implement a conref-like mechanism so that part numbers were authored exactly once wherever they might be mentioned in procedures. This would ensure that if a part number changed, the change would be reflected everywhere that part number was used. It would also enable navigable links from mentions of parts to the parts catalog in an eventual online version of the manuals.

2. Enable publication of interactive, online versions of the manuals, removing the need to manage physical change pages as manuals were updated, and thus ensuring that technicians were always working with the latest procedures.

3. Reduce writer headcount. This was simply a sad fact of the economics at the time: they had to reduce headcount, and technology would enable that.[11]

As you might imagine from requirement (3), the budget was constrained. We had enough scope to do a thorough analysis and implementation design or to buy commercial tools, but not both.

The project was managed by Dave Williams, who is still at Woodward at the time of writing. Dave chose, we thought correctly, to go for the analysis and design and do an inexpensive initial implementation, essentially a proof of concept. A more robust implementation could come later, driven by our solid analysis and design.

At the start of the project, the documents were managed on authors' PCs—there was no existing repository of any sort. They had chosen SoftQuad's Author/Editor SGML editing tool (the precursor to today's XMetal editor). I don't remember how they were going to do print output, but that wasn't a focus of the project. Probably some custom DSSSL implementation or something (this was before XSLT) or maybe some Python code or something. I really don't remember.

Our general implementation approach was to use the open-source CVS code control system as a central versioned repository for the source files. We implemented a simple integration of Author/Editor with CVS to enable checkin and checkout of files to authors' PCs.

The main challenge was link management. In order to enable authoring of the links to part numbers, we needed to implement a little link database that would provide lists of available part numbers to the editing tool so it could both construct the right link markup and resolve the links in the editor to display the part numbers.

As I was starting on the implementation activity I was explicitly instructed by my boss at the time to not do anything that would perform or scale, as this was a proof of concept and we wanted to make sure Woodward came back with more budget to implement a production-quality solution once the value of the approach was demonstrated.

---

[11] This was the one time in my career that I was explicitly a "Bob." However, I never had to ask "what would you say you *do* here?" See the movie "Office Space" if this reference is not immediately obvious.

The link management piece used CVS commit hooks to trigger the grabbing of the relevant part information from the docs and thereby maintained an index of part numbers to part descriptions in the markup for use by the editing tools. I started to implement this index using a flat file and quickly realized that was too much work. So I looked around and found a little in-memory SQL database implemented entirely in Python, Gadfly (*http://gadfly.sourceforge.net/*). I thought "this can't possibly perform or scale, it's just a little in-memory database." The first part of my analysis was correct; using Gadlfy to manage the little index was a piece of cake. The link resolution functions were provided by the GroveMinder product, a HyTime implementation that happened to provide a Python API and was itself easy to integrate.

So I quickly implemented the necessary link management features, closed up the hood, and went home, knowing we'd hear from Woodward soon enough.

The phone never rang.

We maintained contact with Dave over the years, and he consistently reported that he was completely satisfied with the system, they were using it just as they had intended, and everything was great.

My boss was not pleased.

Fast forward 10 years. We finally get that call from Dave saying that Gadfly had *finally* run out of steam, they wanted to replace it with MySQL, and could we help with that? Of course we said yes.

So a system built on two fairly light-weight but very reliable open-source tools, CVS and Gadfly, and a little bit of custom code (none of it rocket science) satisfied the authoring and content management needs of the fuel controls writing team for a decade. What the system itself did from a linking standpoint was fairly sophisticated, but that sophistication was all in the data and in the GroveMinder product, which implemented HyTime linking and address processing (in a way that is analogous to how the Open Toolkit implements DITA linking and addressing processing). The actual data management tools didn't need to be that sophisticated to meet requirements.

Of course, Woodward was not doing some things that really do require more sophistication, such as managing translation workflows or automating complex business processes, but at the same time they're not atypical either.

Just because your data needs to be sophisticated doesn't necessarily mean that your supporting tools must also be sophisticated, at least not to get started.

DITA file organization

Probably the single most important aspect of DITA management is naming things, and in particular, naming and organizing the files that make up your information set.

Clear, well-thought-out naming conventions help everyone find things and predict where things are or should be. Good organization of files into directories or equivalent containers also helps in finding things and keeping them neat and organized.

Because DITA depends on references between files, which of course reflect where the files are relative to each other, moving files around or renaming them is inherently disruptive. So it's important to define appropriate conventions and practices that are likely to stand the test of time.

If you are managing your content within a component management system that does not impose a particular organizational structure, then you will have more flexibility in how you name and organize things. But if not, organization will be an important up-front consideration.

It's impossible to specify a one-size-fits-all file naming and organization convention, but the following general practices and guidelines seem to serve well:

- Use subdirectories to organize content that has a natural hierarchy. Having too many maps or topics in a single directory tends to make the files harder to work with.
- Use submaps to organize related components and have one map per directory.

  For example, if you have a publication organized into parts and chapters, have one directory per part, with a submap for each part and subdirectories under that for each chapter, with a submap for each chapter. With the chapter directories, use subdirectories for different categories of topic or non-DITA components.

- Use subdirectories to organize topics that naturally group together, such as all topics of a particular information type or all topics on a specific subject or associated with a specific product component. The nature of the grouping will be specific to your content.

  The primary concern here is with ease of navigation through the files when presented in typical file system user interfaces like Windows Explorer, Finder, or file-chooser dialogs. However, having too many nested directories becomes annoying and counter-productive.

- Name things semantically, not based on their position within a specific publication. That is "chapter-intro" not "chapter-01."

  The exception is when the position is invariant, mandated such that it will not change, or is the most natural choice for authors. That is, don't abstract when the abstraction causes more confusion than it avoids.

- Name things so they naturally sort together.

  This usually means using prefixes like "authoring-foo," "authoring-bar," rather than "bar-authoring," "foo-authoring."

- Use a "common" directory structure for things that are likely to be used in more than one map.

  In general, you should expect to have a common area that holds most of your content, and per-publication structures that hold those things specific to just those publications.

- Store topics as separate files, except where a set of topics wouldn't make sense in isolation, such as in narrative content where the subordinate topics are part of the narrative flow and would never be used in some other context.

  While DITA doesn't absolutely require one-topic-per-file, following that practice usually makes things easier. The main exception is for content such as narrative content where it just make things harder to have separate files for subordinate topics. If necessary, you can always burst out subordinate topics and generate maps that produce the same structure as the multiple topic file, and you can also do the reverse and combine topics that were authored as single files into multiple topic files.

Even if your initial use of DITA focuses on topics as the unit of reuse, you should expect that over time submaps will become the primary unit of reuse as authors become more comfortable with using submaps to group related topics together into reusable groups, such as the combination of a task and its supporting concepts. This is especially likely if management practices or tools require or encourage having exactly one topic per file.

The naming conventions for files also apply to keys and, to a lesser degree, to element IDs. Keys will become a primary way for authors to point to things within the repository so they will tend to function like filenames. However, because keys are a flat namespace within a given root map, there is no natural way to organize them hierarchically. Therefore, using naming conventions that allow related keys to sort together is very important. I like a convention that uses the type of thing the key points to as a prefix. An example of this is the use of the prefix "gloss-" for the glossary entries in the authoring tutorial.

Given these principles, let's apply them to the resources that make up the authoring tutorial to see how we might improve the organization.

In the authoring tutorial I purposely kept the file organization very simple to keep the focus on the primary task of creating the maps and topics. But by the end of the tutorial you should have started to see that that file organization was not ideal.

At the end of the tutorial, the file organization looked like this:

```
workspace/
  common/
    techniques/
      topics/
        *.dita
  ditavals/
    *.ditaval
    icons/
      *.jpg, *.png, etc.
  intro-to-aikido/
    intro-to-aikido.ditamap
    topics/
      *.dita
    aikido-master-glossary-keydefs.ditamap
```

```
graphics/
    *.jpg, *.png, etc.
aikido-belt-requirements/
    aikido-belt-requirements.ditamap
    topics/
        *.dita
```

This organization does reflect some or our organizational principles, such as one directory per publication and a common area, but it doesn't reflect others.

If you imagine this publication fully realized, you should start to see you would have the following kind of content:

- Hundreds of separate technique description topics
- Several hundred glossary entry topics
- Lots of graphics for the descriptions.
- Lots of videos, ideally one per technique.
- More conceptual content not reflected in the exercise.

For example, the glossary entries are currently in the `intro-to-aikido/topics` directory. Their naming convention, `gloss-*`, causes them to group together, but there will be several hundred entries (the complete glossary included in the sample materials has over 500 separate glossary entries). Managing these within the `topics/` directory is clearly not good. In addition, the glossary is probably best managed as a common resource.

How would you reorganize the glossary content?

My solution would be as follows:

- Create a new directory, `common/aikido-master-glossary`
- Within the `aikido-master-glossary` directory, create a subdirectory for each letter group.
- Move the `aikido-master-glossary-keydefs.ditamap` file to the `aikido-master-glossary` directory.
- Move the glossary entries into their appropriate letter group directory.
- Update the master glossary keydefs map to reflect the new locations of the glossary entries, using `<topicgroup>` elements with navigation titles to organize the key definitions by letter group. This use of navigation titles with topic groups takes advantage of the explicit rule in the DITA specification that a `<topicgroup>` element is always treated as a topic group even if it has a navigation title.

It might be useful to have separate submaps for each letter group, but probably not, since it's unlikely you'd use an individual letter group by itself. So the letter group directories just serve to make navigating the directory tree a little easier.

To complete the glossary rework, I would create a new separate "Master Glossary" publication that uses the master glossary keydef map and creates a navigation tree organizing the glossary entries for publication, something like this:

```xml
<?xml version="1.0" encoding="UTF-8"?>
<!DOCTYPE bookmap PUBLIC "-//OASIS//DTD DITA BookMap//EN" "bookmap.dtd">
<bookmap>
  <booktitle>
    <mainbooktitle>Master Aikido Glossary</mainbooktitle>
  </booktitle>
  <frontmatter>
    <mapref
href="../aikido-master-glossary/aikido-master-glossary-keydefs.ditamap"/>
  </frontmatter>
  <chapter href="master-aikido-glossary.dita">
    <topichead>
      <topicmeta>
        <navtitle>A</navtitle>
      </topicmeta>
      <topicref keyref="gloss-ai"/>
      ...
    </topichead>
    <topichead>
      <topicmeta>
        <navtitle>B</navtitle>
      </topicmeta>
      <topicref keyref="gloss-barai-harai"/>
      ...
    </topichead>
    ...
    <topichead>
      <topicmeta>
        <navtitle>Z</navtitle>
      </topicmeta>
      <topicref keyref="gloss-za"/>
      ...
    </topichead>
  </chapter>
</bookmap>
```

The same sort of rework could be usefully applied to the technique reference topics. It would probably make sense to organize the techniques by principle or by attack (as that's the initial part of each technique name).

But note that in the case of techniques it's less obvious what the best organizational scheme is, because each technique is classified by several different aspects, any one of which could be usefully used for organization (except perhaps pins vs. throws, as that wouldn't do much to create shorter lists of techniques).

One temptation would be to use a deeper directory structure to reflect the classification dimensions or aspects, for example:

```
techniques/
    throws/
       iriminage/
         holds/
            katate-dori/
            kosa-dori/
         strikes/
            munetsuki
            shomenuchi/
       kaitenage
       shihonage/
```

This is a sensible organization, but it would require a lot of navigation to find specific files. In addition, the choice of which aspect to use at each level is arbitrary and might not match authors' expectations. It also requires up-front knowledge of how a given technique should be classified, which not all authors will have.

In my experience, it's usually better to either pick just one level of organization or use a neutral approach such as organizing into letter groups by technique name.

If you are using a component management system where you can have multiple organizations applied to components, you could have multiple organizations applied to the content so you that you don't have to choose. This works especially well if the organization can be dynamic, using searches against metadata to find topics.

But in practice, when the content is this complicated, users tend to prefer a search-based approach to finding things, rather than a tree-navigation-based approach. It is this ability to search that tends to justify moving beyond simple code-control-based management approaches and putting a true component management system in place.

Another question that would need answering for the technique content is how to organize the graphics? It might make sense to put each technique's graphics in the same directory as the technique topic that uses it. However, the graphics might be useful as standalone resources used in other contexts, so it might make more sense to organize the graphics separately, perhaps in a parallel directory structure or in a completely different structure.

For the graphics, having one or more key-definition maps that serve as catalogs would also be useful. Such maps can serve much the same function as a component management system that has the ability to apply different organizing structures to objects. Key-defining maps can also use metadata in the key definitions to impose classifying metadata onto graphics to help with search and retrieval.

Another problem with the Aikido content set is the file naming. You'll notice that the names of the two publications are not consistent: one is "intro-to-aikido," the other is "aikido-belt-requirements." Per the "sort together" practice, it would probably be better to use "aikido-" as a common prefix if there will be other publications for other subjects (say other martial arts like Judo, Kung-Fu, and Tae-Kwon-Do). If the information set will always be exclusive to Aikido then using prefixes that reflect the type of document might make more sense: "intro-," "testing-"," etc. But the current names are clearly not reflective any particular naming approach.

This analysis of the Aikido information set should give you a feel for the sorts of questions and considerations to apply when trying to work out the naming and organizational scheme for a new DITA environment. The main thing is consistency and sensitivity to the culture of your authors and the subject area of the information.

It is also important to experiment and test. Until you actually populate a candidate organizational scheme with realistic data you may not see inherent practical problems. For example, using a taxonomy as the organizing scheme may make sense until you realize that it's too flat and each term will have hundreds or thousands of items under it or it's too deep and navigating it to select things is prohibitively hard. Take the time to mock up proposed ideas with a realistic volume and variety of data before committing your content and systems to a particular approach.

Reacting to Changes in File Location

Despite your best efforts at defining a robust and sensible file organization and naming scheme, there will always come a time when you need to move things around and update all the maps and topics to reflect the new locations of things.

The practical question is, how do you update things so they work again with the least amount of effort?

The first principle is to always use key-based references for all references from topics to things in other topics. This avoids the need to worry about the specific locations of topics relative to each other and simply avoids a whole host of problems.

The second principle is to always use keys for references to topics from maps or to non-key-defining submaps from maps, especially when there is or will be more than one map that uses the same topic or submap. This also avoids problems when topics or submaps have to move around, limiting the scope of any changes to just the key definitions for the topics affected.

But at some point you still have to update @href attributes to modify the URL references to reflect the new locations of the moved topics or maps.

Assuming the URLs you have to modify are limited to maps, then in most cases a simple global search and replace will do the trick. Many editors, including OxygenXML and the Eclipse IDE, support global search and replace over multiple files. Both OxygenXML and Eclipse let you use regular expressions if you need to.

If you're doing a more complex reorganization, such as organizing a flat set of glossary entries into letter-group directories, then XSLT 2 is your friend if you don't already use traditional tools like Perl, sed, and awk.

With XSLT 2 you can generate multiple result files from a single transform, so you can calculate new filenames, copy files to new locations using an identity transform, and generate maps that reference the new files all from a single transform.

The DITA for Publishers Toolkit plugins (*http://dita4publishers.sourceforge.net*) include a generic path-manipulation XSLT library, relpath-utils.xsl, that makes it easy to manipulate and construct relative URLs. You will find it in the net.sourceforge.dita4publishers.common.xslt plugin. The same plugin also provides a general DITA utility function package, dita-support-lib.xsl, that provides functions for resolving topicrefs to topics, among other things.

For example, an XSLT to process the flat list of glossary entries into a new organization using letter groups would look like this:

```
<?xml version="1.0" encoding="UTF-8"?>
<xsl:stylesheet xmlns:xsl="http://www.w3.org/1999/XSL/Transform"
  xmlns:xs="http://www.w3.org/2001/XMLSchema"
  xmlns:xd="http://www.oxygenxml.com/ns/doc/xsl"
  xmlns:df="http://dita2indesign.org/dita/functions"
  xmlns:relpath="http://dita2indesign/functions/relpath"
  xmlns:ditaarch="http://dita.oasis-open.org/architecture/2005/"
  xmlns:local="local-functions"
  exclude-result-prefixes="xs xd df relpath local ditaarch"
  version="2.0">

  <!-- Transform to organize a flat list of glossary entry topics
       into directories by letter group.

       Generates a new map with topicrefs organized by letter
       group within topicgroups.
  -->

  <xsl:import href="relpath_util.xsl"/>
  <xsl:import href="dita-support-lib.xsl"/>

  <xsl:param name="outputDir" as="xs:string"/>

  <xsl:output indent="yes"/>

  <xsl:output doctype-public="-//OASIS//DTD DITA Map//EN"
    doctype-system="map.dtd"
    indent="yes"
  />
```

```
  <xsl:template match="/">
    <!-- Input is a DITA map with one topicref per glossary entry -->
    <map>
      <title>Glossary organized by letter group</title>
      <xsl:for-each-group select="//*[df:isTopicRef(.)]"
        group-by="local:getLetterGroup(.)"
        >
        <xsl:sort select="current-grouping-key()"/>
        <xsl:message>+ [INFO] Creating letter group "<xsl:sequence
select="current-grouping-key()"/>"...</xsl:message>
        <topicgroup>
          <topicmeta><navtitle><xsl:sequence
select="current-grouping-key()"/></navtitle></topicmeta>
          <xsl:apply-templates select="current-group()">
            <xsl:with-param
              name="letterGroup"
              select="current-grouping-key()"
              tunnel="yes"
              as="xs:string"/>
          </xsl:apply-templates>
        </topicgroup>
      </xsl:for-each-group>
    </map>
  </xsl:template>

  <xsl:template match="*[df:isTopicRef(.)]">
    <xsl:param name="letterGroup" as="xs:string"
      tunnel="yes"
    />
    <xsl:variable name="topic" as="element()?"
      select="df:resolveTopicRef(.)"
    />
    <xsl:choose>
      <xsl:when test="$topic">
        <xsl:variable name="filename" as="xs:string"
          select="relpath:getName(base-uri($topic))"
        />
        <xsl:variable name="resultRelpath" as="xs:string"
          select="concat($letterGroup, '/', $filename)"/>
        <xsl:variable name="resultUrl" as="xs:string"
          select="relpath:newFile($outputDir, $resultRelpath)"
        />
        <xsl:message>+ [INFO] Creating result topic "<xsl:sequence
select="$resultRelpath"/>"...</xsl:message>

        <!-- Generate an updated version of this topicref: -->
        <xsl:apply-templates mode="copy" select=".">
          <xsl:with-param name="resultRelpath"
            tunnel="yes"
            as="xs:string"
            select="$resultRelpath"/>
```

```
        </xsl:apply-templates>
        <xsl:variable name="dtdPublicId" as="xs:string"
        >
          <xsl:choose>
            <xsl:when test="df:class($topic, 'glossentry/glossentry')">
            <xsl:sequence select="'-//OASIS//DTD DITA Glossary Entry//EN'"/>

            </xsl:when>
            <xsl:when test="df:class($topic, 'glossgroup/glossgroup')">
            <xsl:sequence select="'-//OASIS//DTD DITA Glossary Group//EN'"/>

            </xsl:when>
            <xsl:otherwise>
              <xsl:sequence select="'-//OASIS//DTD DITA Topic//EN'"/>
            </xsl:otherwise>
          </xsl:choose>
        </xsl:variable>
        <xsl:variable name="dtdSystemId" as="xs:string"
          select="concat(normalize-space(tokenize($topic/@class,
'/')[last()]), '.dtd')"
          />
        <xsl:result-document href="{$resultUrl}"
          doctype-public="{$dtdPublicId}"
          doctype-system="{$dtdSystemId}"
          >
          <xsl:apply-templates select="$topic" mode="copy"/>
        </xsl:result-document>
      </xsl:when>
      <xsl:otherwise>
        <xsl:message>- [ERROR] Failed to resolve topicref <xsl:sequence
select="."/> to a topic.</xsl:message>
      </xsl:otherwise>
    </xsl:choose>
  </xsl:template>

  <!-- =============================
       Mode copy

       Does an identity transform
       ============================= -->

  <xsl:template mode="copy" match="*">
    <xsl:copy copy-namespaces="no">
      <xsl:apply-templates select="@*, node()" mode="#current"/>
    </xsl:copy>
  </xsl:template>

  <xsl:template mode="copy" match="@href" priority="10">
    <xsl:param name="resultRelpath" tunnel="yes" as="xs:string?"
    />
    <xsl:choose>
```

```
   <xsl:when test="$resultRelpath">
     <xsl:attribute name="{name(.)}"
       select="$resultRelpath"
     />
   </xsl:when>
   <xsl:otherwise>
     <xsl:sequence select="."/>
   </xsl:otherwise>
 </xsl:choose>
</xsl:template>

<xsl:template mode="copy" priority="10"
 match="
 keydef/@processing-role[. = 'resource-only'] |
 @domains |
 @class |
 @ditaarch:DITAArchVersion
 ">
 <!-- Suppress these attributes, which should be
   defaulted in the DTD.
   -->
</xsl:template>

<xsl:template mode="copy" match="@*">
 <xsl:sequence select="."/>
</xsl:template>


<!-- =============================
     Mode titleText

     Produces a single string from title
     elements.
     ============================= -->

<xsl:template match="*[df:class(., 'topic/title')]" mode="titleText">
 <xsl:apply-templates mode="#current"/>
</xsl:template>

<xsl:template mode="titleText" match="*">
 <xsl:apply-templates mode="#current"/>
</xsl:template>

<xsl:template match="text()" mode="titleText">
 <xsl:sequence select="."/>
</xsl:template>

<!-- =============================
 Local functions
 ============================= -->
```

```
  <xsl:function name="local:getLetterGroup" as="xs:string">
    <xsl:param name="topicRef" as="element()"/>
    <xsl:variable name="topic" as="element()?"
      select="df:resolveTopicRef($topicRef)"
    />
    <xsl:variable name="titleText">
      <xsl:apply-templates mode="titleText" select="$topic/*[df:class(.,
'topic/title')]"/>
    </xsl:variable>
    <xsl:variable name="letterGroup"
      select="upper-case(substring(normalize-space($titleText), 1, 1))"
    />
    <xsl:sequence select="$letterGroup"/>
  </xsl:function>
</xsl:stylesheet>
```

This transform demonstrates several useful XSLT techniques that you can use for similar types of processing, including map-driven processing in XSLT, generation of multiple result documents, and identity transforms, all important tools for working with DITA content in XSLT.

The root template uses a for-each-group instruction to group the topicrefs in the map by letter group. The local function local:getLetterGroup() determines the letter group by resolving the topicref to a topic, getting the topic's title text, and then getting the first letter of the title text. It uses the DITA support library function df:resolveTopicRef(), which resolves topicrefs.

The direct output of the root template is a new map with the topicrefs grouped by letter group.

The default-mode template for topicrefs constructs both the relative URL and the absolute URL for the result document, using functions from the `relpath_utils.xsl` library, and then generates both a copy of the original topicref and a new result document for the referenced topic.

These templates use the DITA support library convenience function df:class() to match elements on DITA class value. This function is equivalent to the usual `contains(@class, ' topic/title ')` predicate, but is slightly less verbose and removes the need to remember the leading and trailing spaces around the class value.[12] It also anticipates a future where the class declaration mechanism might be different.

The templates in the mode "copy" do a normal XSLT 2 identity transform. There are also templates in this mode to handle @href where a new result URL has been specified. It also handles DITA defaulted attributes so they won't be copied to the new topics or maps.

---

[12] The value of the DITA @class attribute is a sequence of blank-delimited module/tagname pairs. In order to match on them reliably, you must include the leading and trailing space. For example, if you only matched on " topic/p" (no trailing space, you would also match on " topic/ph". The value of the @class attribute must include a trailing space at the end of the value, for example, class="- topic/p " not class="- topic/p".

Note the use of tunnel parameters for the letter group and result URLs. Tunnel parameters are an XSLT 2 feature. Tunnel parameters are automatically passed down to all match templates and named templates, removing the need to explicitly get and re-pass parameters from template to template. If a template needs a parameter it gets it, otherwise it just ignores it.

An exercise would be to extend this transform to also generate a separate publication map that links each glossary entry into an appropriate navigation tree by key reference. Or, perhaps more usefully, create a more generic transform that takes an existing key definition map and generates a publication map with a reference to each key defined in the input map.

DITA-Aware Component Management Systems

What can you reasonably expect from DITA-aware component management systems?

DITA content can be managed in any XML-aware content or component management system, but many component management systems are now claiming to provide DITA-specific features.

What should you expect from a DITA-aware component management system or what can you reasonably expect?

DITA-aware systems may be general-purpose or special-purpose. General-purpose DITA-aware systems should support any valid DITA document or any valid DITA document specialized from a specific set of base vocabulary modules. Special-purpose DITA-aware systems may be tied to specific vocabulary or constraint modules. Both types can be conforming DITA systems. In particular, DITA conformance does not require specialization-awareness nor does it require support for any particular vocabulary module or element types.

This means, for example, that you could have a fully-conforming DITA-aware system that only supports a specific set of vocabulary modules using a specific set of constraint modules. Such a system might be very task specific or be intended for a particular vertical industry that happens to use a DITA-based vocabulary but does not require or anticipate interoperation with arbitrary DITA content. Or a system might only support a subset of the base DITA vocabulary in order to minimize the need for up-front configuration or to provide a "one-size-fits-all" solution or to constrain the DITA vocabulary and features supported to the functions provided by the underlying implementation platform. Provided there is clear documentation about the vocabulary modules supported and the constraint modules required, the system is conforming as long as all mandatory processing—primarily address resolution and conref processing—is otherwise correct.

But most commercial DITA-aware systems will be, or claim to be, general-purpose systems that can handle any conforming vocabulary or constraint modules. The main question for these systems is their degree of specialization awareness.

Specialization Awareness

Specialization awareness means the ability to handle processing of elements and attributes based on their class ancestry, not their direct tag or attribute names.

The ideal DITA-aware system would be able to do everything in terms of DITA class values. The OxygenXML editor is an example of a tool that is very nearly fully specialization aware.

However, most commercial DITA-aware CMS systems were not originally developed with DITA in mind, and they almost always assume that element types or element/attribute values are the only useful way to associate functionality and configuration. Many of the commercial CMS systems predate DITA or at least predate DITA's wider adoption.

So you will probably find that most CMS systems do not allow you to define configuration in terms of class hierarchy, but you should not hold that against them, especially if the tools were not developed in the last couple of years. However, that doesn't mean you shouldn't complain about the lack of that functionality. Part of the point of DITA's class mechanism is that specialized content "just works" in tools that understand the base types.

Many CMS systems were designed around the assumption and misconception that specific DTD files, represented by specific public identifiers, were meaningful. Many, if not most, XML-aware CMS systems bind configuration to specific DTDs or schemas. This was always wrong, for all SGML and XML document types. It was wrong because the external DTD subset a document uses tells you nothing reliable. You can locally map a public identifier to any file you want. You can use internal declaration subsets to change or override the declarations in the external DTD. While people and systems acted as if public IDs meant something, in fact they never did and never will. The fact is, SGML and XML have always lacked a mechanism like the one provided by DITA document types. Namespaces come closer, but since there is no standard way to associate a namespace to its rules, namespaces don't fully solve the problem.

Systems that bind configuration to document type public IDs or namespace names cause a practical problem for DITA, where there many be any number of document type shells for the same logical document type. Each document type shell must have a different public ID or system ID. Such systems make it unnecessarily difficult, or at least annoying, to configure DITA document types.

In the ideal DITA-aware CMS, document-type-level configuration would be bound to DITA document types, that is, to unique sets of vocabulary modules or sets of vocabulary modules and constraint modules. But it is probably unlikely that you will find any DITA-aware CMS systems that do that. Again, you shouldn't hold that against them, but you shouldn't be silent about it either. Such systems were *always broken* but DITA makes it really obvious that that is the case.

Import and Export

A primary challenge with XML management in general is import and export. Most of the complexity with XML management concentrates at the boundaries: moving data from outside the CMS to inside or from inside to outside always involves processing, including rewriting of addresses, determining storage organization, extracting or adding content or metadata, and so on.

Because DITA content almost always involves sets of maps and topics managed as a unit, import and export can be quite challenging. You should expect a DITA-aware CMS to provide tools and supporting components to make importing and exporting DITA content as easy as possible.

For example, you should expect "map import" and "map export" facilities. You should look for features for packaging DITA content into Zip files for interchange or archiving. You should expect some sort of customization library or function package or re-usable scripts that provide the basic tools you'll need for implementing custom import and export of DITA content.

Link, Key, and Dependency Management

You should expect DITA-aware CMS systems to be able to manage, track, and act on the dependencies among maps and topics by, for example, ensuring that all the dependencies defined by a map tree have been imported or exported.

You should expect to find facilities for working with keys, including getting lists of defined keys and the maps that define them and getting "where used" information about keys (what maps or topics refer to a specific key name). The ideal DITA-aware CMS will provide APIs for creating and resolving keys, especially for use by editors.

As for keys, the ideal DITA-aware CMS will recognize and track content reference relationships, letting you quickly determine where a given element is used by reference, whether by key or by direct URL reference.

Searching and Metadata

The ideal DITA-aware CMS will provide, without configuration or customization, built-in searching on all DITA-defined metadata elements and attributes, including specializations of `<data>` and other built-in metadata elements. However, this is hard to implement because the current XML search engines, such as MarkLogic and eXist, are not optimized for searching on elements based only on attribute value matching—they are optimized for searching on elements indexed only by tagname. But it's not impossible.

One of the main justifications for using a CMS system rather than a simple code control system is the ability to search quickly across large volumes of data. DITA's clear distinction of data and metadata provides the opportunity for sophisticated search with little or no configuration. DITA-aware CMS systems should capitalize on that opportunity.

Other Features and Considerations

- The ideal CMS system will be aware of DITA's applicability features and provide functions specifically for acting on DITA applicability, such as filtering search results by applicability.
- Most, if not all, CMS systems require system-specific attributes or elements to manage XML reliably. In particular, they usually need to embed a system-specific object ID into the XML so that the object IDs of the things in the XML that are treated as objects in the CMS can be maintained when the XML is exported from the system. This is usually done with attributes but may require system-specific elements as well. DITA-aware systems should add such markup in the least intrusive way possible. Ideally the system would use a single attribute specialized from @base.[13]

  Where CMS systems must add markup, and that markup cannot be made DITA-conforming, systems should provide out-of-the-box facilities for removing the added markup on export so the exported result is conforming.

- CMS systems might provide ways to create DITA maps within the CMS system. However, there are some limits to how complete a map editor CMS systems can provide without themselves becoming general-purpose XML editors. In general, you should expect to use DITA-aware editors to create and modify non-trivial maps.
- DITA-aware CMS systems should provide out-of-the-box integration with the DITA Open Toolkit, even if they provide their own versions of Toolkit transforms. Ideally you should be able to integrate multiple Toolkit instances, for example, to support different Toolkit versions or different configurations of the same Toolkit with different sets of customizations or incompatible plugins.
- DITA-aware CMS systems should provide out-of-the-box integrations with all the major DITA-aware editors, including Arbortext Editor, OxygenXML, and XMetal.

---

[13] At the time of writing the DITA TC has accepted a proposal for DITA 1.3 to add a new attribute, @resourceid, that would be for the specific purpose of holding one or more system-specific object IDs, labeled by system, as for the existing <resourceid> element allowed within <topicmetada>. This would provide a consistent place for DITA-aware CMS systems to put their object IDs without requiring each CMS implementor to invent their own attribute and corresponding vocabulary module. Look for it in DITA 1.3.

4

Running, Configuring, and Customizing the Open Toolkit

This chapter describes how to run the DITA Open Toolkit and details some basic-but-common transformation type configurations and customizations.

The DITA Open Toolkit is one of the primary DITA processing tools available, and its use is almost universal. The DITA Open Toolkit provides a number of useful output transforms, including HTML, Windows help, Web help, Eclipse InfoCenters, and PDF. However, production use of these tools almost always requires some degree of configuration and customization to tune the output to your specific needs.

This chapter describes how to customize the DITA Open Toolkit to produce HTML and PDF from the example document created in this part. It introduces Open Toolkit configuration and customization, but it is not a complete tutorial on the Open Toolkit. For complete Toolkit information see the Open Toolkit documentation maintained at the main Open Toolkit website (*dita-ot.sourceforge.net*).

This chapter reflects the 1.5.4 version of the Open Toolkit, which was the latest production version at the time of writing. The Toolkit is under constant development and new releases are fairly frequent.

The Toolkit functionality is provided through "transformation types" that reflect different types of output: HTML, PDF, etc. Transformation types are implemented through Toolkit plugins that provide the components that make up the transform, including Ant scripts that manage the overall transformation process, XSLT transforms or other processing, and static components that might be needed. The set of transformation types provided with the Open Toolkit out of the box is only a starter set—you can implement your own transformation types. In addition, other groups maintain Toolkit plugins, including the DITA for Publishers project, which provides plugins for generating EPUB and Kindle electronic books from DITA source.

The two most-commonly used transformation types are for HTML and PDF output.

The HTML transformation type generates HTML or XHTML. It is relatively easy to customize and extend by extending or overriding the base XSLT transforms. It also provides facilities for including custom CSS stylesheets and custom Web page headers and footers. For many uses you can use CSS to do most or all branding and tuning of the output. However, the base HTML transform is limited because each input topic document is processed in isolation, so it is difficult to implement formatting that requires coordination across topics, such as sequentially numbering headings or figures through a publication. The DITA for Publishers project includes an HTML transformation type that uses a map-driven processing framework to enable that type of processing. See the DITA for Publishers project for details (*dita4publishers.sourceforge.net*).

The PDF transformation type generates PDF (or, in fact, any output produced by the XSL Formatting Objects engine you are using). The PDF transformation is not nearly as easy to customize and configure as the HTML transformation. However, it is possible to configure and customize this transformation type with a reasonable amount of effort. If all you want to do is change the fonts and maybe some page layout details, it's not hard to configure. However, the configuration and extension mechanism provided by the PDF transform is different from that used by other transformation types, so it can be challenging to use without some guidance.

The goals of this chapter are the following:

1. Configure the HTML transformation to produce an HTML version of the publication that is branded with a custom CSS stylesheet and has custom headers and footers for each page.
2. Configure the PDF transformation to produce a PDF version of the publication that is branded with custom fonts and has a 7x9 inch page size.

Overview of the DITA Open Toolkit and its transforms

The DITA Open Toolkit is a general-purpose framework for processing DITA maps and topics into a variety of outputs. It provides a flexible plugin framework for integrating extensions to existing transformations and providing completely new transformations.

The DITA Open Toolkit ("Toolkit") is one of the most important tools for the DITA Practitioner. It serves as a reference implementation of the DITA standard, including those parts that are particularly challenging to implement, such as conref, filtering, and key references. It enables production of publication-quality deliverables from DITA content at a reasonable price. Even if you are not using the Toolkit in production you should expect to use it for testing and validation of documents and new vocabulary.

The development of the Open Toolkit is, at the time of writing, managed and largely funded by IBM and closely coordinated with the work of the OASIS DITA Technical Committee. However, the Open Toolkit is an independent open-source project and is not officially connected to OASIS or the DITA Technical Committee in any way. It is a community-supported project made possible largely through the generosity of IBM, which originally developed the technology for its own internal use and has continued to support its development by funding dedicated developers and project managers, most notably Robert Anderson, the long-time Open Toolkit Chief Architect.

Through version 1.6, the Toolkit is implemented as a set of Ant scripts ("build files") that define chains of processes that generate specific outputs. These processes include both Java-based generic pre-processing steps that implement generic processing including conref resolution, filtering on conditional attributes, and map resolution ("map pull"), and XSLT-based processing steps for specific outputs, such as HTML, PDF, Open Document Format, DocBook XML, and so on.

The Toolkit's Ant scripts are rooted at the file `build.xml` in the root Toolkit directory. You can run the Ant scripts either by using the normal "ant" command or by running the Toolkit-provided `dost.jar` Java program, which then sets up and runs Ant. You can run the Toolkit from the command line, from within a Java application, or from within an IDE like Eclipse or Netbeans. Most DITA-aware editing environments integrate the Toolkit and provide ways to run it from within the editor.

Ant is a general-purpose scripting framework that comes out of the Java world. It is an Apache project, *http://ant.apache.org/*. The full Toolkit package includes the Ant executable, but it is often useful to have a separate Ant installation in your development environment if you do not already have one. I recommend at least taking a look at the Ant documentation on the Apache site if you're not already familiar with Ant. It's pretty easy to work with, but there are some non-obvious and non-intuitive aspects that will cause you problems, such as the way properties work. Doing anything non-trivial with the Toolkit almost always involves creating or modifying Ant scripts.

The Toolkit provides a Toolkit-specific plugin mechanism that lets you package both extensions and complete transformation types as standalone modules and deploy them to a Toolkit instance conveniently and easily. Base transforms enable plug ins by defining extension points to which other plugins can add components. For example, the HTML transformation type provides an extension point for adding imports of additional XSLT modules. Toolkit plugins can declare other plugins as dependencies, and the Toolkit's "integrator" process will check the dependencies and ensure that they are all met.

The Toolkit also manages a master entity resolution catalog for all the vocabulary modules deployed to the Toolkit. It uses the same plugin extension mechanism to allow plugins to extend the base catalog for their own vocabulary. This makes it easy to package document type shells, constraint modules, and new vocabulary modules as plugins and then deploy them to the Toolkit. XML processors that can use the Toolkit's master catalog then have immediate access to the new vocabulary modules with no additional configuration required. Even if you don't use the Toolkit's processing, using it to manage your document type shells and custom vocabulary can be quite handy.

The Open Toolkit is well documented at the main Open Toolkit site, *http://dita-ot.sourceforge.net*. Everything you need to know should be found there. This discussion is provided to give you a general overview of how to run the Toolkit. Please see the official documentation for details and the latest options.

The Toolkit is under active development and is updated frequently to provide new features and bug fixes. If you are simply processing documents using the built-in transform types without customization or extension, then it is usually safe to upgrade to newer versions of the Toolkit without worry. However, if you have customizations or extensions you may need to modify them to work with newer versions of the Toolkit because internals and processing details may change from version to version. Be prepared to test new versions before you commit them to production use. Fortunately, it is easy to have multiple versions of the Toolkit on the same development system. Also be aware that a new version of the Toolkit may change the Java jar files it provides or depends on, so you may need to update the Toolkit integration with specific products to reflect those dependency changes.

Extending and customizing the Toolkit involves creating one of the following types of plugin:

- A custom version of a base transformation type that simply sets Ant properties to configure the transform. Doing this is a shortcut that lets you avoid specifying the properties explicitly each time you run the Toolkit. For example, if you have a set of publications that should all use the same PDF settings, it makes sense to define a new transformation type just for them, even though the settings could be specified directly on the Toolkit call.
- A vocabulary-only plugin that provides new document type shells or vocabulary modules but contains no processing code.
- Global extensions to a particular transformation type. For example, generic HTML processing for a new domain module.
- A custom version of a base transformation type that includes custom processing extensions or overrides that are not global. For example, an HTML transformation extension that implements specific HTML markup unique to a given publication or set of publications.
- An entirely new transformation type defined through new base processing code. For example, implementing a new output type that is not provided out of the box with the Toolkit.

The first two forms of plugin are the most common and are relatively easy to set up. The two customizations detailed in this chapter are both examples of the Ant-script-only form of plugin. The specialization tutorials include examples of the vocabulary and global extension forms of plugin. The differences between these types of plugin are the amount of effort required to implement them. The plugin configuration mechanism is the same for all plug ins.

Installing the DITA Open Toolkit

The Open Toolkit is distributed as a Zip file that contains everything you need. To install, simply requires unpack the Zip file into whatever location you want. There is no separate installation process or installer application.

The Toolkit is provided in a number of different packages to suit different requirements. For most purposes you want the "full easy install" package, which includes everything you need to run the Toolkit, including the Ant executable, command-line setup scripts, and so on.

The root directory of the Toolkit is usually "DITA-OT," although that name is not required. Common practice is to include the Toolkit version number in the directory name, especially when you may have different versions of the Toolkit installed, which is common if you are developing and testing Toolkit plugins or testing new versions as part of a potential upgrade.

Having extracted the Toolkit somewhere, it's usually necessary or helpful to set an environment variable to point to the Toolkit. For example, on my development machine I have two environment variables defined, "DITA_OT_HOME" and "DITA_HOME."

Tools that integrate the Open Toolkit will have different requirements for where the Toolkit can or must go and what environment variables you should or must set. For example, OxygenXML puts its built-in toolkit in the directory `frameworks/dita/DITA-OT`, but Oxygen also can be configured to use a different Toolkit location. You should expect similar configuration options from other tools that include or use the Open Toolkit.

If you are using the Toolkit from Eclipse or a similar Java IDE, you may need to copy the Java Jar files included with the Toolkit into another location or update the IDE's configuration to point to the Toolkit's `lib` directory.

The full easy install package of the Toolkit includes Ant in the `tools` directory. Through version 1.6, the Toolkit uses Ant version 1.7, although it should work with later versions of Ant. You are not required to use the Ant distributed with the Toolkit—it is simply provided as a convenience.

Running The DITA Open Toolkit

You can run the Open Toolkit from the command line, from within an Ant-aware development environment like Eclipse, or from editors like OxygenXML that integrate the Toolkit.

The DITA Open Toolkit is based on the Ant scripting language, *http://ant.apache.org*. Ant is a general-purpose facility originally intended to replace the functionality of the Unix "make" command. It is typically used for managing compilation and packaging of Java source code, but it can be used to automate pretty much any task.

Ant is a Java application and therefore is cross-platform, as is the Open Toolkit. The procedure for running the Toolkit is pretty much the same on any platform, except for platform-specific differences in how you construct command-line commands or specify file paths.

The Toolkit is implemented as a set of Ant scripts, rooted at the file `build.xml`. You can run the Ant scripts either by using the normal "ant" command or by running the Toolkit-provided `dost.jar` Java program, which then sets up and runs Ant. You can run the Toolkit from a command line, from within a Java application, or from within an IDE like Eclipse or Netbeans. Most DITA-aware editing environments integrate the Toolkit and provide ways to run it from within the editor.

The Open Toolkit is well documented at the main Open Toolkit site, *http://dita-ot.sourceforge.net*. Everything you need to know should be found there. This discussion is provided to give you a general overview of how to run the Toolkit. Please see the official documentation for details.

Running the Open Toolkit from the Command Line

You can run the Open Toolkit from a command line using Ant or the Toolkit-provided dost.jar.

The DITA Open Toolkit can be run from a command line on any platform that supports Java and Ant, including, Windows, Linux, Unix, or OSX. The procedure is essentially the same for all platforms, differing only in platform-specific details on how you construct command lines.

The key to successfully running the Open Toolkit is to set up the Java environment correctly. The Toolkit provides a number of Java JAR files it depends on, and it also depends on specific directories being in the Java class path. The Toolkit provides two scripts, `startcmd.bat` and `startcmd.sh`, that set up the class path correctly and start a new command window from which you can then run the Toolkit. If you do not use one of these scripts, or manually configure the class path to match them, the Toolkit will not run correctly. It may appear to run, but it will fail in odd ways.

The `startcmd.bat` script should work correctly on any version of Windows. The `startcmd.sh` script should work correctly under Linux, Unix, and OS X.

There are two ways to run the Toolkit from the command line: using the `ant` command directly or using the Toolkit-provided `dost.jar` file with the `java` command. The mechanisms are equivalent but the way you specify command-line parameters is different and the parameter names are different. I usually use the Ant approach, because it's more general and it means I only have to remember the Ant-specific parameters.

If you are continually processing the same documents, it's usually easier to set up Ant scripts or batch files to run the Toolkit or use a tool like OxygenXML that provides a user interface for running the Toolkit.

See the official DITA Open Toolkit documentation on the main Toolkit site (*http://dita-ot.sourceforge.net/*) for the full list of parameters.

Using the `dost.jar` *command line tool*

To use the `dost.jar` command-line tool, start a Toolkit command line using `startcmd.bat` or `startcmd.sh` and then from the root directory of the Toolkit, run this command:

```
c:\DITA-OT > java -jar lib\dost.jar
```

You should see a list of command options, like this:

```
C:\DITA-OT>java -jar lib\dost.jar
java -jar lib/dost.jar [mandatory parameters] [options]
Mandatory parameters:
  /i:                  specify path and name of the input file
  /transtype:          specify the transformation type
Options:
  -help, -h            print this message
  -version             print the version information and exit
  /basedir:            specify the working directory
  /ditadir:            specify the toolkit home directory. Default "temp"
  /outdir:             specify the output directory
  /tempdir:            specify the temporary directory
...
```

This establishes that you have things set up correctly and can now process something.

Parameters are specified as `/param:value`. As you can see, there are many options, but the key options are:

- /i

    The path and filename of the input file to process. Usually a map document, but can also be a topic.

- /transtype

    The transformation type, for example, "xhtml," "pdf," "epub," etc. The value is a transformation type name as defined by a plugin or one of the Toolkit's built-in transforms.

- /generatecopyouter

    For XHTML-based transforms, indicates whether or not output directories that would be outside the scope of the main output directory should be generated. The allowed values are:

    - 1—(default) Do not generate outer files. Any topics outside the map's directory tree will to be reflected in the output.
    - 2—Generate outer files. Outer files will be generated above or next to the main output directory.
    - 3—The output directory is adjusted so that all output files are underneath the main output directory.

- /outdir

  The output directory to use for the content. Note that if your map is not above all the files used from the map, some of the output files may be output *above* this directory.

For example, to process the map file `c:\workspace\doc-one\doc_src\doc-one.ditamap` to HTML you would use a command line like:

```
c:\DITA-OT > java -jar lib\dost.jar /transtype:xhtml
   /i:c:\workspace\doc-one\doc_src\doc-one.ditamap
   /outdir:c:\workspace\doc-one\output\html
```

Using the Ant command line

Using the `ant` command, you run the Toolkit's `build.xml` file, setting properties for the different Toolkit Ant properties you need for the transformation type you want to run. All of the Toolkit's command-line parameters correspond directly to Ant parameters.

For the `ant` command, the default Ant script is `build.xml`, so you don't need to specify the Ant script to run, just the parameters. If you want to specify a script file to run, you do so with the -f Ant parameter, for example:

```
ant -f build-doc_one.xml
```

Ant parameters are specified on the command line as `-Dparam=value`. If a value has spaces the entire parameter can be put in double quotes. Filenames can be specified using forward slashes on both Windows and non-Windows systems.

The parameters you specify on the Ant command line are exactly the same as you set in Ant scripts that run the Toolkit.

The key parameters are:

- transtype

  The transformation type to run, for example, "xhtml," "pdf," "epub," etc.

- args.input

  The path and filename of the input file. Usually a map but can be a topic.

- output.dir

  The output directory to put the transformation result in. Note that if your map is not above all the files used from the map, some of the output files may be output *above* this directory.

- generate.copy.outer

  For XHTML-based transforms, indicates whether or not output directories that would be outside the scope of the main output directory should be generated. The allowed values are:

  - 1—(default) Do not generate outer files. Any topics outside the map's directory tree will not be reflected in the output.
  - 2—Generate outer files. Outer files will be generated above or next to the main output directory.
  - 3—The output directory is adjusted so that all output files are underneath the main output directory.

For example, to process the map file c:\workspace\doc-one\doc_src\doc-one.ditamap to HTML you would use a command line like:

```
c:\DITA-OT > ant -Dtranstype=xhtml
  -Dargs.input=c:/workspace/doc-one/doc_src/doc-one.ditamap
  -Doutput.dir=c:/workspace/doc-one/output/html
```

If the input directory has a space in it, quote the entire parameter, like the following:

```
c:\DITA-OT > ant -Dtranstype=xhtml
  "-Dargs.input=c:/workspace/doc one/doc_src/doc-one.ditamap"
  -Doutput.dir=c:/workspace/doc-one/output/html
```

Setting Up Custom Toolkit-Running Ant Scripts

You can create Ant scripts to run Toolkit transforms against documents. This is a handy way to set all the parameters you need or to run several transforms in one go. Your Ant script can be for a single document or can use parameters you set on the command line. You can also use separate properties files to set Ant properties that configure the transform, making it possible for users to configure the transform without having to directly modify the Ant script. Unlike Windows batch script and Linux and OS X shell scripts, Ant scripts are cross-platform, so you can maintain one script file for all users.

There are lots of effective ways to construct Ant scripts that run the Toolkit, but the pattern that I've arrived at is the following:

```
<project name="doc-one-toolkit" default="html" basedir=".">
  <property file="build.properties"/>                          [1]
  <property file="${user.home}/.build.properties"/>
  <property file="${user.home}/build.properties"/>

  <property name="dita-ot-dir" location="c:\DITA-OT"/>         [2]

  <property name="source.dir" location="${basedir}"/>         [3]
```

```
    <property name="map.filename" value="doc-one"/>          [4]
    <property name="base.output.dir"
                         location="${basedir}/output"/>      [5]

    <property name="output.dir.html"
                    location="${base.output.dir}/html"/>      [6]


    <target name="html"                                       [7]
       description="build the map to HTML">
       <mkdir dir="${output.dir.html}"/>
       <ant antfile="${dita-ot-dir}/build.xml"                [8]
           inheritAll="false"
       >
         <property name="transtype" value="xhtml"/>
         <property name="args.input"
           location="${source.dir}/${map.filename}.ditamap"/>
         <property name="output.dir"
           location="${output.dir.html}/${map.filename}"/>
         <property name="generate.copy.outer" value="3"/>
       </ant>
    </target>

</project>
```

The lines labeled in italics are:

[1]   Inclusion of properties files. These three lines look for a file named build.properties in
       the same directory as the script, then for .build.properties and build.properties
       in the user's home directory (for example, c:\users\ekimber under Windows,
       /Users/ekimber under OS X).

       In Ant, the first definition of a property wins, so properties set in the build.properties file
       in the same directory as the script take precedent over any properties set by the user-specific
       property files or within the main script. Only properties set on the command line can take
       precedence over those in build.properties.

       The user-specific properties files make it easy to set machine-specific properties that will be used
       by any scripts that follow this pattern, in particular, the property dita-ot-dir, which defines the
       location of the Open Toolkit to use.

[2]   Definition of the property dita-ot-dir. The value of the property is the location of the root directory
       of the Open Toolkit. As this value will usually be machine specific, it needs to be settable from a
       property. In this example, I've set the default to be c:\DITA-OT, which is a typical location.
       Typically, users would set this property in their personal .build.properties or
       build.properties file.

The attribute @location tells Ant that this is a file system location and that it should be interpreted appropriately for the operating system. You can use forward slashes for both Windows and non-Windows operating systems and it should work. Relative values are made absolute relative to the project's base directory (as set by the @basedir attribute on the root <project> element).

Properties set with the attribute @value are simple string values.

[3]   Definition of the property source.dir. This is the directory under which the input document source will be found. This reflects the common file organization pattern of having a directory that contains the root maps for many publications. By making this value a property, it can be easily set on the command line or in a properties file.

[4]   Definition of the property map.filename. This is the filename part of the map. By capturing just the filename part, it makes it easy to do things such as constructing the output directory name, as shown in line [9]. Ant can also get the filename from a full path and filename, but since you have to specify something anyway, it's easier to just specify the name part of the filename, since DITA maps almost always have the extension .ditamap.

[5]   Definition of the property base.output.dir. This is the base output directory, from which the final output directory path will be constructed. Again, making this a property makes it easy to parameterize. I specifically chose the name "base.output.dir" to distinguish it from the Toolkit parameter output.dir.

[6]   Definition of the property output.dir.html, which will be used as the value of the Toolkit's output.dir parameter. By including ".html" in the property name, it sets the stage for producing other outputs from the same script.

[7[The Ant <target> element, which defines the Ant target "html". Ant targets are what do the actual work within an Ant script. An Ant script is a set of one or more targets. Targets can be dependent on other targets or can call other targets within the same or other scripts. In this case, the Ant script has just one target, but you could use this target as a pattern to create other targets for other transformation types.

Every Ant script can have a default target that is run automatically if no specific target is specified. This target is defined as the default target through the @default attribute of the root <project> element.

The @description attribute contains a short description of the target, making it a "public" target. Target descriptions are displayed when you use the -projecthelp parameter with the ant command. For example, if you do ant -projecthelp from the Toolkit directory, you should see output like this:

```
Eliots-MacBook:DITA-OT ekimber$ ant -projecthelp
Buildfile: /Applications/oxygen/frameworks/dita/DITA-OT/build.xml

Main targets:

 check-arg                            Validate and init input
arguments
 chunk                                Process chunks
 clean-temp                           Clean temp directory
 coderef                              Resolve coderef in input
files
 ...
```

An Ant target can contain many different Ant tasks, which do different things. This target does two things:

1. Creates the output directory as specified by the output.dir.html property (the <mkdir> task).
2. Calls the main Toolkit Ant script, providing the appropriate parameters (line *[8]*).

[8]   An <ant> task, which calls the main Toolkit build.xml file. The @antfile attribute points to the build file to run, in this case the main Toolkit build.xml file.

The @inheritAll value of "false" keeps the Toolkit Ant script from inheriting any properties defined in this Ant script. This avoids any unexpected interference between the properties in this script and the properties used by the Toolkit script. Only the properties set explicitly in the <ant> task will be passed, meaning you know exactly what you're telling the Toolkit to do.

The parameters defined within the <ant> task should be familiar from the command-line discussion. The parameter names are same.

To run this script, run the Toolkit's startcmd.bat or startcmd.sh script to create a Toolkit command environment, then run the ant command with the -f parameter:

```
c:\workspace\doc-one > ant -f doc-one-html.xml
```

The process should run and produce the same result as if you had run the main Toolkit Ant script directly from the command line.

Running the Open Toolkit from OxygenXML

The OxygenXML editor includes the DITA Open Toolkit and provides facilities for running it against files open in the editor or on the file system. OxygenXML usually includes the latest release that is stable at the time the OxygenXML release is produced. You can also swap in a different Toolkit version or reconfigure OxygenXML to use a different Toolkit installation. The Toolkit included with the OxygenXML distribution may reflect customizations or bug fixes developed by SynchroSoft, although these are usually minor. Historically, SynchroSoft has contributed bug fixes and enhancements to the Open Toolkit project, which minimizes their need to maintain OxygenXML-specific versions of the Toolkit.

OxygenXML has the general concept of "transformation scenarios", which are transformation configurations you can create and save through the OxygenXML user interface. It has built-in scenarios for the main DITA transformation types and you can use those directly or as a base for custom transforms. You can run any transformation type by setting the value of the transtype parameter explicitly. When you run a transform through OxygenXML, it captures the log output in a separate window.

To create a custom DITA transformation scenario, follow these steps:

1. Open a DITA map or topic in the editor.

    This will automatically make DITA transformation scenarios the default scenario type.

2. Select the **Configure Transformation Scenario** (🔧) button to bring up the **Configure Transformation Scenario** dialog.

    You should see at least the pre-defined DITA transformation scenarios, plus any custom ones you may have created.

3. Select the "DITA XHTML" pre-defined transform and click **Duplicate**.

    This opens the **Edit DITA Scenario** dialog with the name "DITA XHTML Duplicate".

4. Change the name to something like "Doc One XHTML"

5. Look at the various parameters. The dialog shows you the default values for parameters that are not set.

    The args.input should be set to "${cf}", which means the current file open in the editor. You could change this to be the specific file you want to always process. If you double-click in the field you will get a dialog that lets you choose a file or choose different Oxygen-defined variables.

    For the built-in DITA transformation types, the transtype parameter is set by default, for example, "xhtml" for the DITA XHTML transforms. However, you can add the transtype parameter to the scenario if you want to change it to something else, for example, to a custom transtype that extends the base XHTML transformation type.

6. In the **Edit DITA Scenario** dialog, choose the **Output** tab.

   Here you can specify the details of the output location. The default is to use the current file's directory ("${cfd}") as the base output directory. You can have the output automatically opened in the appropriate application or opened in the OxygenXML editor.

7. When you're satisfied with the parameter settings, click **OK** to go back to the **Configure Transformation Scenario** dialog. From here you can simply save the scenario or run it immediately. For this exercise, click **Save and close**.

8. With your DITA document still open in the editor, click the **Apply Transformation Scenario** (▶) button.

   If you haven't run a transform yet, this will ask you to select one. If you have already run one it will run that scenario again.

   The log output of the transform will go into a window in the message area, which is usually at the bottom of the OxygenXML window, labeled "DITA Transformation". There may also be a separate message window labeled "Transformation problems".

Running the Open Toolkit from Eclipse

Eclipse is a general development environment that offers many handy features for doing DITA development, including the ability to develop and run Ant scripts. Eclipse includes both an Ant editor for editing Ant scripts and an Ant "view" that makes it easy to run different Ant scripts.

I use Ant scripts from Eclipse mostly for development-related activities such as developing scripts for compiling, packaging, and deploying project components to my local working environment. For example, for all my DITA-related projects I have a standard Ant target that deploys that project's Toolkit plugins to my local Toolkit instance (which is normally the Toolkit that Oxygen uses).

You can set up Eclipse to run the Open Toolkit's Ant scripts. For example, you can create Ant scripts that will run multiple Toolkit transformations on a given input DITA map, or process a whole set of documents, and then do something with the generated results, such as publish them to a website.

To set this up you must add the Toolkit's custom Java jar files to the list of jar files that Ant uses when it is run by Eclipse. This does essentially the same thing as the Toolkit's `startup.sh` and `startup.bat` scripts do, namely set up the appropriate Java class path so the custom Toolkit Ant processing will work.

You must also configure an Ant property that specifies the location of the Open Toolkit on your machine. By convention I call this property *dita-ot-dir*, and that's the name used in all the samples in this book. While you can hardcode this property in the various Ant scripts you use, it's much better to set up your Ant scripts to get the property from a separate configuration file so that you can change it in one place.

This also makes collaborative development of DITA projects easier when scripts are managed in a common code repository, but each developer needs to have a different value for the Toolkit location.

To set up a property file to define the *dita-ot-dir* Ant property, do the following:

1. Create a file named `build.properties` or `.build.properties` in your home directory. If you are on a Unix or Linux system, using `.build.properties` offers more security because the file will be hidden by default, making it safer to hold sensitive values like passwords.
2. Edit the `build.properties` file and add a line like this:

```
dita-ot-dir=/Applications/oxygen/frameworks/dita/DITA-OT
```

Where the value to the right of the "=" is the actual location of the Open Toolkit you want to use on your machine. For Windows you can replace "/" with "\" in paths.

3. In your Ant scripts include these three lines before any other property definitions:

```
<property file="build.properties"/>
<property file="${user.home}/.build.properties"/>
<property file="${user.home}/build.properties"/>
```

These three property file inclusions will look for `build.properties` in the same directory as the Ant script itself, `.build.properties` in your home directory, and `build.properties` in your home directory, in that order. Whichever of these files has the first definition of a given property will set the value of that property. This organization allows you to have global defaults for properties in your user-specific properties file and override those defaults in a project-specific properties file.

To add the Toolkit-related jar files to Eclipse's Ant configuration, do the following:

1. Go to **Preferences** > **Ant** > **Runtime** to bring up the Ant runtime settings. Select the **Classpath** tab.
2. Select "Global Entries" item in the classpath list. Expand the item to see what jar files are already listed.
3. Assuming that the Toolkit's jar files are not listed, with "Global Entries" selected in the tree view, select "Add external JARs" and navigate to the `lib` directory underneath the Toolkit installation you want to use (for example, the Toolkit installed with OxygenXML).
4. Select all the .JAR files in the lib directory add them to the list under "Global Entries."
5. Select "Add external JARs" again and navigate down into the `saxon` directory under the `lib` directory.
6. Select all the .JAR files in the `saxon` directory and add those to the list under "Global Entries."

You may also need to add the two jars, `xercesImpl.jar` and `xml-apis.jar`, which are part of the Apache Xerces2 Java project. If you don't already have them on your system somewhere, you can download them from *http://xerces.apache.org* and put them in the `lib` directory of your Toolkit installation.

With this Ant configuration in place you should be able to run Ant scripts that use the Open Toolkit from within Eclipse. This Ant script tests the ability to run the Toolkit from Ant:

```xml
<?xml version="1.0" encoding="UTF-8" ?>
<project name="dita.build.demo" default="demo.book" basedir=".">
  <!-- Simple Build script to test the ability to call the
       DITA Open Toolkit from Ant.
    -->

  <property file="build.properties"/>
  <property file="${user.home}/.build.properties"/>
  <property file="${user.home}/build.properties"/>

  <property name="dita-ot-dir" location="c:\DITA-OT1.5"/>
  <property name="dita.demo.book.dir"
      value="${dita-ot-dir}${file.separator}samples"/>

  <property name="dita.output.demo.book.dir" location="${basedir}/temp/demo"/>


  <target name="demo.book" description="build the book demo">
    <mkdir dir="${dita.output.demo.book.dir}"/>
    <ant antfile="${dita-ot-dir}/build.xml" target="dita2xhtml">
      <property name="args.input"
        value="${dita.demo.book.dir}${file.separator}taskbook.ditamap"/>
      <property name="output.dir"
        value="${dita.output.demo.book.dir}"/>
      <property name="transtype" value="xhtml"/>
    </ant>
  </target>

</project>
```

To run this script yourself you will need to either create a `build.properties` file that sets the value of the *dita-ot-dir* Ant property or change the value in the script itself. (The first definition of a property is the effective value in Ant, so a value for *dita-ot-dir* set in one of the included `build.properties` files would take precedence over the value specified in the Ant script itself.)

If you want to run this type of Ant script from the command line outside of Eclipse, you must either use a command window created using the Toolkit-provided `startcmd.sh` or `startcmd.bat` script or configure Ant's classpath using normal Ant configuration facilities. For this type of configuration there are many possible approaches, all of which are beyond the scope of this book.

You can find all the code examples used in this book at the DITA for Practitioners website, *http://dita4practitioners.com.*

Introduction to Open Toolkit Customization and Extension

The DITA Open Toolkit is customized and extended through plugins[14]. A plugin consists of an XML plugin descriptor (plugin.xml) and one or more files that make up the plugin itself. The files for a plugin are organized within a directory under the Toolkit's plugins directory.

Plugins contribute new code, which is added to base files through a process called *integration*. You perform integration by running the integrator.xml Ant script that is in the root Toolkit directory.

 Note: See the main DITA Open Toolkit site, *http://dita-ot.sourceforge.net/*, for complete documentation on the Toolkit's extension facilities.

The integration process uses files that act as templates as the basis for generating working files, where the working files reflect the code added to the templates by plugins.

For example, in the root Toolkit directory is the file build_template.xml. This is the template for the main Ant build script. When you run the integrator.xml Ant script, the integrator looks in the template for elements that define extension points, finds all the plugins that contribute to that extension point, and adds their contributions to the resulting file, build.xml. Within the Toolkit files, files whose names end with _template are template files that can be extended by plugins. Plugins may also define their own template files.

It is safe to rerun the integrator.xml process at any time. You must run it any time you change the contents of your Toolkit's plugins directory.

You run the integration script using the Ant command:

```
c:\DITA-OT > ant -f integrator.xml
```

from the root directory of the Open Toolkit (for example, c:\DITA-OT). You should be able to run the integrator.xml script from any command line without first running the startcmd.bat or startcmd.sh script.

You would normally develop your plugin in a work space separate from any Toolkit instance and then *deploy* the plugin to a Toolkit instance by copying the plugin's directory into the Toolkit's plugins

---

[14] While the Toolkit's PDF plugin can be customized by adding files directly to its customization directory, it is possible to package PDF customizations as Toolkit plugins and I suggest that as being the best practice.

directory and rerunning the `integrator.xml` script. This deployment process can be manual or automated through Ant scripts, for example.

For plugins that will be distributed for use by others, normal practice is to package the plugins as Zip files so that when the Zip file is unpacked in the `plugins` directory, the plugin's directory is created, ready to be integrated.

Plugin Descriptors (`plugin.xml`)

An Open Toolkit plugin is defined through a plugin descriptor file, named `plugin.xml`. The plugin descriptor defines the plugin's unique ID, any plugins on which it is dependent, any extension points it extends, and any extensible templates it provides. The plugin files are organized within a directory within the Toolkit's `plugins` directory. You can use any directory name you want, but standard practice is to use the plugin's ID value as the directory name.

A plugin's ID and directory name must be unique across all the plugins installed in a given Toolkit instance. Standard practice for plugin IDs is to use reverse domain names as for Java classes, for example, `org.example.myplugin`. This ensures that your plugin's ID and directory name will be unique across all possible plugins, as you presumably own the domain name you use as the base for your plugin's ID and directory name.

A typical `plugin.xml` file for a custom transformation type looks like this:

```
<plugin id="net.sourceforge.dita4publishers.epub">

  <require plugin="org.dita.xhtml"/>
  <require plugin="net.sourceforge.dita4publishers.common.mapdriven"/>
  <require plugin="net.sourceforge.dita4publishers.common.xslt"/>

  <feature extension="dita.conductor.transtype.check"
     value="epub"
     type="txt"
  />
  <feature extension="dita.conductor.target.relative"
     value="build.xml"
     type="file"
  />

  <template file="build_transtype-epub_template.xml"/>

  <template file="xsl/map2epub_template.xsl"/>

</plugin>
```

All the plugin integration mechanisms let you hook into extension points using relative paths so that you don't have to hard-code the location of your plugin as deployed anywhere within your plugin.

The `<require>` element names other plugins your plugin is dependent on.

The `<feature>` element points to extension points in other plugins or in the base Toolkit code that your plugin is extending.

The `<template>` element declares files provided by your plugin that may themselves be extended by other plugins.

Defining Plugin Dependencies

If a plugin extends another plugin or uses components of that plugin, then the plugin has a dependency on the plugin it extends or uses.

You can formally declare these dependencies in the `plugin.xml` and the integration process will check the dependencies and not integrate any plugin for which the dependencies are missing.

Dependencies are defined using the `<require>` element, like so:

```
<plugin id="net.sourceforge.dita4publishers.epub">

  <require plugin="org.dita.xhtml"/>
  <require plugin="net.sourceforge.dita4publishers.common.mapdriven"/>
  <require plugin="net.sourceforge.dita4publishers.common.xslt"/>

  <template file="build_transtype-epub_template.xml"/>

  <template file="xsl/map2epub_template.xsl"/>

  <feature extension="dita.conductor.transtype.check"
     value="epub"
     type="txt"
  />
  <feature extension="dita.conductor.target.relative"
     value="build.xml"
     type="file"
  />

</plugin>
```

The value of the @plugin attribute is the required plugin's ID, as specified on its @id attribute in its plugin.xml file.

For example, if you wanted to extend the DITA for Publishers EPUB transformation type plugin, you would specify this `<require>` element in your `plugin.xml` file:

```
<plugin id="org.example.myepubextension">
  <require plugin="net.sourceforge.dita4publishers.epub"/>
  ...
</plugin>
```

Starting with version 1.5.3 of the Open Toolkit, all the base transformation types are defined as plugins, so you can indicate dependencies on them as well, for example:

```
<plugin id="org.example.myhtmlextension">
  <require plugin="org.dita.xhtml"/>
  ...
</plugin>
```

Toolkit Extension Points

Extension points are indicated by `<extension>` elements in the namespace "http://dita-ot.sourceforge.net", using the prefix "dita:" by convention, for example, from the `build_template.xml` file:

```
  ...
  <condition>
    <and>
      <dita:extension
        id="dita.conductor.transtype.check"
        behavior="org.dita.dost.platform.CheckTranstypeAction"
        xmlns:dita="http://dita-ot.sourceforge.net"/>
    </and>
  </condition>
  ...
```

Any XML file may include `<dita:extension>` elements, including Ant build scripts and XSLT transform modules.

Each extension point has an ID that is unique across all template files for a given `@behavior` value, defined by the `@id` attribute of the `<dita:extension>` element, for example, `dita.conductor.transtype.check` in the example above.

Within a plugin descriptor, you use `<feature>` elements to point to a particular extension point and specify the data to use at that point, which can be either a reference to a file or literal text.

For example, to define a new transformation type in a plugin, you point to the
`dita.conductor.transtype.check` extension point, like so:

```
<?xml version="1.0" encoding="UTF-8"?>
<plugin id="org.example.mypub.html">
  <require plugin="org.dita.xhtml"/>

  <template file="build_mypub-transtype-html_template.xml"/>

  <feature extension="dita.conductor.transtype.check"
    value="html-mypub"
    type="txt"/>
  <feature extension="dita.conductor.target.relative"
    value="build.xml"
    type="file"/>
</plugin>
```

In this example, the `<feature>` element is adding the value "html-mypub" to the extension point
`dita.conductor.transtype.check`. The `@type` attribute value of "txt" indicates that the plugin
is adding the value of the `@value` attribute.

The next line, which points to the `dita.conductor.target.relative` extension point, is adding
the contents of the file `build.xml` from the plugin's directory to the extension point, as indicated by
the value "file" for the `@type` attribute. When `@type` is "file", then the value of the `@value` attribute is
taken as a filename. You can also use the attribute `@file` rather than `@value` to point to files. In this
example, the extension point `dita.conductor.target.relative` takes the value "build.xml" as
a filename relative to the location of the plugin itself.

Plugins may provide their own template files and extension points, which allows plugins to be extended
by other plugins. To provide templates, you use the `<template>` element in the plugin descriptor to
name template files, for example:

```
<plugin id="net.sourceforge.dita4publishers.epub">

  <require plugin="net.sourceforge.dita4publishers.common.mapdriven"/>
  <require plugin="net.sourceforge.dita4publishers.common.xslt"/>

  <feature extension="dita.conductor.transtype.check"
    value="epub"
    type="txt"/>
  <feature extension="dita.conductor.target.relative"
    value="build.xml"
    type="file"/>
  <template file="build_transtype-epub_template.xml"/>
  <template file="xsl/map2epub_template.xsl"/>
</plugin>
```

For a given template file, you can determine what extension points it provides by simply looking for the `<dita:extension>` elements within it. For example, the `map2epub_template.xsl` file from the EPUB transformation type has this extension point:

```
<xsl:stylesheet version="2.0"
                xmlns:opf="http://www.idpf.org/2007/opf"
                xmlns:dc="http://purl.org/dc/elements/1.1/"
                xmlns:xsl="http://www.w3.org/1999/XSL/Transform">

  <xsl:import href="map2epubImpl.xsl"/>

  <dita:extension id="xsl.transtype-epub"
    behavior="org.dita.dost.platform.ImportXSLAction"
    xmlns:dita="http://dita-ot.sourceforge.net"/>


</xsl:stylesheet>
```

The ID of the extension point is `xsl.transtype-epub`, so you would use that ID to contribute additional XSLT code from another plugin.

Extensions that add XML markup to the template file always ignore the root element of the file pointed to by the `<feature>` element.

Extension Point Behaviors

The Open Toolkit provides the following extension point behaviors:

- org.dita.dost.platform.InsertAction

  Inserts XML elements from the specified XML file into the template document.

  The root element is of the input file is ignored. The typical use of the insert action is to add Ant `<param>` elements to base Ant tasks. For example, the `build_dita2xhtml_template.xml` file has this extension point:

```
  . . .
  <param name="OUTPUTCLASS" expression="${args.xhtml.toc.class}"
if="args.xhtml.toc.class" />
  <dita:extension
      id="dita.conductor.xhtml.toc.param"
      behavior="org.dita.dost.platform.InsertAction"
      xmlns:dita="http://dita-ot.sourceforge.net"/>
  . . .
```

To add a parameter, you would create a file like:

```
<?xml version="1.0" encoding="utf-8"?>
<project>
  <param name="MyParam" expression="some value/>
</project>
```

The `<project>` element is ignored, so the result is that the `<param>` element is added to the Ant file produced from the template.

- org.dita.dost.platform.ImportXSLAction

  Produces an `<xsl:import>` element that points to the specified XSLT module. Used within XSLT modules.

- org.dita.dost.platform.ImportStringsAction

  Adds string definitions to XML files that define localized strings, such as the `xsl/common/strings.xml` file.

- org.dita.dost.platform.ImportAntLibAction

  Adds Java class path entries to an Ant script.

  The value of the `<feature>` element is the path, relative to your plugin, of the Java JAR file to add to the class path, for example:

```
  ...
  <feature
     extension="dita.conductor.lib.import"
     file="lib/myJavaLibrary.jar"/>
  ...
```

- org.dita.dost.platform.CheckTranstypeAction

  Adds a transformation type check an Ant task. The transformation type check verifies that a given transformation type is available.

  The `<feature>` element specifies the name of the transformation type to check for, for example:

```
   <feature
      extension="dita.conductor.transtype.check"
      value="epub"
      type="txt"/>
```

- org.dita.dost.platform.ListTranstypeAction

  Adds a transformation type to the list of available transformation types. The value of the `<feature>` element is the name of the transformation type, for example:

  ```
  <feature extension="dita.conductor.transtype.check"
    value="epub"
    type="txt"/>
  ```

- org.dita.dost.platform.ImportPluginInfoAction

  Inserts plugin information into an Ant script. You don't have to explicitly use this extension, it is automatically applied for each plugin. In particular, it defines an Ant property of the form "dita.plugin.*pluginId*.dir", where *pluginId* is the value of the `@id` attribute on the `<plugin>` element in the plugin's `plugin.xml` file and the value of the property is the path to the plugin's directory.

  For example, if your plugin's `plugin.xml` file looks like this:

  ```
  <plugin id="org.example.myplugin">
    ...
  </plugin>
  ```

  Then the `build.xml` file produced from the template `build_template.xml` file will include a property definition like:

  ```
  <property name='dita.plugin.org.example.myplugin.dir'
      location='${dita.dir}/plugins/org.example.myplugin'/>
  ```

  You can then use this property in Ant scripts to refer to files within your plugin's directory, for example:

  ```
    ...
    <param name="data-file"

  location="${dita.plugin.org.example.myplugin.dir}/data/data-file-01.xml"
    />
    ...
  ```

- org.dita.dost.platform.InsertAntActionRelative

  Inserts Ant XML code into an Ant script, rewriting any file references so that they are correct in the result. File references are interpreted as being relative to the location of the plugin-provided file. This is typically used to add imports to plugin-provided Ant modules to the main `build.xml` file. The root element is of the input file is ignored. This behavior is used primarily with the extension point `dita.conductor.target.relative`.

- org.dita.dost.platform.InsertCatalogActionRelative

  Inserts references to XML catalogs relative to the location of the contributing plugin. Used to add catalogs provided by vocabulary plugins to the main Toolkit plugin. The value of the `<feature>` element is the path, relative to the plugin, of the catalog file to add:

```
<plugin id="com.planetsizedbrains.dita4practitioners.doctypes">
  <feature
    extension="dita.specialization.catalog.relative"
    file="catalog.xml"
  />
</plugin>
```

The root element of the referenced catalog is ignored. In this example, the `catalog.xml` file looks like this:

```
<?xml version="1.0" encoding="UTF-8"?>
<catalog xmlns="urn:oasis:names:tc:entity:xmlns:xml:catalog"
prefer="public">

  <nextCatalog catalog="doctypes/catalog.xml"/>

</catalog>
```

The original value of the `@catalog` attribute on the `<nextCatalog>` element is rewritten to add an `@xml:base` attribute reflecting the location of the plugin, resulting in the entry:

```
<nextCatalog

xml:base="plugins/com.planetsizedbrains.dita4practitioners.doctypes/doctypes/"

  catalog="catalog.xml"></nextCatalog>
```

in the main Toolkit catalog file (`catalog_dita.xml`).

- org.dita.dost.platform.InsertDependsAction

  Used on Ant `<target>` elements, indicates that all the dependencies required by Toolkit transformation types should be added to the `<target>` element in the result build file. This is part of the general pre-processing extension support provided by the Toolkit, as the set of dependent pre-processing tasks can be modified by plugins that extend the preprocessing framework.

Customizing the Open Toolkit HTML Transform

The HTML transformation type can be extended and customized through Toolkit plugins that either override or extend the base XSLT transformations. You can also use custom CSS style sheets and other normal Web technologies to further customize the content as delivered for the Web.

The Open Toolkit's HTML transformation type is implemented as a set of XSLT transforms that generate HTML from the topics used by the input root map. It also generates a table of contents page from the input map. The separate TOCJS plugin (within the demo directory of the Toolkit) generates a dynamic JavaScript-based table of contents. The DITA for Publishers HTML2 transformation type extends the base HTML transformation type to add map-driven features such as a dynamic table of contents (similar to the TOCJS table of contents), cross-topic numbering, and a back-of-the-book index.

Like most Open Toolkit transformation types, the HTML transform depends on the generic pre-processing the Toolkit does for resolving content references, applying conditional filters, chunking topics, resolving map-to-map references, and cascading map metadata down the map hierarchy and from maps to topics. Thus the input to the transforms is a single, resolved map and a set of chunked topics.

Each topic is transformed separately, so there are some limitations on what processing you can do without additional work. In particular, during processing, there is no good way to determine where a topic is in the map, which makes it essentially impossible to number things across topics.

The actual XSLT processing is reasonably straightforward, which makes it relatively easy to override or extend. While it requires some knowledge of XSLT, many customization requirements can be met with very simple XSLT. The specialization tutorial sections provide simple examples of extending and overriding the base XSLT processing for HTML output.

For this exercise the goal is to use a custom CSS stylesheet for brand-specific styling and provide custom headers and footers for each HTML page.

The implementation requires the following actions:

1. Define the CSS stylesheet
2. Define the HTML markup for the headers and footers.
3. Set up a new Toolkit plugin that will package the stylesheet and footers and set the appropriate Ant parameters for the HTML transform.

The use of a plugin is not strictly required in this case, as you can do everything with run-time Toolkit parameters, but the presumption is that this customization is something that will be used by multiple users or on multiple servers, or that it otherwise needs the convenience and manageability of a plugin.

HTML Customization: Step 1—Create new customization plugin

To set up the customization plugin, perform the following steps:

1. Create a directory called `org.example.mypub.html` in your workspace, for example, `c:\workspace\org.example.mypub.html`. This will be the root directory of the new Toolkit plugin.

2. In the `org.example.mypub.html` directory create the file `build_mypub-transtype-html_template.xml` with this content:

```xml
<project name="org.example.mypub-transtype-html" default="dita2html-mypub">


    <!-- ==========================
         Build file for use with the DITA Open Toolkit.

         Configures the base HTML plugin to use
         the MyPub customizations.

         ========================== -->

  <property name="transtype" value="html-mypub"/>


    <target name="dita2html-mypub"
      xmlns:dita="http://dita-ot.sourceforge.net"
      dita:extension="depends org.dita.dost.platform.InsertDependsAction">
      <property name="args.copycss" value="yes"/>
      <property name="args.css" value="myPub.css"/>
      <property name="args.cssroot"
                value="${dita.dir}/plugins/org.example.mypub.html/css"/>

      <property name="args.ftr"
value="${dita.dir}/plugins/org.example.mypub.html/html/myPub-footer.html"/>

      <property name="args.hdr"
value="${dita.dir}/plugins/org.example.mypub.html/html/myPub-header.html"/>


    <antcall target="dita2xhtml"/>
  </target>
</project>
```

This is a template Ant script that defines a new transformation type, `html-mypub`, and configures it to use the various Ant properties that configure the CSS stylesheet and the HTML headers and footers. The Toolkit's integration process will copy this file to `build_mypub-transtype-html.xml`. (You could avoid the use of the template, but creating a template build script in this way is the normal Toolkit plugin pattern.)

common-error: Note that the property definitions for the transform are *inside* the `<target>` element for the transformation type. This is essential. If the property settings are outside the `<target>` element, they act as global property settings and will either set the values for all transformation types or will have no effect because another included build file has set the properties first (for example, this can happen if you have two HTML customization plugins deployed). This is a subtle error because you will only notice it when there are two transformation types that use the property. If that doesn't happen, you won't see the error.

3. In the `org.example.mypub.html` directory create the file `build.xml` with this content:

```
<project>
  <import file="build_mypub-transtype-html.xml" />
</project>
```

This file will be integrated into the master Toolkit `build.xml` file to hook this plugin into the Toolkit proper. All it does is create a reference to the main Ant script for the transformation type (`build_mypub-transtype-html.xml`).

4. In the `org.example.mypub.html` directory create the file `plugin.xml` with this content:

```
<?xml version="1.0" encoding="UTF-8"?>
<plugin id="org.example.mypub.html">
  <require plugin="org.dita.xhtml"/>

  <template file="build_mypub-transtype-html_template.xml"/>

  <feature extension="dita.conductor.transtype.check"
           value="html-mypub"
           type="txt"/>
  <feature extension="dita.conductor.target.relative"
    file="build.xml"/>
</plugin>
```

This is the plugin descriptor that makes this directory into a Toolkit plugin. It names the template file you created above and connects the transformation type and its build file into the main Ant build scripts.

5. Create the directories `css` and `html` under the plugin's directory.

You can test the plugin by deploying it to your Toolkit: copy the directory org.example.mypub.html to your Toolkit's plugins directory and run the integrator.xml Ant script:

```
c:\DITA-OT > ant -f integrator.xml
```

You can then try to run the transform by running the Toolkit with the Ant property "transtype" set to the value html-mypub. It should fail with messages about missing the CSS and header and footer files, since you haven't created those yet.

For example, to run the transform against the "garage" sample provided with the full Toolkit installation, start a Toolkit command line and do this command:

```
c:\DITA-OT > ant -Dtranstype=html-mypub
    -Dargs.input=samples\hierarchy.ditamap
    -Doutput.dir=temp\output\mypub-html
```

The output should be in the directory temp\output\mypub-html.

To run the transform from OxygenXML, duplicate the built-in DITA XHTML transformation scenario, giving the new scenario a name like "DITA XHTML MyPub." Add the transtype parameter, giving it the value "html-mypub". It should work. Because the plugin specifies all the parameters for the CSS and HTML headers and footers, you don't need to set any other parameters, just the transformation type.

HTML Customization: Step 2—Create CSS and HTML headers and footers

The HTML transform includes built-in CSS stylesheets for left-to-right and right-to-left content. You can override or extend the base CSS with your own.

The easiest way to determine what you want to modify is to generate HTML from your publication, see what it looks like, and then code the CSS to match that.

For this exercise you will simply change the heading and body fonts to emulate the PDF style, using a sans-serif font for headings, ideally Myriad, and a serif font other than Times for the body, ideally Minion. Both Myriad and Minion are fairly common fonts and are likely to be available for most users.

The headers and footers are HTML fragments that get added to the generated pages. They can hold anything you want that is valid within an HTML page. Typical use is to put the publication title or some branding in the header and a copyright statement in the footer. You can, of course, also use JavaScript to achieve more sophisticated effects, but that is beyond the scope of this book.

For the headers, create the file `org.example.mypub.html/html/myPub-header.html` with this content:

```
<div class="header">
  <span class="pubtitle-header">My Publication's Title</span>
</div>
```

For the footers, create the file `org.example.mypub.html/html/myPub-footer.html` with this content:

```
<div class="footer">
  <span class="copyright">Copyright © 2012 example.org</span>
</div>
```

For the CSS, create the file `org.example.mypub.html/css/myPub.css` with this content:

```
body {
    font-family: Minion, serif;
}

h1, h2, h3, h4, h5 {
    font-family: Myriad, sans-serif;
}

.header {
    text-align: right;
    font-size: 9pt;
    font-family: Minion, serif;
    border-bottom: blue 1pt solid;
    margin-bottom: 2em;
}

.footer {
    text-align: center;
    font-size: 9pt;
    font-family: Minion, serif;
    border-top: blue 1pt solid;
    margin-top: 2em;
}
```

Note that the CSS is providing styling for classes defined in the header and footer, which would require a custom CSS in any case.

Redeploy the transform and run it as you did in Step 1. You should see the result of the CSS and the headers and footers.

If something isn't working, the first thing to check is the Toolkit log to make sure the parameter values are correct. Starting with version 1.5.3, the Toolkit log echoes all Ant properties near the start of the log so you can check to see what was actually used. This is an easy way to spot typos in the properties. Also look for error messages in the log. An annoying aspect of the Toolkit is that an error in an earlier step doesn't always end the Ant process, so you sometimes get a "Build successful" message even though the processing wasn't successful. When things don't work, you always need to look up in the log to see if something went wrong in an earlier step.

It should be clear from this exercise that it's pretty easy to customize the HTML output with little effort as long as you can do it with CSS, which is often the case. This example just scratches the surface of what you can do for re-branding and improving the presentation from the rather blah built-in styling.

Customizing the Open Toolkit PDF Transform

The Open Toolkit's PDF transformation type provides its own configuration and customization facility that is different from the general Toolkit extension and override mechanism.

To generate PDF for our DITA publication the goals are:

1. Change the page design to a 7"x10" trim size from the default 8.5" x 11" trim size.
2. Change the fonts used for the document body and headings from the default.

These changes can be done completely through configuration or non-programming modifications to XSLT files. More involved changes, such as adding custom covers or changing the chapter opener treatment, require more involved XSLT programming, which is beyond the scope of this section.

The typographic requirements are as follows:

Table 1: Layout and Typography Requirements

Property	Value
Heading font	Myriad
Body text font	Minion
Page header font	Myriad
Sidebar font	Myriad
Footnote font	Minion
Chapter label font	Papyrus
Trim size	7" width by 10" height

Property	Value
Header region	0.5" high, 0.375" from bottom of header to top of main text area.
Footer	0.3in high, 0.5" from bottom of main text area to top of footer.
Outside margin	0.75"
Inside margin	0.8755"
Top margin	0.5" (above header region)
Bottom margin	0.375" (below footer region)
Body point size	10pt
Pager header point size	10pt
Index point size	9pt
Footnote point size	8.5pt
Line height (leading)	120%
Chapter title	32pt
Chapter label (number)	72pt
Appendix title	32pt
Appendix label	72pt
Index title	32pt
Colophon title	16pt centered
Level 1 headings	13pt bold
Level 2 headings	12pt bold italic
Level 3 headings	10pt bold
Index pages	two columns

Implementing these requirements requires doing the following:

1. Create a new "customization" Toolkit plugin to hold your customizations. While it's not always obvious from the PDF plugin documentation, you can store and deploy a customization, separate from the PDF plugin itself, that defines a new transformation type. This new transformation type really just sets a number of properties for your customizations that make them easier to use—it does not implement a new transformation process.

2. Customize the page masters to define the page layout details.
3. Customize the appropriate XSLT attribute sets to reflect the typographic details.
4. Set up the font configuration for your FO engine (for this example, FOP).

Additional resources for the PDF transformation type customization and configuration include:

- *Customizing the DITA Open Toolkit for Print* , by Leigh White, XML Press.

  How-to information on customizing the Toolkit's PDF transformation type.

- *www.scriptorium.com/whitepapers/ditaotpdf/DITA-PDF-tweaks.pdf*

  White paper on general PDF customization.

- *http://www.scriptorium.com/whitepapers/fop_fonts/index.html*

  A detailed discussion of configuring fonts for use with FOP and the Open Toolkit.

- *www.ditausers.org/tutorials/lone-dita/ditaguide.pdf*

  A general introduction and how-to guide to DITA targeted at writers working alone or in very small teams. Includes a good introduction to customizing the PDF transformation type.

- The `README.txt` file in the `plugins/fo` and `plugins/fo/Customization` directories of the Open Toolkit.

  Describes the contents of the plugin and provides some guidance on setting up configurations and customizations.

About the Open Toolkit PDF Transform

The PDF transformation type has a long and storied history.

The transform type named "PDF" in the 1.5 version of the DITA Open Toolkit was originally implemented by Idiom Inc. (since acquired by SDL) as part of their larger translation support system. It replaced the much less functional original "pdf" transformation type included in earlier versions of the DITA Open Toolkit.

Thus, you will sometimes see the PDF transformation referred to as the "Idiom PDF transform," and you will still find references to Idiom in the materials that make up the transformation type.

For a time the Idiom transformation type was called "PDF2" to distinguish it from the original PDF transformation type. As of version 1.5 of the Toolkit, the old PDF transformation type has been completely replaced by the Idiom transform and so is now just the "PDF" transformation type.

The company Scriptorium (*www.scriptorium.com/*) also produces a commercial variant of the Idiom PDF transform they refer to as "PDF3."

The PDF transform uses the W3C standard "XSL Formatting Objects, "usually referred to as "XSL-FO" or just "FO," to generate the PDF. The general process is that something, usually an XSLT transform, generates a formatting objects document that defines the pages and content of the final document. The formatting objects document is then processed by a Formatting Objects "engine" to generate the final pages, normally as PDF. There are three main FO engines in common use, all of which are supported by the PDF transform. All are cross-platform. Formatting objects are by convention given the namespace prefix fo:, for example, <fo:simple-page-master>.

The following FO engines are the best known of those available at the time of writing:

- Apache FOP (*http://xmlgraphics.apache.org/fop/*) is a free, open-source FO implementation written in Java. The latest version at the time of writing is version 1.0. It implements much, but not all, of the FO 1.1 recommendation. For example, FOP does not support any of the FO indexing features or floats. In general, FOP is not useful for production page generation unless your typographic requirements are fairly restricted. A version of FOP is included with the Open Toolkit full distribution and should reflect the latest FOP version at the time the Toolkit version is released.
- Antenna House XSL Formatter (*http://www.antennahouse.com/*) is a commercial FO engine. It is distinguished by its support for Asian languages, and it includes a number of extensions for typographic and layout effects not available with standard formatting objects. It includes a graphic user interface under Windows.
- RenderX XEP (*http://www.renderx.com/tools/xep.html*) is a commercial FO engine. It is distinguished by its processing speed. Like XSL Formatter, it provides a number of extensions for specific typographic and layout effects.

Both XSL Formatter and XEP are solid, mature products in wide use, and they are comparable in features and price. Both Antenna House and RenderX provide evaluation licenses. If you are doing production PDF generation, you will almost certainly want one of these products.

PDF Customization: Step 1—Create a new customization plugin

You can package a set of PDF customizations as an Open Toolkit plugin, making it easy to manage and deploy. This also allows you to have different sets of customizations within the same Toolkit installation. The Open Toolkit PDF transform includes extension points that let you globally extend the PDF generation processing. For example, you can use them to implement general support for new vocabulary modules. For this exercise, you are customizing the PDF processing rather than extending it, so you will not use any extension points.

The PDF transformation type provides for two customization files, which are included into the main XSLT transforms, one for "attributes," meaning static settings, and for "XSL," meaning overrides or extensions to XSLT templates. Your PDF customization plugin can contain either or both of these files. Both files are actually XSLT stylesheets, but they are intended to be used in different ways. These files are included from the topic2fo_shell_*.xsl files in the demo/fo/xsl/fo directory, using URNs that are mapped through a `catalog.xml` file that you define. This bit of indirection makes it possible for different customization plugins to provide different customization files in the same Toolkit instance without interfering with each other and without you needing to set up your own top-level XSLT shell, which is what you need to do to accomplish the same goal for the HTML transformation type.

Once you have the basic customization framework set up you can do pretty much whatever you want in terms of customizing the PDF processing. The challenge is figuring out what to do and how to do it. Simple things can be done by just setting variables, but more complicated things will require some knowledge of XSLT and XSL-FO. That knowledge outside the scope of this book. A good XSL-FO resource is Ken Holman's *Practical Formatting Using XSL-FO* (*http://cranesoftwrights.com*). You can also find a number of online XSL-FO tutorials if you need them. And. of course. you can read the XSL-FO recommendation, *Extensible Stylesheet Language (XSL) Version 1.1* (*http://www.w3.org/TR/xsl11/*).

To set up the customization plugin, perform the following steps:

1. Create a directory called `org.example.mypub.pdf` in your workspace, for example, `c:\workspace\org.example.mypub.pdf`. This will be the root directory of the new Toolkit plugin.
2. Copy directory `demo/fo/Customization` from the Toolkit into the `org.example.mypub.pdf` directory.
3. In the `org.example.mypub.pdf` directory create the file `build_mypub-transtype-pdf_template.xml` with this content:

```xml
<project name="org.example.mypub-transtype-pdf" default="dita2pdf-mypub">


    <!-- ==========================
         Build file for use with the DITA Open Toolkit.

         Configures the base PDF2 plugin to use
         the MyPub customizations.

         ========================== -->

  <property name="transtype" value="pdf-mypub"/>

  <target name="dita2pdf-mypub"
    xmlns:dita="http://dita-ot.sourceforge.net"
    dita:extension="depends org.dita.dost.platform.InsertDependsAction"
    >
    <property name="customization.dir"
location="${dita.dir}/plugins/org.example.mypub.pdf/Customization"/>
    <property name="pdf.formatter" value="fop"/>
    <antcall target="dita2pdf2"/>
  </target>
</project>
```

This is the template Ant script that defines a new transformation type, "pdf-mypub" and configures it to use the customization directory in the plugin. It also sets the FO engine to FOP. The only purpose of this file is to set the *customization.dir* Ant property to point to the correct customization directory. You could set this property as a parameter to an invocation of the base "pdf" transformation type, but setting up the separate transformation type can make it easier to use, especially if this is something that will be used by many authors. The Toolkit's integration process will copy this file to build_mypub-transtype-pdf.xml. (You could avoid the use of the template, but creating a template build script in this way is the normal Toolkit plugin pattern.)

common-error: Note that the property definition for *customization.dir* is *inside* the `<target>` element for the transformation type. This is essential. If the property setting is outside the `<target>` element then it acts as a global property setting and will either set the value for all transformation types, or it will have no effect because another included build file sets the property first (for example, if you had two of these PDF customization plugins deployed. This is a subtle error because you'll only notice it when there are two transformation types that use the property, which you may never have in your local environment, so you may never notice the problem.

4. In the `org.example.mypub.pdf` directory create the file `build.xml` with this content:

```
<project>
  <import file="build_mypub-transtype-pdf.xml" />
</project>
```

This file is what is integrated into the master Toolkit `build.xml` file in order to hook this plugin into the Toolkit proper. All it does is create a reference to the main Ant script for the transformation type (`build_mypub-transtype-pdf.xml`).

5. In the `org.example.mypub.pdf` directory, create the file `plugin.xml` with this content:

```
<?xml version="1.0" encoding="UTF-8"?>
<plugin id="org.example.mypub.pdf">
  <require plugin="org.dita.pdf2"/>

  <template file="build_mypub-transtype-pdf_template.xml"/>

  <feature extension="dita.conductor.transtype.check"
           value="pdf-mypub" type="txt"/>
  <feature extension="dita.conductor.target.relative"
           value="build.xml" type="file"/>
</plugin>
```

This is the plugin descriptor that makes this directory into a Toolkit plugin. It names the template file you created above and connects the transformation type and its build file to the main Ant build scripts.

6. Find the file demo/fo/Customization/catalog.xml.orig in the Toolkit and copy it under org.example.mypub.pdf/Customization as file catalog.xml. This file will hook your custom PDF settings and XSLT overrides or extensions into the main PDF processing.

Test the plugin by deploying the org.example.mypub.pdf directory to your Toolkit's plugins/ directory and running the integrator.xml Ant script. You should not see any error messages. You should be able to then use the transformation type "pdf-mypub" in place of the base "pdf."

☞   **Note:** Don't confuse the Open Toolkit plugins directory, within the DITA-OT directory, with the separate OxygenXML plugin directory directly under the OxygenXML installation directory. The OxygenXML plugins directory is for extensions to OxygenXML itself and has nothing directly to do with the Open Toolkit.

If you are using OxygenXML, an easy thing to do is to set up a new transformation scenario by copying the base DITA Map PDF transformation type and setting the "transtype" parameter to "pdf-mypub":

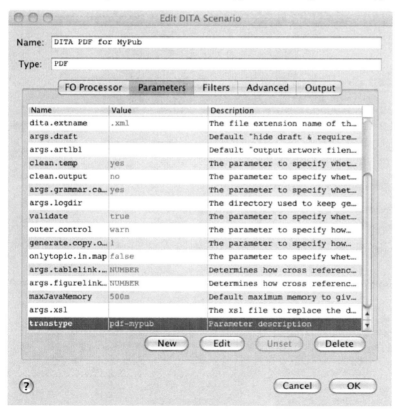

Figure 5: Setting transtype to "pdf-mypub" in OxygenXML

You will probably need to add the "transtype" parameter to the dialog.

Run the transform against a document and inspect the Toolkit log to verify that it is using the pdf-mypub transform, which you will see in the messages from the "check-arg" stage of the Toolkit processing:

```
check-arg:
    [mkdir] Created dir:
/Users/ekimber/workspace/mypub/doc_src/body/part-end-to-end/temp
    [echo] *****************************************************************

    [echo] * basedir = /Users/ekimber/workspace/mypub
    [echo] * dita.dir = /Applications/oxygen/frameworks/dita/DITA-OT
    [echo] * input = /Users/ekimber/workspace/dita-for-mypub/mypub.ditamap

    [echo] * transtype = pdf-mypub
```

You should get the same output you would get from the normal PDF transform since you haven't modified the customizations yet.

PDF Customization: Step 2—Setup the basic layout configuration

The basic page layout and overall document processing options are defined in the file base-settings.xsl in the demo/fo/cfg/fo/attrs directory of the PDF transformation type. To customize these settings you create a copy of the file, naming the copy custom.xsl, in your customization plugin and then modify the settings appropriately.

To set up the basic page layout, perform the following steps:

1. Create the directory Customization/fo/attrs within the org.example.mypub.pdf directory of your Toolkit plugin.
2. Copy the file demo/fo/cfg/fo/attrs/base-settings.xsl into this new directory as the file custom.xsl.
3. Edit the file org.example.mypub.pdf/Customization/catalog.xml and uncomment this line:

```
...
<!--uri name="cfg:fo/attrs/custom.xsl" uri="fo/attrs/custom.xsl"/-->
...
```

Removing "!--"and "--" leaves this result:

```
...
<uri name="cfg:fo/attrs/custom.xsl" uri="fo/attrs/custom.xsl"/>
...
```

This hooks the file `custom.xsl` into the main PDF processing.

4. Edit `fo/attrs/custom.xsl` and find the line that starts:

```
<xsl:variable name="page-width">
```

This is an XSLT variable declaration. The variable name is *page-width* and the value is in the content of the element. The value can also be in the `@select` attribute. You will see both forms of variable declarations in the XSLT files for the PDF transformation.

5. Change the content of this variable to "7in" and the line following, which should be the *page-height* variable, to "10in," like the following:

```
...
<!-- The default of 215.9mm x 279.4mm is US Letter size (8.5x11in) -->

<xsl:variable name="page-width">7in</xsl:variable>
<xsl:variable name="page-height">10in</xsl:variable>
...
```

You can also put the value in `@select` attributes, like the following:

```
<xsl:variable name="page-width" select="'7in'"/>
<xsl:variable name="page-height" select="'10in'"/>
```

Note that the value of the `@select` attributes are literal strings delimited with single quotes (') and the `<variable>` elements are now empty tags. The two forms are equivalent.

6. Find the variable named *mirror-page-margins* and set the value from false() to true():

```
...
<xsl:variable name="mirror-page-margins" select="true()"/>
...
```

This turns on the use of the odd and even page masters.

7. Update the page margin variables to reflect the margin specifications:

```
    <!-- Change these if your page has different margins on different
sides. -->
    <!-- legacy parameter -->
    <xsl:variable name="page-margin-left"/>
    <!-- legacy parameter -->
    <xsl:variable name="page-margin-right"/>
    <xsl:variable name="page-margin-inside" select="'0.8755in'"/>
    <xsl:variable name="page-margin-outside" select="'0.75in'"/>
    <xsl:variable name="page-margin-top" select="'0.5in'"/>
    <xsl:variable name="page-margin-bottom" select="'0.375'"/>
```

Note that the values in the @select attributes are enclosed in single quotes within the double quotes, for example, '0.8755in'.

8. Set the *side-col-width* variable to "0pt":

```
    <xsl:variable name="side-col-width">0pt</xsl:variable>
```

9. Deploy your plugin and test it by running the pdf-mypub transformation type. You should get a PDF that reflects the page dimensions and margins.

At this point you know that you have your customization plugin hooked up correctly with the custom variables file in place and working. You can now proceed with the additional customization needed to fully implement the custom presentation specifications.

If your plugin isn't working, the error result you get from the Toolkit may not be that helpful. Often the real error causes a failure later in the process, so the error report is not always pointing at the real problem. You may also need to look through the processing log to find the real issue.

If the process runs to completion, but you do not get the custom layout, check the following:

- Make sure you set the transtype parameter to "pdf-mypub." You can see the value of the parameter you specified near the top of the Toolkit log.
- Make sure the *customization.dir* parameter is set correctly in the build_mypub-transtype-pdf_template.xml file.
- Make sure the catalog.xml entry correctly points to the custom.xsl file. You can check this OxygenXML by using the "open file at cursor" function from the catalog file.

If all those things check out, then it should work.

If it's still not working, one technique is to add <echo> elements to the base Toolkit build files to confirm that a given target is being called and to report the values of specific properties. For example, in the process of developing this section, I was not getting the customization I expected. I debugged the problem by modifying the file demo/fo/build_template.xml to add an <echo> element at the start of the target "transform.topic2pdf.init," which was the first place that the *customization.dir* property was used. My modification looked like this:

```
  ...
  <target name="transform.topic2pdf.init">
    <echo message="*** customization.dir=${customization.dir}"/>
    <property name="customization.dir"
 value="${dita.plugin.org.dita.pdf2.dir}/Customization"/>
    <property file="${customization.dir}/build.properties"/>
  ...
```

This produces a message showing the value of the *customization.dir* property at that point. With that information I was able to see that I had another customization plugin that was setting the property globally rather than locally.

Note that I modified the "build_*template*.xml" file, not the build.xml file. That's because the build.xml file is regenerated from the template file any time you run the integrator.xml Ant script.

PDF Customization: Step 3—Setup page layout details

You now have the basic trim size configured, but you still need to define the various page regions to set up the header, footer, and main text areas appropriately.

The general challenge here is figuring out what to modify. All the base settings for the PDF transform are somewhere under demo/fo/cfg. The attrs directory contains all the statically-set properties, and most of what you need to do is done with those attributes. The details of the page layouts is ultimately defined through <fo:simple-page-master> elements, which define the details of each different page layout, such as even body pages, or odd index pages, or whatever.

The page masters are in turn defined through the use of named attribute sets, which you can override and modify to set specific properties on the page masters. The default page master setup provides most of the page master's you would need for a typical document: frontmatter, body pages, index pages, and glossary pages. However, it doesn't provide page masters for covers, inside title pages, and other miscellaneous pages that you might need. Thus, you may need to override the default page master template to add additional page masters depending on the needs of a specific type of publication.

To configure the page masters, perform the following steps:

1. Find the file demo/fo/cfg/fo/attrs/layout-masters-attr.xsl and open it in your editor.
2. Open the file org.example.mypub.pdf/Customization/fo/attrs/custom.xsl

3. In `layout-masters-attr.xsl`, find the `<xsl:attribute>` sets named "region-before" and "region-after" and copy them into `custom.xsl` before the `<xsl:stylesheet>` end tag:

```
  . . .

  <xsl:attribute-set name="region-before">
    <xsl:attribute name="extent">
      <xsl:value-of select="$page-margin-top"/>
    </xsl:attribute>
    <xsl:attribute name="display-align">before</xsl:attribute>
  </xsl:attribute-set>

  <xsl:attribute-set name="region-after">
    <xsl:attribute name="extent">
      <xsl:value-of select="$page-margin-bottom"/>
    </xsl:attribute>
    <xsl:attribute name="display-align">after</xsl:attribute>
  </xsl:attribute-set>

</xsl:stylesheet>
```

4. As defined, these attribute sets make the top and bottom regions the same size as the page margins, but for your page you want a 0.5 inch margin above the header region and after the footer region plus the vertical extent of each region. There are two ways to do this in XSL-FO: define margins on the page itself, or make the top and bottom regions big enough to include the page margin and put the margins in the regions. The second approach is the better practice because it allows you to still place things up to the edge of the physical page, which you cannot do if you define actual page margins.

To get the geometry right, set the value of the `@extent` attribute for the region-before to 0.5in + 0.5in or 1.0in:

```
  . . .
  <xsl:attribute-set name="region-before">
    <xsl:attribute name="extent" select="'1.0in'"/>
    <xsl:attribute name="display-align">before</xsl:attribute>
  </xsl:attribute-set>
  . . .
```

Note that I've put the attribute value in a `@select` attribute directly on the `<xsl:attribute>` element; using a nested `<xsl:value-of>` is not necessary and just makes the code more verbose.

5. Now add an `<xsl:attribute>` for the attribute named "margin-top" with a value "0.5in," which gives us the effective page margin of 0.5 inches:

```
...
<xsl:attribute-set name="region-before">
  <xsl:attribute name="extent" select="'1.0in'"/>
  <xsl:attribute name="margin-top" select="'0.5in'"/>
  <xsl:attribute name="display-align">before</xsl:attribute>
</xsl:attribute-set>
...
```

Note that for edge regions (region-before, region-after, region-start, region-end), the region always extends from the corresponding page margin inward toward the middle of the page. If there are no page margins, as there are not in this case, then the regions extend from the physical edge of the page.

6. The base setting for the region-before sets the "display-align" property to "before," which makes everything start at the top of the region. But for this design, you want the header contents to sit on the bottom of the region's area. So change @display-align from "before" to "after":

```
...
<xsl:attribute-set name="region-before">
  <xsl:attribute name="extent" select="'1.0in'"/>
  <xsl:attribute name="margin-top" select="'0.5in'"/>
  <xsl:attribute name="display-align" select="'after'"/>
</xsl:attribute-set>
...
```

I set the value of @select as a literal string in single quotes. If you decide later to set the value using an XSLT variable, you have to use the @select attribute, so I find it easier to use this form. However, if you leave off the single quotes, the value of @select is interpreted as an XPath expression selecting the element named "after" (in this example), which of course will result in a null string. This is not a syntax error, which makes it hard-to-find. Therefore, you may prefer not to use @select.

7. To make it easy to verify that you're actually modifying the page layout, set a background color on the region so it will show up on the page even if there's no content:

```
...
<xsl:attribute-set name="region-before">
  <xsl:attribute name="extent" select="'1.0in'"/>
  <xsl:attribute name="margin-top" select="'0.5in'"/>
  <xsl:attribute name="display-align" select="'after'"/>
  <xsl:attribute name="background-color" select="'teal'"/>
</xsl:attribute-set>
...
```

8. Redeploy the plugin and rerun it. You should see something like this on most of the pages:

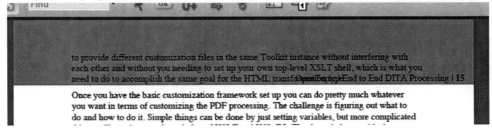

Figure 6: Custom region-before with teal background color

Note that the body text overlaps the heading text, which you can tell by finding the page number.

This is because you haven't changed the margins for body region to account for the "page" margins and the header and footer region extents. In XSL-FO, edge regions can overlap the body region, so you have to make sure that all the margins are correctly specified.

9. Rework the "region-after" attribute set to mirror the region-before attribute set, but using a "margin-bottom" value of "0.5," an extent of 0.5 + 0.3 (0.8), and a "display-align" of "before":

```
...
<xsl:attribute-set name="region-after">
  <xsl:attribute name="extent" select="'0.8in'"/>
  <xsl:attribute name="margin-bottom" select="'0.5in'"/>
  <xsl:attribute name="display-align" select="'before'"/>
  <xsl:attribute name="background-color" select="'teal'"/>
</xsl:attribute-set>
...
```

10. Redeploy the plugin and run it again. You should see a teal area at the bottom of the page as well. Again, the body text will likely overlap that region.

11. In the custom.xsl file, find the variables named *page-margin-top* and *page-margin-bottom*. You can see that I gave you the wrong value. The value needs to be the nominal page margin (0.5in) plus the region extent (0.5in or 0.3in) and the gap between the inner edge of the edge region and the start of the body region: 0.25in, or 1.25 inches for the top margin and 1.05 inches for the bottom margin. Update the variables to reflect these new values:

```
...
<xsl:variable name="page-margin-top" select="'1.25in'"/>
<xsl:variable name="page-margin-bottom" select="'1.05in'"/>
...
```

12. Redeploy the plugin and run it again. You should now see that the body text does not overlap the edge regions.

At this point, the page geometry reflects the specs and is good enough for now. A more complete solution would probably require tuning the first chapter pages. If you needed to define additional page masters you would need to override the "createDefaultLayoutMasters" template from the base `demo/fo/cfg/fo/layout-masters.xsl` file by copying it into your customization and reworking it. That level of customization is beyond the scope of this book, but at this point you should be familiar enough with the overall process to at least know what questions to ask, if not puzzle out a working solution.

PDF Customization: Step 4—Configure typographic details

With the page layout under control, the next challenge is configuring the typographic details, meaning the fonts and sizes for the different document elements: headings, body text, footnotes, and so on. The challenge here is to find the variables or attribute sets that control the properties you want to modify. That can take a bit of poking about, but in general the attribute sets and variables have been named in a fairly clear way. The other challenge is configuring the fonts to work with your FO engine. The PDF transform provides a general font configuration mechanism, but you may need to also adjust the configuration of your FO engine as well.

To start you will set the default font for titles to "Myriad," per the spec. To do this, perform the following steps:

1. Find the file `demo/fo/cfg/fo/attrs/commons-attr.xsl` and find the attribute set named "common.title":

```
...
<!-- titles -->
<xsl:attribute-set name="common.title">
  <xsl:attribute name="font-family">Sans</xsl:attribute>
</xsl:attribute-set>
...
```

2. Copy and paste this attribute set at the bottom of your `custom.xsl` file:

```
...
<!-- titles -->
<xsl:attribute-set name="common.title">
  <xsl:attribute name="font-family">Sans</xsl:attribute>
</xsl:attribute-set>

</xsl:stylesheet>
```

3. Change font name "Sans" to "Myriad":

```
...
<xsl:attribute-set name="common.title">
  <xsl:attribute name="font-family" select="'Myriad'"/>
</xsl:attribute-set>
...
```

4. Deploy the plugin and run it. Look in the Toolkit log for the section starting "transform.topic2fo.i18n:," you should see messages like the following:

```
transform.topic2fo.i18n:
      [xslt] Processing /Users/dita/temp/stage3.fo to
             /Users/dita/pdf/part-end-to-end/topic.fo
      [xslt] Loading stylesheet
/Applications/oxygen/frameworks/dita/DITA-OT/demo/fo/xsl/fo/i18n-postprocess.xsl

      [xslt] [PDFX008W][WARN]: Font definition not found for the logical
name or alias 'Myriad'.
      [xslt] [PDFX008W][WARN]: Font definition not found for the logical
name or alias 'Myriad'.
```

That indicates that your configuration change was successful, and you now need to configure the font mapping.

5. Find the file `demo/fo/cfg/fo/font-mappings.xml` and copy it to `org.example.mypub.pdf/Customization/fo/font-mappings.xml`.

6. Edit the file `org.example.mypub.pdf/Customization/catalog.xml` and uncomment the line pointing to the font-mappings file:

```
...
<!-- FontMapper configuration override entry.-->
<uri name="cfg:fo/font-mappings.xml" uri="fo/font-mappings.xml"/>
...
```

7. Edit the `font-mappings.xml` file and add the following after the `<aliases>` elements:

```
...
<logical-font name="Minion">
  <physical-font char-set="default">
    <font-face>Minion</font-face>
  </physical-font>
</logical-font>
```

```
<logical-font name="Myriad">
  <physical-font char-set="default">
    <font-face>Myriad</font-face>
  </physical-font>
</logical-font>
...
```

You have now registered the font names Minion and Myriad and mapped them to the font face names Minion and Myriad. The font names are used in the XSL-FO @font-family values, for example, <fo:root font-family="Minion"/>, and are used to find the appropriate font files.

For FOP, you must separately define the mapping between the logical font names in the <font-face> elements and the real font files. On non-Windows platforms, you must do a similar configuration for Antenna House XSL Formatter and RenderX XEP, as there is no standard way for Java applications to find fonts on non-Windows systems.

On Windows, XEP and XSL Formatter should be able to find fonts as long as the font names match the XSL-FO @font-family values. Refer to the documentation for your FO engine for details.

PDF Customization: Step 5—Setup FOP font configuration

FOP depends on a configuration file to tell it where the font files it requires are located. This font configuration file can go anywhere, but for this exercise you will include it in the mypub customization plugin. In practice it probably makes sense to have a separate Toolkit plugin that manages the FOP configuration or put the configuration somewhere on the machine and point the Toolkit to it.

FOP does not completely support the OpenType font specification and may not support some TrueType fonts. You may need to either generate TrueType fonts from OpenType fonts or find TrueType versions of the fonts you want. For some TrueType fonts, you may need to generate FOP-specific font metrics files using a utility provided with FOP. The open-source FontForge tool can generate TrueType versions of OpenType fonts that will work with FOP (*http://fontforge.sourceforge.net*).

For general information on configuring FOP font usage, see the FOP documentation at the Apache FOP site (*http://xmlgraphics.apache.org*).

To set up the font configuration, perform these steps:

1. Edit the FOP configuration file demo/fo/fop/conf/xconf. Note that through version 1.5.3 of the Open Toolkit, there is no Ant mechanism for pointing FOP at a different configuration file, so you must modify the configuration file within the Toolkit itself. Once you get the font configuration working, it's a good idea to save a copy of the configuration file so you don't lose your changes when you update your Toolkit installation.

2. Find the line `<renderer mime="application/pdf">`. This is the start of the configuration for PDF output. Find the `<fonts>` element. This contains the font configuration details:

```
...
<renderers>
 <renderer mime="application/pdf">
  <filterList>
   <!-- provides compression using zlib flate (default is on) -->
   <value>flate</value>
<!-- encodes binary data into printable ascii characters (default off)
     This provides about a 4:5 expansion of data size -->
<!-- <value>ascii-85</value> -->
<!-- encodes binary data with hex representation (default off)
     This filter is not recommended as it doubles the data size -->
<!-- <value>ascii-hex</value> -->
  </filterList>
  <fonts>
    ...
  </fonts>
...
```

3. Configure the Myriad and Minion fonts by adding `<font>` entries similar to these:

```
...
<fonts>
  <!-- Minion: -->
  <font kerning="yes"
    embed-url="file:////Library/Fonts/MinionPro-Regular.ttf">
    <font-triplet name="Minion" style="normal" weight="normal"/>
  </font>
  <font kerning="yes"
    embed-url="file:////Library/Fonts/MinionPro-Bold.ttf">
    <font-triplet name="Minion" style="normal" weight="bold"/>
  </font>
  <!-- Myriad: -->
  <font kerning="yes"
    embed-url="file:////Users/ekimber/Library/Fonts/MYRIADAT.TTF">
    <font-triplet name="Myriad" style="normal" weight="normal"/>
  </font>
  <font kerning="yes"
    embed-url="file:////Users/ekimber/Library/Fonts/MYRIADAB.TTF">
    <font-triplet name="Myriad" style="normal" weight="bold"/>
  </font>
  <font kerning="yes"
    embed-url="file:////Users/ekimber/Library/Fonts/MYRIAABI.TTF">
    <font-triplet name="Myriad" style="italic" weight="bold"/>
  </font>
  ...
```

The `@embed-url` is the absolute path to the font on your system.

The `<font-triplet>` element specifies the base font name, as used in the XSL-FO `@font-family` attribute, the font style, and the font weight. Those values are matched against the `@font-style` and `@font-weight` values used in the XSL-FO to select the appropriate font file. Thus, for each different combination of font weight and style you will need a separate `<font>` entry in the FOP configuration.

4. Run your plugin (you don't need to redeploy it because you are modifying a file in the Toolkit itself). If your font configuration is correct and the fonts are usable by FOP, then you should see them reflected in the PDF. If you have Acrobat Pro or a similar PDF viewer, you can inspect the PDF to verify that it is using the fonts. In the case of Minion and Myriad, they are sufficiently different from Times and Helvetica that it is easy to see if your configuration is correct.

   If the font configuration is not correct or the fonts are not usable, FOP will give you reasonably helpful error messages. The configuration shown here is the configuration that works for me under OSX. Font configuration can be pain so don't be surprised if you have to spend some time fiddling with the fonts to make them work with FOP. On my machine I had use FontForge to generate TrueType versions of the Adobe Minion Pro fonts, but I did not need to generate font metrics for them.

The lack of support for OpenType fonts in FOP is annoying, but there are usable workarounds, such as FontForge. The FOP developer discussion indicates that work to implement support for OpenType is ongoing, but it's not a particularly easy thing to implement.

The commercial FO engines all support OpenType fonts directly. For example, here is my font configuration for XSL Formatter:

```
<font-config>
  <!--otf-metrics-mode mode="typographic"/-->
  <!-- add your font folder here -->
  <!--font-folder path="~/Library/Fonts"/-->
  <font-folder path="/System/Library/Fonts"/>
  <font-folder path="/Library/Fonts">
    <font-alias file="MinionPro-Regular.otf">
      <alias family-name="Minion" />
    </font-alias>
    <font-alias file="MinionPro-Bold.otf">
      <alias family-name="Minion" weight="bold"/>
    </font-alias>
  </font-folder>
  <font-folder path="/Users/ekimber/Library/Fonts">
    <font-alias file="MyriadPro-Regular.otf">
      <alias family-name="Myriad" />
    </font-alias>
    <font-alias file="MyriadPro-Bold.otf">
      <alias family-name="Myriad" weight="bold"/>
    </font-alias>
```

```
    </font-folder>
    <font-folder path="/Users/ekimber/apps/AHFormatterV5/fonts">
      <glyph-list file="ZapfDingbats-glyphname.txt" afm="ZapfDingbats.afm"/>
    </font-folder>
  </font-config>
```

If you think you have the font configuration correct, but you're still not getting the fonts you want, the best thing is to look at the generated FO instance and verify the values being used in the @font-family attributes. You can do this by setting the Ant parameter retain.topic.fo to "yes." This will keep the PDF process from deleting the intermediate FO file. You can then look for @font-family attributes. You should see code like the following:

```
<fo:root
  xmlns:fo="http://www.w3.org/1999/XSL/Format"
  xmlns:opentopic-i18n="http://www.idiominc.com/opentopic/i18n"
  font-size="10pt"
  line-height-shift-adjustment="disregard-shifts"
  font-family="Minion">
```

Note also that the PDF transform uses the literal value of the @font-family attribute to look up fonts in the font mappings file, so you can't specify a sequence of font names as is often done in XSL-FO. The values of all @font-family attributes need to be single font names.

Part II

An Overview of the DITA Architecture

DITA has several key architectural features that make it fundamentally different from all other XML applications and standards. These features are:

- Vocabulary composition, which enables the interchange and management of markup vocabularies irrespective of how they are combined into specific document types.
- Specialization, which enables blind interchange of DITA documents, regardless of the element types used in any given document, through controlled extension of the vocabulary.
- Modularity of processing, which is enabled and rewarded, though not mandated, by the modular nature of DITA vocabularies.

No other aspect of DITA is particularly distinguishing, although many are innovative. In particular, there is no single aspect of DITA's markup design that cannot be found in other well-known XML applications, such as DocBook, IBM ID Doc, or S1000D. While DITA's design integrates a set of features that support modular documents more completely than other designs, it does not do anything that couldn't be done by other XML applications.

This means that the distinguishing aspects of DITA, in particular specialization, could be applied to any markup design. Here I'm specifically thinking of DocBook, which is both very widely used and not generally structurally compatible with the current DITA markup design.

Thus it's useful to think of DITA as a combination of two technologies: first, the specialization facility and second, the vocabulary, that is the base topic and map types and the built-in domains. The latter defines a starter vocabulary optimized for general-purpose documents and reflects a set of more or less arbitrary design decisions that lead to specific content model patterns (for example, requiring a wrapper element around the body content of topics).

While it doesn't directly drive DITA's markup design, the specialization facility requires the more general element types to have very loose content models. This allows specialized elements to be built with more options, for example, for leaving things out or changing the order of elements. This means that the base content models tend to be much more open than would normally be used in typical authoring document types.

Keep in mind that DITA provides facilities for both constraining base content models without doing specialization (configuration) and defining new, more-constrained elements types (specialization). This means that you can adapt otherwise-generic element types to reflect your authors' specific needs for constraint without having to do specialization. Thus you should not be concerned about DITA's loose base content models.

However, the DITA markup design is unique, reflecting a set of considered design decisions driven primarily by DITA's general requirement to support modular information authoring. In particular, DITA's map and topic dichotomy reflects a fundamental separation of concerns between content authoring (topics) and the organization of that content (maps). Compare that with book-centric markup designs, like DocBook, where the normal practice is to have a single XML document that both contains the content and defines the publication structure.

Once you get to content, DITA is, by design, as familiar and natural as it can be, especially if you are familiar with HTML. The content of any prose document essentially breaks down into some combination of paragraphs, lists, figures, and tables, salted with various inlines and annotated with metadata as needed. If you are familiar with any other documentation or publishing document type, there will be few, if any, surprises in DITA's content markup design, with one notable exception, the `<section>` element, about which more later.

5

Vocabulary Composition and Specialization

DITA turns traditional XML practice on its head with regard to document types.

In traditional XML applications, you define a single, monolithic document type that is expected to be used by all documents within a given body of documentation. You may have a family of related document types that include common declaration sets, but each document type is a separate artifact with a specific, invariant name (its public ID or namespace name or URI). This thing is *the* document type.

DITA was specifically designed to enable the creation of new markup without breaking interchange. This cannot be done using the monolithic document type approach: we've tried for more than 20 years and have consistently failed.

The reason is simple: if you have an invariant document type definition, it cannot be extensible. Any extension is no longer the same document type and referring to it by the public name of the extension base is incorrect and leads to pain.

By the same token, any monolithic document type intended for wide use and interchange must, by necessity, be so loose as to offer little assurance of consistency of application to content.

An example of this is the National Library of Medicine Journal Article Tag Sets (JATS) document type (nee NLM), which is used by a large number of publishers to interchange scientific and medical papers with the National Library of Medicine. Given two JATS documents from two different publishers it is highly likely that those publishers will have applied the JATS elements differently for equivalent information content.

Many publishers use JATS as a starting point for developing their own document types. These document types are all JATS-based but, because JATS does not impose any real constraints on extension or customization, there is no knowable relation between any two publisher-specific JATS-based document types or between those document types and JATS itself because there is nothing in the declarations or the elements they govern that says *how* a given element relates to the original JATS base. This means that smooth interchange of nominally JATS-based documents is impossible in the general case. One symptom of this is that Pubmed Central, the publishing organization that takes articles from publishers and makes them available in a normalized JATS XML form, maintains at least 40 different transforms to manage the transformation from publisher-specific documents to JATS documents.

DITA's approach is to turn the problem around and put the focus on the element types that are used by a given document rather than on a single use of those element types in an invariant schema. DITA also defines a controlled extension mechanism, *specialization*, that allows the creation of new markup while ensuring interchangeability and interoperability.

Vocabulary Modules and DITA Document Types

Each topic type is defined in a separate, invariant *vocabulary module* that defines all the element types specific to that topic type. Likewise each map type is defined in a separate module. Domains, which provide "mix in" elements or attributes, are also defined in modules.

Each module has at least one invariant public name by which it is known and a short name that is likely to be unique in any use context. The markup declarations within the module are invariant, and can only be modified through the configuration and extension facilities defined by the DITA specification. This means that all copies of a given vocabulary module should be identical. This is very important.

A vocabulary module is simply a definition, by whatever means, of a set of DITA element types and attributes. In practice vocabulary modules are implemented as DTD declaration sets or XSD schema modules, along with documentation for humans. Thus, when you talk about the "concept vocabulary module" you are referring to the idea of the concept topic type as well as all concrete expressions of it, which include a set of concrete DTD declaration sets, XSD documents, and documentation in the DITA Language Reference.

The DITA specification allows you to configure vocabulary modules for use in specific contexts, but constrains those configurations so that processors can determine whether two different uses of a given module in two different documents are compatible, where compatibility means that elements from one document can be reliably combined with elements from the other. This means, for example, that processors can determine whether a content reference should be allowed or not.

Because vocabulary modules are invariant, the processing specific to a particular module can also be invariant. From a practical standpoint this means you can package a vocabulary module and its supporting processing modules together as a unit of deployment, for example, as a plugin or set of plugins for the DITA Open Toolkit. It also means that software that enables modular extension (for example, plugins for the DITA Open Toolkit) is easier to configure and adapt to new vocabulary modules.

The result of this focus on vocabulary modules (topic types, map types, and domain modules) is that you end up with a collection of modules that can be "composed" (in the formal sense of making a new thing out of smaller bits) in different ways. Likewise, the processing that supports these modules can be composed from individual modules as long as your processing technology supports at least some modular functionality.

Vocabulary modules may be defined by the DITA specification (topic, map, concept, task, reference, etc.), other standards, or created for use by specific communities (for example, specializations created within a company or department). Regardless of the source of the module, all conforming modules must follow the same rules and patterns.

Any given DITA document uses one or more vocabulary modules. Because vocabulary modules are invariant, two documents that use the same set of vocabulary modules necessarily have the same "document type" in the traditional XML sense: a unique set of element types in a specific combination.

Because a document type is determined by the set of modules used, the only thing you need to know to see if they use the same document type is which modules are used, that is, the names of the modules. If Document A uses the modules topic, concept, and ui-d and Document B uses the modules topic, concept, and ui-d, then they must have the same document type.

Documents declare their module usage through the `@domains` attribute, which must occur on the root element of a conforming DITA document, for example:

```
<?xml version="1.0"?>
<concept id="mytopic"
   domains="(topic concept) (topic ui-d)"
>
 ...
</concept>
```

The `@domains` attribute simply lists the modules used and how they relate to each other. The value is a sequence of parenthesized groups naming the modules. In this example, the first group indicates that the document uses the concept topic type module, which is a specialization of the topic module. The second group indicates that the document also uses the ui-d topic domain module.

Such a set of vocabulary modules (and constraint modules, which will be discussed later) is called a *DITA document type* to distinguish it from any particular syntactic implementation of the document type.

Note that the declaration of the set of vocabulary modules used has nothing to do with whether the document has a DOCTYPE declaration or references an XSD schema. All that is required is the list of module names provided by the @domains attribute. This means, in part, that DOCTYPE declarations and schemas are *never required* by the DITA specification. Of course, DTDs and schemas are a useful convenience, particularly for authoring and validation, but they are never required for processing as long as the documents to be processed include all the attributes that DITA uses to convey the module usage and express the specialization of elements and attributes.

Of course, in practice it is useful to have DTDs or XSDs that reflect a given set, or "integration," of modules so you can edit and validate documents using normal XML technology. However, you could, if it made sense to do so, build software components that have intrinsic knowledge of the rules defined by a given vocabulary module and thus enable editing or validation of documents that use that module.

For example, you could construct a schematron that validates a vocabulary module or DITA document type. That schematron could then be used to validate documents that have no DOCTYPE declaration or schema reference. The details for using DTDs and XSD schemas with DITA documents is defined in the document type coding requirements section of the DITA architectural specification.

Given DITA's concept of DITA document type it follows that there is not **a** DITA document type in the way there is a DocBook document type or JATS document type. Rather, there is a set of DITA vocabulary modules. While OASIS provides a set of DTD and XSD document type shells for use with DITA documents, those shells are simply conveniences or examples—they have no normative force, meaning that there is no requirement that conforming DITA systems include or support those document type shells and no requirement that DITA users use them.

It should go without saying that for a document to be a conforming DITA document the first (leftmost) module listed in its @domains value must be "topic" or "map," since all conforming DITA documents are either topics or maps and their root elements must be specializations of <topic> or <map>.

Constraints and Vocabulary Module Integration

The simplest DITA document consists of exactly one topic type or map type with no additional domains, for example, a document that simply uses the "concept" module with no additional domains. In that case, the @domains attribute value would be "(topic concept)." In fact, the simplest possible DITA topic document would use only the "topic" topic type module and no domain or constraint modules. The @domains attribute value for such a topic would be "(topic)".

In practice, it would be rare for any production use of DITA to use base topic types without any additional domains. In part, this is because the base topic types intentionally have very loose content models to make them suitable as a base for specialization.

For example, both the base `<body>` and `<section>` elements allow PCDATA where most users of DITA would never want PCDATA. Likewise, the `<section>` element allows `<title>` to occur multiple times, anywhere within the `<section>`.

The base content model for `<section>` is a direct consequence of the limitations of DTDs, in particular, the requirement that if a content model includes #PCDATA it must be defined as a repeating OR group. Thus, if sections must allow #PCDATA (which they must, since a specialized section that allows only #PCDATA or only phrase-level elements is perfectly sensible) then the only choice is to have a repeating OR group, and if sections must also allow (but not require) `<title>` elements (which they must, since a `<section>` is a titled unit of content, where the title is either explicit or generated), then there is no way to avoid having a content model for `<section>` that allows both #PCDATA and multiple `<title>` elements anywhere within the `<section>`.

DITA's solution to this problem is to allow adjustment of the base content models. These adjustments are called *constraint modules*. They are called constraint modules because they can only constrain content models, they cannot extend them. That is, you can use a constraint module to disallow elements allowed by the base content model, but you cannot use it to allow elements not allowed by the base content model.

DITA constraints are fundamentally different from the extension facilities of traditional XML applications like DocBook and JATS, which simply provide parameter entities (or the XSD or RelaxNG equivalent) that you can modify in whatever way you need to, without constraint.

By only allowing constraint, DITA ensures that no conforming DITA document can contain things that would be completely unexpected by a processor that understands the modules involved.

For example, a processor that understands the DITA "topic" topic type must handle sections that directly contain #PCDATA or have multiple titles or anything else allowed by the very loose base content models. Such a processor will then be able to handle any DITA topic document no matter how constrained, because it knows about everything that *could* occur in those documents.

It doesn't matter if some of those documents locally disallow things that are allowed in the base. On the other hand, if DITA allowed the use of elements not allowed by the base content models, then the generic topic processor would not be able to reliably process all topic documents. That would largely destroy any hope of interchange or interoperable processing.

Like vocabulary modules, constraint modules are also declared in the `@domains` attribute and thus contribute to the DITA document type used by the document.

A processor need not be able to process topics in a fully general way. A processor is free to say "I only understand topics with this specific set of constraints applied to it." That might allow, for example, a much simpler implementation if the constraint removes a number of hard cases that users don't need in a given documentation set. Because constraint modules are declared in the `@domains` attribute, a non-general processor can determine immediately whether or not it can process a particular document.

The main practical implication of constraints involves content references or cutting and pasting of content across topics with different DITA document types. In particular, the DITA specification disallows content references from a more-constrained document to a less-constrained document, since the less-constrained document may allow elements that are not allowed by the more-constrained document. The same constraint applies to cut and paste: You cannot paste from less constrained to more constrained without risking making the result invalid.

Specialization

Specialization is the process of creating new structural or domain vocabulary modules that provide new markup for specific requirements.

The essential aspect of specialization is that every element type or attribute defined in a vocabulary module must be based on and consistent with an element type or attribute defined in a more-general vocabulary module or in the base topic or map type.

This requirement ensures that any element, no matter how specialized, can always be mapped back to some known type and therefore understood and processed in terms of that known type. This ensures that all DITA documents, no matter how specialized, can always be processed in some way. That is, new markup should never break existing specialization-aware DITA processing.

Every element type exists in a *specialization hierarchy*, which goes from the base type through any intermediate types to the element itself.

For example, if you defined a specialization of <concept> called <myConcept>, its specialization hierarchy would be <topic> -> <concept> -> <myConcept>. A processor given a <myConcept> document would be able to process it either as a concept topic or as a generic topic.

The magic of specialization is the @class attribute.

Every DITA element must have a @class attribute. The value of the class attribute defines the specialization hierarchy for the element. The syntax of the @class attribute is:

- A leading "-" or "+" character: "-" for structural types, "+" for domain types.
- One or more space-separated module/element-type pairs: "topic/p," "topic/body," "hi-d/i," etc.
- A trailing space character on the last term in the hierarchy to ensure accurate string matching.

For the <myConcept> topic type the @class value would be

```
"- topic/topic concept/concept myConcept/myConcept "
```

Which you read right to left as:

> The `<myConcept>` element in the "myConcept" module,
> which specializes `<concept>` from the "concept" module,
> which in turn specializes `<topic>` from the "topic"
> module.

If the `<myConcept>` topic type defined a specialized body element, say `<myConceptBody>`, then the `<myConceptBody>` element's @class value would be:

```
"- topic/body concept/conbody myConcept/myConceptBody "
```

Looking at an instance of the `<myConcept>` element you would find these @class attributes:

```
<myConcept id="topicid"
  class="- topic/topic concept/concept myConcept/myConcept "
>
  <title>My Concept</title>
  <myConceptBody
    class="- topic/body concept/conbody myConcept/myConceptBody "
  >
</myConcept>
```

Note that these are attributes on element instances. While we tend to think of the @class attribute as something that is set in DTDs or XSDs, that is merely a convenience. What's really important is that the attributes are available to XML processors, which will be the case whether they are defaulted in DTDs or specified explicitly in instances—the two are identical to XML processors.

The magic of the @class attribute is that specialized DITA documents will "just work" when processed by general-purpose specialization-aware processors, such as the DITA Open Toolkit.

One implication of this magic is that you can define new markup without the need to also implement all the different forms of processing that might be applied to that markup—it will just work. To the degree that your specialized markup doesn't require any specialized processing, then you will *never* need to implement any new processing for it.

If your specialized markup does require specific processing, adding that processing will generally be easier because DITA-aware tools are usually modular, too. For example, the DITA Open Toolkit plugin mechanism makes it easy to implement specialization-specific processing that extends the out-of-the-box processing using the smallest amount of custom code possible.

Specialization also let's you define new *global* attributes specialized from @base or @props.

Specialization allows for extension of the base DITA vocabulary by adding new element types and attributes. However, this is a *controlled* extension mechanism, meaning that you can't just add anything without restriction. There are three restrictions to specialization:

1. All new markup must be based, ultimately, on a base type defined in the DITA standard.
2. Specialized elements can only be allowed where their base types are allowed. For example, if you define a specialization of <p>, that element type can only be allowed where <p> is allowed. That means, for example, that you can't use your new element directly within <p> elements, because <p> does not allow <p> within its content. The base DITA markup design is intentionally loose and inclusive so that specializations are not limited inappropriately.
3. You cannot add arbitrary attributes to specialized element types. Because of DITA's attribute-based specialization declaration mechanism, the declaration syntax for mapping new attributes to base attribute types would be unusably complex. You can, however, define specializations of the <data> element and then allow or require them in the content of specialized elements. <data> elements can function as attributes because the semantic of <data> is metadata and because the default presentation of <data> is to hide it, and also because you can put the value of <data> elements in the @value attribute of the <data> element.

These restrictions ensure interoperability and interchangeability of DITA documents.

The specialization facility and the design and implementation of specialized vocabulary is covered in detail in *Volume 2*.

DITA and Namespaces

An important feature of XML is *namespaces*. An XML namespace is a globally-unique name that is used to construct the names of element types and attributes within XML documents. Namespace names are URIs, which means that they can be guaranteed to be globally unique because the rules for assigning URNs and URLs are managed through global name registries, namely the authorities responsible for assigning Internet domain names. If you own the domain name "example.com," then you can use "example.com" as part of a namespace URI. Because you own the domain name, it's presumed that you can manage the assignment of the remaining parts of namespace URIs you create so that they are unique. For example, you might define a namespace name like "urn:namespace:example.com:vocabulary-01."

Note that per the XML namespace standard, a namespace name is just a string. While it is syntactically a URI, it is not intended to be resolvable to a resource. This is one reason that it's appropriate to use URNs, rather than URLs, for namespace URIs—you should never need to actually resolve it to something. XML takes advantage of the managed nature of URIs to enable creation of globally-unique strings.

An XML element or attribute is either in a namespace or is in no namespace. If an element or attribute is in no namespace, then its name is simply the *local name*, and it has no namespace name. If an element or attribute is in a namespace, then its name is the namespace name plus the local name. A namespace name and local name pair is a *qualified name* or "qname" for short. Namespace names may be bound to prefixes to make it possible to qualify tagnames and attribute names in the XML syntax, as it would be both impossible and inconvenient to use URN or URL strings as literal parts of start tags.

For example, if you have the namespace name "urn:namespace:example.com:vocabulary-01," you could bind it to the prefix "vocab01" like so:

```
<root xmlns:vocab01="urn:namespace:example.com:vocabulary-01">
  <vocab01:foo>...</vocab01:foo>
</root>
```

The xmlns:vocab01 namespace declaration binds the namespace name to the prefix. The prefix you choose is arbitrary—it's simply a local binding to the namespace name. Two different elements could use different prefixes for the same namespace. You could even use different prefixes for the same namespace in the same document. While there are conventions for prefixes used for some well-known vocabularies, you should never assume that a given prefix means a particular namespace. You always have to look at the namespace declaration.

In the example above, the element with the tagname "vocab01:foo" has the qualified name "{urn:namespace:example.com:vocabulary-01}foo," that is, the local name "foo" in the namespace "urn:namespace:example.com:vocabulary-01." (The "{*namespacename*}" syntax is a convention for writing out qualified names. It is used by some tools and processing languages where it would be difficult or inconvenient to go through a prefix binding.)

Note that attributes that start with "xmlns" are not true XML attributes, they are namespace declarations. XML parsers should not report namespace declarations as attributes but as namespace declarations. However, DTD-based validation does treat them as attributes, which means you have to declare all namespace declaration attributes in DTDs, and you can set them as defaulted attributes in the DTD.

For XSD-based validation, you do not, and in fact cannot, declare namespace declarations as attributes. While XSDs can define default attributes, they cannot define default namespace declarations. One implication of this is that XSD-based documents must always have the required namespace declarations in the document instance, while DTD-based documents may have them implied by the DTD and not present in the instance.

An element does not need to use a prefix in order to be in a namespace. You can declare a namespace to be the default namespace for the element that declares it and all of its descendants that do not themselves define a default namespace. The previous example could be rewritten as:

```
<root>
  <foo xmlns="urn:namespace:example.com:vocabulary-01">...</foo>
</root>
```

In this example, the element with the tagname "foo" still has the qualified name "{urn:namespace:example.com:vocabulary-01}foo." Note also that the namespace declaration is now on the `<foo>` start tag, not on the `<root>` start tag. If the default namespace declaration was on the `<root>` start tag, it would put the `<root>` element in that namespace, which would be different from the previous example.

In both examples, the `<root>` element is in no namespace, meaning its qualified name is "{}root."

Because an element name with no prefix may still be in a namespace, you cannot make any assumptions about elements and namespaces without knowing the namespace declarations in the document. If a document is DTD-based, you have to either examine the DTD or parse the document with respect to the DTD to know what the namespace declarations are. If a document is XSD-based, or has no associated schema, then all the namespace declarations will be in the document instance. But for any specific element you still need to inspect its ancestry to see what the effective namespace bindings are for that element.

Attributes are a little different from elements in that attribute names with no prefix are always in no namespace—there is no way within a document to define the default namespace for attributes.

Using the previous example as a starting point, if you wanted to have an attribute in the "urn:namespace:example.com:vocabulary-01" namespace you would have to bind it to a prefix:

```
<root>
  <foo xmlns="urn:namespace:example.com:vocabulary-01"
       xmlns:vocab01="urn:namespace:example.com:vocabulary-01"
   >
     <bar vocab01:baz="something"
          fred="something else">...</bar>
   </foo>
</root>
```

Now the namespace "urn:namespace:example.com:vocabulary-01" is both the default namespace for elements and is bound to the prefix "vocab01." The element `<bar>` is in the namespace and its attribute @baz is also in that namespace. The attribute @fred is not in any namespace.

It should be clear that the `<bar>` element's tagname could be either "vocab01:bar" or "bar" and it would have the same qualified name, "{urn:namespace:example.com:vocabulary-01}bar."

That's namespaces in a nutshell.

So what does all that have to do with DITA?

The question really is, "why doesn't DITA use namespaces for element or attribute names?"

The answer is that because of prefixes, it would be difficult or impossible to have both namespace-qualified names and an easy-to-process syntax for the @class attribute.

An original design requirement for DITA was that the @class attribute be easy to check, in particular with CSS selectors. The syntax of the @class attribute was driven entirely by that requirement.

If you could have namespace-qualified names in @class attribute values, you'd either have to use prefixes or you'd have to use the full namespace name. The former would require you to declare the prefix bindings, and processors would have to dereference prefixes to namespace names. This would make it impossible to use CSS selectors unless you had pre-defined prefix names, which would violate a general principle of namespaces (that prefixes are local and arbitrary). And this would not be enforceable since many tools modify or generate namespace prefixes as a normal part of their processing.

So DITA 1.x is unable to allow the use of namespace-qualified names for DITA elements (meaning any element that is a specialization from a DITA-defined base type). DITA can allow foreign elements in namespaces because those elements don't use the DITA @class mechanism. In fact, having foreign elements in a namespace helps clearly distinguish them from DITA elements.

There is one place that DITA uses namespaces: the @DITAArchVersion attribute.

Every conforming DITA document must have an attribute named @DITAArchVersion that is in the DITA-defined namespace "http://dita.oasis-open.org/architecture/2005/," for example:

```
<chapter
  id="topic-id"
  ditaarch:DITAArchVersion="1.2"
  xmlns:ditaarch="http://dita.oasis-open.org/architecture/2005/"
>
```

This use of a DITA-defined namespace for this attribute makes DITA documents self-describing as being DITA documents because they declare a DITA-defined namespace.

Any document that declares the DITA architecture namespace and has a @DITAArchVersion attribute is almost certainly a DITA document. Any document that does not have both of those things cannot be a *conforming* DITA document, although it may still be a DITA document. Processors are free to assume that documents without the namespace declaration are not DITA documents and reject them or otherwise not apply DITA processing to them.

If a document has the namespace declaration, the @DITAArchVersion attribute, and a @domains attribute with a value that conforms to the syntax for @domains, then processors can both process it as DITA and report against that document any failure to conform to DITA-defined rules.

This self-describing aspect of DITA documents is unique, because it depends only on the use of a specific namespace and a couple of attributes, not on the use of a specific DTD or schema document. Remember that the DITA standard explicitly allows for conforming DITA documents to have no directly-associated DTD or schema or other formal document grammar. This is what makes that possible.

Because DITA documents may use a unique, specialized vocabulary, it is essential that DITA documents be self-describing in this way, otherwise there would be no way for general-purpose tools like XML editors and content management systems to automatically associate DITA processing with DITA documents.

Because one of the points of DITA is that all conforming DITA documents can be understood and processed regardless of their markup details, it follows that DITA-aware processors should be able to usefully process any DITA document without the need for any up-front configuration or customization. The self-describing nature of DITA documents enables that.

If your DITA documents are DTD or XSD-based then you will need to make the DTDs or XSDs findable by your tools, but in practice that's usually done by packaging the DTDs or XSDs as DITA Open Toolkit plugins and deploying them to whatever tool your processor uses (assuming that all modern DITA-aware tools will use the Open Toolkit at least for DTD and schema resolution, if not for other processing). But that should be it.

You see this at work in the OxygenXML editor. OxygenXML will recognize all DITA documents as DITA if they have the @DITArchVersion attribute and the namespace declaration. If the documents have no associated DTD or XSD, then they just work. If they have a DTD or XSD, when you have to deploy the Toolkit plugins for them to Oxygen's built-in (or configured) Toolkit, and then they just work. No further configuration is required. This makes it as easy as it could possibly be to work with specialized documents, because there is essentially no extra work needed to edit those documents as DITA within OxygenXML.

The fact that DITA cannot use namespaces for DITA elements is an annoyance and a limitation in DITA 1.x, but in practice it's not a big deal.

For maps and topics, there is less concern with name collision because map documents and topic documents will never be literally combined together (maps with topics, that is) and because most topic documents are managed separately and therefore having two topic types with the same name but different semantics is not a huge problem (although it should be avoided if possible). In general, the base vocabulary for map types and topic types is managed and defined in a way that is unlikely to result in name collisions.

Domains are another matter.

For domains, name collisions are a concern because the whole point of domains is that they can be combined with other domains in any topic or map type, which makes name collisions more likely.

The solution is to include a "prefix" in your specialized tagnames to help ensure they are globally unique. For example, the Learning and Training domains use "lc" ("learning content") as the first characters of all tagnames. For example, <lcSingleSelect> is an element from the learning domain. DITA for Publishers uses "d4p" as a prefix. As long as the prefix is more or less obviously associated with the owner of the vocabulary, it's as good as using a namespace prefix but avoids the complexity of actually being a namespace prefix with a separately-declared binding to a namespace name.

The TC has been wracking its collective brain to try to figure out a way to use namespaces in DITA, but so far we haven't thought of anything. For DITA 2.0, where backward compatibility will not be a concern, it is likely that we'll define a specialization declaration mechanism that does allow for namespaces. For example, it could make sense to have each vocabulary module be a separate XML namespace rather than using the DITA 1.x convention of "module name.".

The challenge is how to do that so the declaration is manageable and processing with common tools is efficient. I suspect that we will decide that the CSS-selector requirement is not compelling, since it appears that people rarely deliver DITA XML content directly to Web browsers, which was the original driver for that requirement.

If DITA processing were always in the context of transforms, then resolving prefixes to namespaces as part of determining an element's DITA class would not be a problem since all modern XML processing languages can do that easily.

But for now, DITA cannot use namespaces for DITA-based vocabulary.

6

Maps and Topics

DITA's markup design is based on an approach to content authored characterized by standalone units ("topics") organized into different structures by separate documents ("maps").

In most traditional XML applications for documents, a "publication" is represented by a single XML document that contains all the content and defines the hierarchical organization of the publication. With few exceptions, before the publication of the XInclude specification, there was no standard way to do anything else. XInclude allows for a weak form of separation of structure from content but does not really do more than you could always do with external parsed entities.

Neither external parsed entities nor XInclude are useful for re-use because they are both use-by-copy, not use-by-reference. For example, the XInclude specification does not provide for rewriting IDs and references to them in included content. That means that an XInclude is equivalent to copying the content referenced literally, which is no different from using external parsed entities. In addition, XInclude only supports direct URI references and does not support indirect addressing. That makes it inappropriate for authoring in a re-use context. Thus, for DITA's purposes, where re-use and modularity are primary driving requirements, external parsed entities and XInclude have no value.

DITA's design was driven by the need to have a clear and complete separation between the content used in a publication and the structure of that publication. The idea was that content should be organizable into reusable chunks that could then be organized into structures for different purposes. Because, in this environment, content would necessarily have no knowledge of where it was or how it might be used, it would be necessary for the users to impose information onto the content: titles, metadata, additional content, and so on.

Because DITA was designed initially to support the technical documentation practice of modular writing, the content chunks are called "topics," meaning roughly a "a single rhetorical topic or subject" This implies that the content more or less stands alone and is thus inherently reusable. This idea makes general sense in a technical documentation context, though it cannot always be achieved in that context. Divorced from any particular writing practice or editorial policy, topics are simply titled units of content.

Because the primary use of the content is to produce published information for human use, and those publications usually need some sort of navigation structure, the publication structuring component was called a "map," meaning roughly a map of navigation structures onto content.

Thus in DITA there are two types of XML document:[15] map documents and topic documents. Map documents are documents whose root element is `<map>` or a specialization of `<map>`. Topic documents are documents whose root element is `<topic>` or a specialization of `<topic>`. No document with any other element type as its root can be a conforming DITA document. Thus, even though XML allows any element type defined within a DTD or any global type defined in an XSD schema to be the root of a document governed by that DTD or schema, the DITA standard requires all conforming DITA documents to be either map documents or topic documents.

For practitioners used to more freedom in how content is organized for storage, this may seem like a bit of a severe restriction. However, there are good reasons for this design approach.

- It ensures, in part, that all DITA documents have a consistent structure and are consistently described in terms of their structural requirements (that is, their DITA document types).
- It ensures that all DITA documents are objects in the general computer science sense.
- It means that DITA-aware component management systems only need to know about two things: maps and topics—they don't need to manage elements below the topic or map level as storage objects.
- It means you can practically manage DITA content on a file system or in a simple code control system.

One practical implication of this requirement is that you may have topic documents that serve only to hold elements intended for use by reference from other topics. For example, you might have a topic that contains nothing but warnings used by reference or phrase elements that contain product-specific terms or whatever. This is perfectly natural in DITA and should not bother you at all.

While DITA does not require the use of maps—you could represent an entire publication as a single XML document containing a tree of topics—it definitely rewards it and in most cases there is no reason not to use maps and many reasons to use them. Many people (and tools) assume that maps are required.

---

[15] In fact there are really four types defined by the DITA specification: map, topic, ditabase, and DITAVAL. However, ditabase and DITAVAL do not directly apply to the DITA architecture.

Topics

The "topic" is the primary unit of content in DITA—all content must be in a document whose root element is, or is specialized from, `<topic>`.

A topic is a titled unit of content. A topic must have a title (`<title>`) and topics that consist of only titles are perfectly fine (these are referred to as "title-only topics"). A topic may have a separate navigation title, a separate search title, a short description (`<shortdesc>`), an abstract (`<abstract>`), a prolog (`<prolog>`) (containing metadata for the topic), and a body (`<body>`). A topic may have child topics following the body.

The topic's body contains the direct content of the topic: paragraphs, lists, figures, and tables. The body may contain one level of arbitrarily-titled containers ("sections") or any level of untitled containers ("body divisions"). See *Sections and Divisions: Organizing Topic Body Content* on page 225.

A topic may have alternate titles (`<titlealts>`): one for use in navigation contexts (`<navtitle>`) and one for searching (`<searchtitle>`).

Navigation titles are intended to be used in tables of contexts or other navigation aids. When specified within the topic itself, navigation titles usually provide a shorter version of the title. Because navigation is necessarily a function of where a topic is used, navigation titles are usually imposed by maps rather than being specified by the topic itself. A topic reference to a topic may specify the navigation title to use for that reference to the topic (see *Maps* on page 200).

Search titles are intended to provide a form of the title for use in search results, usually because the topic's main title would not be distinct in isolation. For example, this topic's title, "Topics" is clear in the context of this chapter , but would be ambiguous in a list of search results. A better search title would be "Architectural overview of DITA topics."

A topic element must have an `@id` attribute. The `@id` attribute on topic elements is an XML ID, meaning that it must be unique within the XML document that contains the topic. This means that if you have nested topics within the root topic, they must all have unique IDs within the scope of that XML document.

There is no general requirement that topic IDs be unique beyond the scope of the XML document that contains them. However, some tools assume global ID uniqueness or impose that requirement. They should not and any that do are, I assert, broken. The identity of a topic is established by the identity of the XML document that contains it, that is, the storage location of that document. Making topic IDs globally unique doesn't add anything. It just complicates authoring and implementation and adds an opportunity for error that you don't need.

DITA provides, through maps, more than sufficient facilities for naming topics uniquely. There is no need for globally-unique IDs on topic elements.

See *Topic Structural Patterns* on page 217 for a deeper discussion of topic markup.

Maps

Maps use hyperlinks (topic references) to organize topics into arbitrary structures. Maps may impose titles and metadata onto topics. Maps bind names ("keys") to topics to enable indirect addressing.

A DITA map is nothing more than a set of hyperlinks pointing to topics (or non-DITA things). The base hyperlink element type is `<topicref>`. The name "topicref" is a slight misnomer because `<topicref>` elements may point to things that are not topics, including DITA maps, graphics, and non-DITA resources such as websites, PDF documents, and so on, or they may not point to anything. A more accurate name would be something like "map component link," but "topicref" is the name DITA uses.[16]

A map may also have a title (`<title>`) and metadata (`<topicmeta>`). It may also include three other element types that are not specializations of `<topicref>`: `<anchor>`, `<navref>`, and `<reltable>`.

We usually think of maps as representing complete publications or as defining a subcomponent of a publication, such as a complete chapter or part or set of related tasks and supporting concept and reference topics. However, maps may be used to collect topics or non-DITA resources for any reason, including simply to define a related set of content objects or to organize content objects by topic, product, subsystem, or whatever.

A DITA map does not necessarily represent a thing to be published. So when we talk about maps and their processing we have to be careful to specify the type of thing a given map represents. The DITA map mechanism is very general, so you should plan to use specializations of maps and topic references to represent specific uses of maps. DITA's built-in BookMap type is a typical example of a map specialization that reflects a specific purpose, in this case, book publications.

The simplest map for a publication will have a `<title>` element that contains the title for the overall publication and one or more `<topicref>` elements that link to the topics that provide the content of the publication:

```
<map>
  <title>An Introduction to Aikido</title>
  <topicref href="topics/chapter-01.dita"/>
  <topicref href="topics/chapter-02.dita"/>
  <topicref href="topics/chapter-03.dita"/>
  <topicref href="topics/chapter-04.dita"/>
</map>
```

---

[16]   There are many places where a more complete abstraction of DITA markup could be defined. That activity will have to wait for DITA 2.0, where the need for backward compatibility with DITA 1.x is removed.

In practice, your maps will usually be much more sophisticated, taking advantage of some or all of the features of DITA maps.

Nominally, a map defines a "navigation tree" for a set of topics, that is a table of contents (ToC) or similar hierarchical navigation structure. However, maps can also organize topics non-hierarchically through sets of extended links defined in relationship tables or even simply collect a set of topics with no particular relationship among any of the topics.

One map may include other maps, forming a "map tree." The root of such a map tree is the "root map" and has some special processing considerations. The input to DITA processing is generally a root map and, conversely, a map used as the input to some process is, by definition, the root map for that processing instance. There is no specific property of a map that makes it be or not be a root map. However, most maps are intended to exclusively be root maps or subordinate maps. While it is possible for a map intended to be a root map to also be used as a subordinate map, usually a map is only useful as root or a subordinate map but not both. In particular, by the rules of DITA, the titles of subordinate maps are ignored by output processors and do not contribute to the navigation tree defined by the root map.

Map Components

The base map content model allows an optional `<title>`, an optional `<topicmeta>`, and then any combination of the following base element types:

- `<anchor>`
- `<data>` or `<data-about>`
- `<navref>`
- `<reltable>`
- `<topicref>`

In practice, `<data>` elements are not used within maps except within `<topicmeta>` elements. That is, it is not general practice to mix topic references and `<data>` elements directly.

The `<topicref>` element is the primary base element type used to construct maps. Topicrefs have a processing role of either "normal" or "resource only" and are "normal" by default. Normal-role topicrefs that point to topics or maps establish the main "navigation tree" for the map. Resource-only topicrefs do not contribute to the navigation tree. If resource-only topicrefs point to topics or other resources, they establish dependencies on those resources, for example, topics that contain elements to be used by reference.

The `<anchor>` element identifies points within a map where another map can impose additional topic references, similar to the conref push feature of content references.

The `<navref>` element creates a reference to another map where the reference is intended to be resolved as late possible, such as by a browser or online delivery system, rather than during the base map processing.

A typical use is in Eclipse InfoCenters, where the Eclipse system resolves and combines maps using `<navref>` elements in compiled InfoCenters.

The `<reltable>` element defines sets of links among topics, effectively defining a "relationship graph" over some or all of the topics used by a map.

The DITA vocabulary includes a map domain, "map group," that defines a number of specializations of `<topicref>` that support common uses of `<topicref>`. These elements are so convenient that most people don't even realize that their use is optional. Therefore, you will see them in nearly all map documents.

The `<topicmeta>` element contains metadata. `<topicmeta>` within `<map>` defines the metadata for the map as a whole and, for root maps, the publication as a whole (when the map is treated as a publication). `<topicmeta>` within `<topicref>` defines the metadata for the topicref and, depending on the rules that apply, to any resource referenced by the topicref.

The rules for maps include rules for propagating metadata down the map tree, down the topicref tree, and from topicrefs to the topics they reference.

Topic references

The primary use of topic references is to point to *resources*, where a resource may be a DITA topic, a map, or a non-DITA object of any type, including graphics, websites, PDF files, etc.

A topicref may point directly to a resource using the `@href` attribute, or indirectly using the `@keyref` attribute. See *Pointing to Things: Linking and Addressing in DITA* on page 227 for details. From the standpoint of the overall meaning of a given topic reference, it doesn't matter whether it uses `@href` or `@keyref`, the meaning and processing results should always be the same.

The type of resource pointed to is indicated by the `@format` attribute of `<topicref>`.

The value of `@format` depends on the data type of the resource. For DITA resources, the required values are:

dita   DITA topics. This is the default value for `@format`, since pointing to topics is the main use of `<topicref>`.

ditamap   DITA maps.

For non-DITA resources, the convention is to use the extension or common name of the format, e.g., "html" for HTML pages, "jpg" or "JPEG" for JPEG graphics, etc. The processing of non-DITA resources is necessarily processor-specific, but most DITA-aware processors will understand this convention.

All topicrefs have a processing role determined by the value of the `@processing-role` attribute. The value is either "normal" or "resource-only," with the default being "normal." A topicref with a processing-role of normal contributes to the map's navigation tree or relationship graph. A topicref with a processing-role of resource-only points to a resource that is not directly part of the navigation tree. For example, topics that only contain elements used by conref would be resource-only topics.

Another use for resource-only topicrefs is to define keys used for indirect addressing. The resource-only processing role allows a map to point to all the resources it requires, removing the need to process every topic just to determine the set of topics needed by the map. This is especially useful if you need to package maps for interchange, provide content to translators, or import or export content from a component management system.

Finally, as with other DITA links, a topic reference has a "scope" (@scope), which indicates whether the referenced resource is part of map's direct content ("local"), is part of a closely-related map ("peer"), or is a completely separate resource ("external"). The default value of @scope is "local."

You use "external" for things like Web pages or PDF documents that you're linking to but that you don't produce as part of your general DITA processing.

You use "peer" for documents that are part of your environment but that are published as separate publications. For example, the installation and operation manuals for a product would likely be peers. The "peer" value generally implies that processors should know about the peer resources and might be able to do things like creating working links to those resources in generated output (for example, because they are all published to the same website or produced as PDFs intended to be delivered together). The "local" and "external" scopes are pretty easy to handle: the resources are either part of your map or completely separate from it. The "peer" scope is more complicated because it brings in processor-specific processing that is outside the scope of the DITA specification.

A scope value of "external" would normally not be used on direct topic references, as it wouldn't make much sense to include an external resource into a map. The value of "external" is normally used for things like cross-references inside a topic to external websites, for example, the following:

```
<p>See <xref href="http://dita-ot.sourceforge.net"
scope="external">The DITA Open Toolkit project page</xref>
for more on the DITA Open Toolkit.</p>
```

However, it can make sense to use "external" for key definitions that bind keys to external resources, such as Web sites:

```
<keydef keys="dita-ot-site"
    href="http://dita-ot.sourceforge.net"
    scope="external"
    format="html"
/>
```

With a key of this form, the cross-reference could be reworked to use a key reference rather than a direct URI reference:

```
<p>See <xref keyref="dita-ot-site"> The DITA Open Toolkit project page</xref>
for more on the DITA Open Toolkit.</p>
```

Topicrefs may contain nested topic references, by which you can create a structural hierarchy:

```
<topicref keyref="topic-01">
  <topicref keyref="topic-02">
    <topicref keyref="topic-03"/>
    <topicref keyref="topic-04"/>
  </topicref>
  <topicref keyref="topic-05">
    <topicref keyref="topic-06"/>
    <topicref keyref="topic-07"/>
  </topicref>
</topicref>
```

A topicref may specify a navigation title. While `<topicref>` provides a `@navtitle` attribute, it is deprecated in favor of the `<navtitle>` subelement, which goes in the `<topicmeta>` child of topicref. The `@navtitle` attribute, being an attribute, cannot contain any markup and many translation tools do not allow, or make it difficult, to modify the contents of attributes.

A topicref with a navigation title looks like:

```
<topicref>
  <topicmeta>
    <navtitle>Some Topic Heading</navtitle>
  </topicmeta>
  ...
</topicref>
```

If you want to impose a navigation title onto a topic you must specify the `@locktitle` attribute, otherwise the navigation title specified in the map is ignored in preference to the title or navigation title defined by the topic:

```
<topicref href="some-topic.dita"
    locktitle="yes">
  <topicmeta>
    <navtitle>Some Topic</navtitle>
  </topicmeta>
</topicref>
```

Here the navigation tree will use the value "Some Topic" as the title of the referenced topic rather than the value of the `<title>` element in that topic. The title of the topic as presented in the main content presentation will reflect the value of the `<title>` element in the topic.

In addition to linking to topics, maps, or non-DITA resources, topicrefs can do the following things:

- Create titled groups of topicrefs ("topic heads")
- Create untitled groups of topicrefs ("topic groups")
- Define sets of topicrefs intended to be used by reference from other maps (`<topicset>`)
- Impose sets of topicrefs onto maps (`<anchorref>`)
- Bind keys used for indirect addressing to resources ("key definitions")

Topicref Configuration Attributes

Topicref elements take a number of attributes. These can be classified as follows:

- Linking and addressing attributes: `@chunk`, `@copy-to`, `@format`, `@href`, `@keys`, `@keyref`, `@linking`, `@scope`, and `@type`. These attributes serve to define or characterize the resource the topicref links to, if any.
- Selection attributes: `@audience`, `@importance`, `@otherprops`, `@platform`, `@print`, `@product`, `@props` and its specializations, `@rev`, and `@status`.
- Topicref configuration attributes: `@collection-type`, `@locktitle`, `@processing-role`, and `@toc`. These configure how the topicref behaves either with respect to its peer topicrefs and the map it's part of or with respect to the resource it references.

The linking and addressing attributes are covered in the sections on linking and addressing. The selection attributes are covered in the sections on conditional processing. The `@locktitle` attribute is covered in the section on metadata cascade.

The `@processing-role` attribute indicates whether the resource pointed to by the topicref is part of the main navigation tree or navigation graph ("normal") or if it acts as a resource used by other topics or topicrefs via key reference ("resource-only"). See *Topicrefs, Navigation Trees, and Navigation Graphs* on page 207.

The `@collection-type` attribute indicates what, if any, relationship exists among topics referenced directly by the topicref that contains the `@collection-type` attribute or any included topicrefs.

unordered   There is no significance to the order of the topics and no implicit relationship among them. In particular, there is no expectation or requirement to generate previous and next topic links between the topics. This is the default value.

sequence   The order of the topics is significant and they explicitly represent a sequence or reading order. Processors usually generate previous and next links or otherwise ensure that the sequence is apparent and navigable.

choice   Indicates that one of the topics out of the set should be chosen. The way this choice is made is processor dependent. For example, you might match selection attributes, such as experience level, with values specified by the reader. The main point of "choice" is to indicate that only one of the set should be presented to a given reader.

family   Indicates that each of the referenced topics is closely related to each of the others. This is usually represented by having "related links" from each member of the set to every other member of the set.

Note that the meaning of `@collection-type` when specified on `@reltable` and `@relcolspec` is undefined and should not be taken as cascading to topicrefs within relationship table cells.

The `@toc` attribute indicates whether or not the topicref should contribute to the navigation table of contents. A value of "no" indicates it should not contribute, a value of "yes" that it should. The default is yes.

Specializations of Topicref

Most of the different uses of `<topicref>` have a corresponding specialization provided by the DITA-defined map group domain vocabulary module:

- `<topicsetref>`: References a `<topicset>` in order to use the topic set by reference.
- `<mapref>`: References another map. Sets the default value for the `@format` attribute to "ditamap."
- `<topichead>`: Represents a titled group of topicrefs within the map. Requires a title but does not allow a reference to a resource. Topic heads contribute to the navigation tree of the map. Any normal-role `<topicref>` element that has a title but no resource reference acts as a topic head.
- `<topicgroup>`: Represents an untitled group of topicrefs. Topic groups never contribute to the navigation tree, even if they have titles. Any topicref with no resource reference and no title acts as a topic group. The specialized element type `<topicgroup>` has the additional rule that even if it does have a title, it still acts as a topic group and not a topic head. This lets you use the `<topicgroup>` element to organize topicrefs for whatever purpose and give those groups titles that are meaningful for authors, without affecting the navigation tree. For example, I often use `<topicgroup>` in this way to organize groups of key definitions.
- `<keydef>`: Defines a key definition. Requires the `@keys` attribute and sets the default value for the `@processing-role` attribute to "resource-only." (See *Pointing to Things: Linking and Addressing in DITA* on page 227).

A common use of specialization is to define new topicref types that reflect specific publication structures. For example, the DITA BookMap map type defines topicref types like "chapter" and "part" and the DITA for Publishers publication map domain defines topicref types like "dedication," "article," and "front-cover."

The use of specialized topicrefs lets you impose publication-specific semantics onto otherwise generic topics. For example, if you use a `<chapter>` topicref to point to a generic `<topic>` topic or to a `<concept>` topic, you are saying explicitly that, in the context of this publication, the generic topic is playing the role of "chapter." Processors can then apply chapter style and processing to the topic.

This is an important use of topicrefs because it creates a clear and complete separation between the concern of information typing—for example, concept, task, and reference—and publication structure—part, chapter, subsection, appendix, etc. In particular, you don't necessarily have to change the element type of a topic simply to use it in an new context where it is playing a different structural role. For example, the same concept might be a chapter in one publication, an appendix in another, and subsection in yet another. The topic itself doesn't change, only the way it is used.

Because the processing and presentation implications of a given topicref or topic are necessarily a matter of style and details of a particular output type, the precise implications of the combination of topicref type and topic type are, of course, processor specific. However, in general, you should expect the tagname of the topicref element to take precedence over the topic type when determining structural role within a publication, except for generic `<topicref>` elements.

In the purest use of DITA, topics always reflect an information type that says nothing about its possible structural role (e.g., "concept," "task," and "reference"), leaving it to maps to define structural roles. In practice, not all topics are quite so pure. For example, the DITA for Publishers vocabulary includes topic types like "chapter" and "part" largely because Publishing users coming to XML for the first time or coming from non-DITA XML applications expect to find those topic types. Over time, as their sophistication grows, they would likely move to topic types that are more descriptive of the content and less descriptive of their original structural roles. DITA for Publishers also provides the topic type "division," which represents a titled publication component with no inherent structural role.

Specializations of `<topicref>` are fairly easy to define because usually all you're doing is changing the tagname and not modifying the base content model or attributes at all.

Topicrefs, Navigation Trees, and Navigation Graphs

The concepts of "navigation tree" and "navigation graph" are not formally defined in the DITA specification through DITA 1.2, but they are inherent in the distinction between normal and resource-only topic references and between topicrefs outside of relationship tables and inside relationship tables. The DITA 1.2 specification uses the term "navigation tree" but does not formally define it. The term "navigation graph" is not used in the DITA 1.2 specification.

Before DITA 1.2, when the @processing-role attribute was introduced, all topicrefs contributed to the navigation tree or relationship graph, meaning that a map existed primarily to define a navigation tree. Therefore, there was no need to formally define the concept of navigation tree. Because relationship tables required distinct markup, there was no need to define the abstraction of navigation graph.

However, with the introduction of resource-only topicrefs there is now a need to talk about the difference between normal-role topicrefs and resource-only topicrefs and describe what they do. That leads to the need to distinguish the navigation tree and navigation graph from resource-only topicrefs.

The *navigation tree* is the table-of-contents structure defined by the normal-role topicrefs in the map (and not within relationship tables). While DITA provides some markup control over how the normal-role topicrefs translate into a literal table of contents or equivalent navigation structure, in general there is a one-to-one correspondence between the normal-role topicrefs and the navigation structure produced from the map for maps used to produce some sort of navigable output. I have to be vague here because the variety of possible uses for maps is unbounded. But in practice, maps are mostly used to generate things like books, websites, and online help with familiar TOC-like navigation trees. More generally, maps are a form of "virtual document," such as provided by many content and component management systems.

The *navigation graph* is the set of links among topics defined in any relationship tables in the map. Each row of a relationship table is effectively an extended link (in the XLink sense), where each cell of the row represents one anchor or end of the link. Each cell of a row contains one or more normal-role topicrefs that link to the resources that act as that anchor of the link. Each column in the relationship table has an associated role. A typical example is a relationship table with the columns "concept" and "reference," which relate concept topics linked from cells in the "concept" column to reference topics linked from cells in the "reference" column. (See *Relationship Tables* on page 263.) A relationship table may have any number of columns.

The typical rendition effect of relationship table links is to generate "See also" links at the ends of the topics linked.

Creating Compound Maps

The simplest map is a single XML document that contains all the topic references and relationship tables that define a single publication.

But in practice, most publications are constructed from multiple maps, creating a "compound map."

DITA defines several ways to combine maps and topicrefs together to construct a compound map and an effective navigation tree.

The most direct way to combine maps is a map-to-map reference using a topicref with a `@format` value of "ditamap":

```
<map>
  <title>My Publication</title>
  <topicref href="chap-01.ditamap"
    format="ditamap"
  />
  <topicref href="chap-02.ditamap"
    format="ditamap"
  />
</map>
```

The referenced maps are usually referred to as "submaps" or "subordinate maps." All the topic references and relationship tables in the subordinate maps are combined with the root map and processed together. This processing results in an effective map that can be represented as a new single map document. The "map pull" processing stage of the DITA Open Toolkit does exactly this: it processes the root map to pull in all referenced maps, applies the DITA rules for combining maps, and produces a single map document as a temporary file.

You can also pull in separately-marked sets of topicrefs from a larger map using the `<topicset>` and `<topicsetref>` elements, which are both specializations of `<topicref>`.

For example, you might have a map that organizes the content for a number of re-usable tasks and associated concept and task topics. Each group of topics forms a reusable unit of structure, but for whatever reason it was easier or more effective to define these in a single map document rather than as individual maps. Such a map would look something like:

```
<map>
  <title>Task and Related Content Topic Sets</title>
  <topicset id="task-01-topicset>
    <topicref href="task-01.dita">
      <topicref href="concept-01.dita"/>
      <topicref href="ref-01.dita"/>
      <topicref href="ref-02.dita"/>
    </topicref>
  </topicset>
  <topicset id="task-02-topicset>
    <topicref href="task-02.dita">
      <topicref href="concept-02.dita"/>
      <topicref href="ref-03.dita"/>
      <topicref href="ref-04.dita"/>
    </topicref>
  </topicset>
</map>
```

From another map you can use individual topic sets using the `<topicsetref>` element:

```
<map>
  <title>My Publication</title>
  ...
  <topicsetref href="topicsets.ditamap#task-02-topicset"/>
  ...
</map>
```

The processed result is that the referenced topicset is included in the referencing map. Note, however, that it is not a content reference, so this map processing is performed *after* any content reference processing or filtering. Processors may delay resolution of topicset references if appropriate, doing the resolution in the rendition system rather than as part of the output processing. Processors can also treat topicset references as equivalent to referencing a map with a `@format` value of "ditamap." By "rendition system" I mean interactive presentation systems like Eclipse InfoCenters or online help systems, where the final rendering of the content to a reader is done by the rendition system, so there is opportunity for additional processing beyond that applied to the DITA source.

You can also "push" subordinate maps onto another map through the use of anchors and anchor references. The `<anchor>` element defines a potential "push" target within a map.

You can use the `@anchorref` attribute of a map or an `<anchorref>` element to point to an anchor and impose the contents of the map or `<anchorref>` onto the anchor. The intent is that the imposition be processed as late as possible, ideally in the delivery system.

Finally, you can use content references with map elements just as you can with topic elements. You can use pull conrefs to pull topicrefs into a map and push conrefs to impose additional topicrefs into a map. However, since you can include maps or individual topicrefs in maps and you have the anchor/anchorref facility, the use of content references within maps is fairly rare. And because content references are always processed before any semantic processing, conref offers much less flexibility in controlling when map composition is done. In particular, it doesn't allow it to be done in the delivery system.

Chunking and Copy-To

You can generate two broad classes of output from a map: monolithic single-file output like PDF and modular, multi-file output like HTML and online help.

For multi-file outputs there is normally a one-to-one relationship between input topic files and result files. That's the obvious way to produce multi-file outputs, but the DITA specification doesn't require it.

Generating output files from input topics presents two potential challenges:

1. Using the same topic in different places in the map to result in different result files.
2. Combining multiple topics into one output file or splitting one topic into multiple output files.

For the first challenge, you can use the @copy-to attribute of <topicref> to specify the effective topic filename for that use of the topic.

For example, say you use a common subtask twice in the same map under different main tasks, but you want each use of the task to result in a different HTML file in HTML outputs. You can force this by specifying @copy-to on each topicref:

```
<map>
  ...
  <topicref href="main-task-A.dita">
    <topicref href="subtask-01.dita"
      copy-to="task-a-subtask-01.dita"/>
    ...
  </topicref>
  <topicref href="main-task-B.dita">
    <topicref href="subtask-01.dita"
      copy-to="task-b-subtask-01.dita"/>
    ...
  </topicref>
  ...
</map>
```

Note that the value of @copy-to specifies the effective *source* filename, not the effective *output* filename. That's because the mapping from source files to output files is still processor dependent. The only knowable thing at authoring time is the source filenames.

You can use @copy-to in this way to enable cross references to specific uses of a topic by putting a key on the topicref that specifies @copy-to. References to that key will then be reliably associated to that specific use of the referenced topic and not to any other, as though you had a made a literal copy of the topic in your source repository. For example, the preceding example can be extended to add keys:

```
<map>
  ...
  <topicref keys="main-task-A" href="main-task-A.dita">
    <topicref keys="task-a-subtask-01"
      href="subtask-01.dita"
      copy-to="task-a-subtask-01.dita"/>
    ...
  </topicref>
  <topicref keys="main-task-B" href="main-task-B.dita">
    <topicref keys="task-b-subtask-01"
      href="subtask-01.dita"
      copy-to="task-b-subtask-01.dita"/>
    ...
  </topicref>
  ...
</map>
```

Note: When you specify @copy-to, you can also specify a short description (<shortdesc>) in <topicmeta> within the topicref to set the short description of the topic as copied. Implementation of this behavior is optional for processors.

For the second challenge, you can use the @chunk attribute of <topicref> to indicate how the input should map to output files, and the @copy-to attribute to specify the effective filename to use when constructing the output result. The @chunk attribute can also be specified on <map>. When specified on a map, the @chunk applies to all the normal-role topicrefs in the map.

The value of the @chunk attribute is a list of blank-delimited tokens that indicate the topics to be chunked, how those topics should be split or combined, and whether the result affects navigation or content.

The selection options are:

select-topic

> Selects just the topic referenced by the topicref, but not any of its ancestor, peer, or descendant topics. This allows you to treat topics that are part of larger topic documents as though they were stand-alone topic documents.

select-document

> Selects the entire document that contains the referenced topic.

select-branch

> Selects the referenced topic and all of its descendant topics.

The combination and split options are:

by-topic

> Splits each topic in the set of selected topics into a separate result file. This lets you create multiple output files from topics that are authored in the same XML document. You don't have direct control over the output filenames because @copy-to only applies to the result of a single-file effective chunk.

by-document

> Combines the topics in the selected set into a single result document. This lets you create a single output file from topics are authored in separate XML documents. Here, @copy-to should determine the effective source filename of the chunk.

The rendering options are:

to-content

> Indicates that the result should be rendered as a new content object in the output, e.g., a new HTML file for HTML-based outputs. When the topicref is a topic head, it means that the output should be as though the topichead had referenced a title-only topic with the topic head's title.

to-navigation

Indicates that a new chunk of navigation should be created to reference the specified chunk, such as a separate table of contents or set of related links. If a topichead has a @chunk value of to-navigation and that topichead is the target of a cross-reference, then the cross reference should go to the navigation structure itself, whatever that might be in a given rendition (for example, an entry in a table of contents or a node in a tree control reflecting the navigation structure). The exact meaning of to-navigation is necessarily highly dependent on the details of the rendition.

You can use @chunk in combination with @copy-to to control the effective filename of chunks.

See the section "Chunking" in the *DITA Architectural Specification* for a full explanation of chunking.

Metadata Cascade In Maps

Maps and topics may have metadata, which can be stored in attributes on those elements or in a <topicmeta> child element.Some of the metadata defined on maps and topicrefs cascades or propagates down the map hierarchy to descendant topicrefs and maps and, for topicrefs that point to DITA topics, to the topics themselves.

The rules for metadata cascade are necessarily complex. See the topic "Cascading of attributes and metadata in a DITA map" in the *DITA Architectural Specification* for complete details.

Here is a summary of the rules:

- Directly-specified values always take precedence over cascaded values for propagation within map documents and from map-to-map. For example, if an ancestor topicref specifies toc="yes" and a descendant topicref specifies toc="no", the value specified on the descendant topicref takes precedence and sets the value cascaded down to its descendants, if any.
- Metadata on topicrefs cascades to referenced topics unless the @lockmeta attribute on <topicmeta> is set to "no." The default value for @lockmeta is "yes," meaning that the topicref's metadata overrides or extends the referenced topic's metadata.
- All the selection attributes and topicref-configuring attributes (@toc, @type, @format, etc.) cascade from <map> to <topicref> and from <topicref> to <topicref> within the map document.
- The metadata elements <author>, <source>, <publisher>, <copyright>, <critdates>, <permissions>, <audience>, <category>, <prodinfo>, <othermeta> all cascade from <map> to <topicref>, from <topicref> to <topicref> within the map document, and from <topicref> to referenced topic.

- Cascading is additive for attributes and metadata elements that allow multiple values. For attributes and elements that allow a single value, the value defined on the nearest ancestor element takes precedence.
- Notabletop attributes that do not cascade are @chunk, @copy-to, and @outputclass, along with the addressing attributes @href, @keyref, and @keys.

In general, the metadata cascade behavior gives you the results you would expect. However, sometimes you get surprising results. For example, in a publication that consists of chapters or articles authored by different people, if you specified author metadata in the map and did not also specify lockmeta="no" on the map's <topicmeta> element, the publication-level authors would also become, effectively, the authors of each chapter, which may not be what you want.

Another important implication of metadata cascade is in component management systems and search and retrieval systems, where the system may need to create a special DITA-aware index or "materialized view" of the maps and topics in order to provide accurate and fast searching on metadata imposed by maps onto topics. It also implies that you may need to select a specific root map before performing a cascade-aware search in order to establish the correct metadata context. Or search results may need to indicate which map imposes a specific bit of cascaded metadata onto a topic.

Finally, note the utility of <topicgroup> as way to set default values for descendant topicrefs. For example, if you want to set the default value of the @collection-type attribute to "sequence," you can do it with a topic group:

```
. . .
<topicgroup collection-type="sequence">
   <topicref keyref="topic-345"/>
   <topicref keyref="topic-143"/>
   <topicref keyref="topic-261"/>
</topicgroup>
. . .
```

7

General Structural Patterns in DITA

If you understand DITA's basic structural patterns you can understand at least the basic intent of any new DITA elements you encounter. Likewise, you will be well prepared to define your own specializations with a minimum of mental effort.

Most XML vocabularies reflect consistent patterns for how to construct and organize common types of structures: titled divisions, publications, figures, lists, etc. Ideally a given document type is rigidly consistent in its structural patterns, although few actually are. By contrast, DITA must be, with very few exceptions, rigidly consistent in its patterns because of the need to enable specialization.

The basic structural patterns of DITA are essentially those patterns inherent in the structures defined by the base vocabulary, that is, all the elements that are base types (and not specialized from a more-general type). Because specializations must have content models that are no less constrained than their base type's content model, all conforming specializations must reflect the same basic structural patterns as defined by the base DITA types. If you understand these patterns then you understand the basics of all possible DITA specializations. This is part of the point of specialization: it conserves and interchanges knowledge about markup rules.

Tip: The DITA 1.2 distribution includes a set of "base" document type shells that only include the base vocabulary modules. These shells can be useful when learning about the base vocabulary because documents that use them will only allow base elements.

An important thing to keep in mind: the normative definition of DITA's structural rules is the *prose* of the DITA standard, not the DTDs or schemas. Likewise, the XSD schema definitions take precedence over the DTD definitions when they are different. This means that just because a DITA DTD or XSD allows a particular combination of elements doesn't necessarily mean that combination of elements is conforming. This is because there are many things you cannot say in a DTD or XSD schema that are still disallowed by the text and intent of the DITA standard.

For example, <p> allows nearly anything in its content, so through a nested <p> element you can do all sorts of things. For example, you could have a <fig> that contains a <p> that contains another <fig>:

```
<fig>
  <p>
    <fig/>
  </p>
</fig>
```

But figures are not intended to nest, and the nesting of <fig> violates the general DITA principle that titled things should not nest. And certainly most, if not all DITA-aware processors would not know what to do with a nested figure like this.

So "but the DTD allows it" is never a valid argument for why a particular combination of markup should be considered correct.

Valid arguments include:

- My reading of the standard indicates it is allowed
- It is a sensible markup structure and here's why...
- A constraint imposed by the DITA standard is arbitrary, unnecessary, or unjustified
- The standard structure is sensible, but there is a missing level of generality that, if provided, would cover my case.

The DITA standard is not perfect in its design. DITA was originally developed by IBM, and it reflects a specific set of initial requirements specific to IBM's hardware and software documentation and authoring practices. The original DITA architects and the DITA Technical Committee have strived to make things appropriately general and to accommodate as many requirements as possible, but there is always room for improvement.

For example, DITA 1.2 reflects several refinements of the base vocabulary to address instances of all of the foregoing arguments. The DITA 1.2 general task reflects the realization that the original task was too constrained and that a more general task model was required. For DITA 1.3 I've proposed allowing figure within table and table within figure because not allowing it is arbitrarily constrained and I have what I think are solid use cases that need it (in particular, documents where tables are represented by images and figures whose display content happens to be tabular data).[17]

I encourage thoughtful questioning of the DITA markup design—that's how standards grow and improve and DITA exists to serve its users—but the questioning has to be thoughtful, which means a simple "but the DTD allows it" is not going to pass the "is this a thoughtful critique?" test. However, "the DTD allows it *and here's why it should*," with a presentation of a reasoned argument or documented user requirements, does pass the test.

It's also important to make sure that your requirement isn't already supported in some way by the existing markup design. There are many ways to do things in DITA, and some things are done in a way that long-time XML and SGML practitioners will not expect. One example is the use of attributes. DITA does not (cannot) allow the definition of element-type-specific attributes on specialized element types. This means you have to use nested `<data>` elements or specializations of `<data>`. This is definitely not the way most XML practitioners would normally work—defining new attributes to capture element-type-specific metadata is second nature for most of us. So it is best to ask the community how best to solve a particular markup question before spending too much time working out a new solution—it's very likely that there's a reasonable but non-obvious way to do what you want.

Topic Structural Patterns

The primary unit of information organization in DITA is the topic. A topic is a titled, potentially-hierarchical container of content and metadata.

Topics correspond to titled divisions in other document types, for example, chapter, section, subsection in more traditional documentation document types.

A topic must have a title—that is the only required content of a topic. That's why I stress the titled aspect of topics. Topics are the only hierarchical titled construct in DITA. That means that if you want to create a titled hierarchy in a publication you must do it with topics. Any other way of creating a hierarchy of titled things is, by definition, wrong. This is why `<section>` cannot nest.

There are other titled elements in DITA: `<section>`, `<fig>`, and `<table>` all allow `<title>`. (Lists allow `@spectitle` but not `<title>`.) But they are not hierarchical, meaning they are not intended to be nested. Lists can nest but using nested lists simply to get a hierarchy of titles would be misuse of the markup. Figures and tables cannot directly nest and should not be nested even though the schema cannot prevent their nesting.

You might be saying "but I can have a hierarchy of topicheads—those are titled and they create a hierarchy." Yes and no. Yes, you can create the hierarchy, but topicheads are really just a shortcut for topicrefs to

---

[17] As it happened, the TC rejected my argument after I had written this paragraph. The agreed upon solution is to use single-cell tables to hold the table graphic.

title-only topics. So I maintain that such a hierarchy is, in fact, a hierarchy of topics. That is, there is no functional difference between a hierarchy of topicheads and the equivalent hierarchy of topicrefs to title-only topics. In fact, DITA 1.2 makes it clear that authors can indicate that processors explicitly treat specific topicheads this way by specifying specific @chunk values on topicheads.

Topics must have titles and may contain any of the following substructures after the title, in this order:

1. `<titlealts>`. Contains alternative navigation or search titles for the topic.
2. `<shortdesc>` or `<abstract>`.

   `<shortdesc>` contains a short description of the topic, in general what would be the first sentence or two of the first paragraph of the topic.

   `<abstract>` contains one or more block-level elements that serve as the abstract of the topic and may also contain a short description element.

3. `<prolog>`. Contains the metadata for the topic as a whole, including authorship information, classifying metadata, keywords, and index entries.
4. `<body>`. Contains the *non-hierarchical* content of the topic, that is, the paragraphs and such that occur before any nested topics. By definition, any titled elements, such as `<section>`, that occur within `<body>` do not affect or contribute to the hierarchy of titles the topic participates in.

   In particular, `<section>` elements should not be reflected in tables of contents and similar navigation structures, and the formatting of `<section>` titles should be the same regardless of the hierarchical level of the topic that contains it. For example, in HTML, `<section>` titles should always map to the same `<hn>` element or to an HTML @class value that will result in consistent styling for all `<section>` titles.

5. `<related-links>`. Contains links to other resources (topics, publications, or non-DITA resources) to which this topic is related in some way. Usually intended to be generated from relationships established in maps or by other means.
6. `<topic>`. A topic may contain nested topics. Nested topics form a hierarchy of titles. There should be no functional difference between a hierarchy of topics created using nested `<topicref>` elements and one created by directly nesting topics within a single XML document. However, even though there is absolutely no requirement in the DITA standard for each topic to be in its own XML document, some processors may treat them differently.

Every topic, no matter how specialized, must reflect this pattern. Specialized topics may omit anything except the title and may require anything that is optional, but they may not add things or change the order of things. Likewise, except for nested topics, none of the child elements of `<topic>` are repeatable, so you may not have a specialized topic that has multiple bodies or multiple abstracts, for example.

If you need to have multiple distinct containers within any of the children of `<topic>` you have several choices:

- Within `<title>` or `<shortdesc>` use `<ph>` to contain distinct text. For example, to have two different title values with different conditional attributes, you would use `<ph>` like so:

```
<title
 ><ph audience="beginner">DITA is Fun!</ph
 ><ph audience="expert">Getting Started with DITA</ph
></title>
```

- Within `<abstract>` use multiple `<p>` elements.
- Within `<prolog>` use `<data>` to create groups of `<data>` elements.
- Within `<metadata>` within `<prolog>` use multiple `<data>` elements or multiple `<keywords>` elements.
- Within `<body>` use `<bodydiv>` to create separate, untitled groups of elements.
- Within `<section>` within `<body>` use `<sectiondiv>` to create separate, untitled groups of elements. See *Sections and Divisions: Organizing Topic Body Content* on page 225.

There are many schools of thought about the "right" rhetorical use of topics. The discussion here is concerned only with the markup rules.

What is appropriate rhetorically depends entirely on the nature of the information and the purpose of the publications that use it. Whether you use a strict minimalist and modular approach or treat DITA as though it were a markup language for narrative documents is entirely a matter of local policy. The DITA standard does not require the former nor disallow the latter. Depending on the circumstances, topics consisting of nothing but titles are just as sensible and correct as topics with deeply nested subtopics in a single document. There is no DITA-defined requirement that each topic be a separate XML document, although that is a fairly typical practice.

Data and Metadata in DITA

DITA makes a fundamental distinction between data and metadata and provides general elements (`<data>`, `<data-about>`, `<indexterm>`, etc.) for capturing arbitrary metadata in almost any context.

In philosophical terms, what is "data" and what is "metadata" is often a matter of opinion, and it is certainly the case that what is metadata in one context is data in another. DITA tries to make the distinction by saying that information intended *primarily* to be presented to readers for direct consumption is "data" and information that serves to classify, identify, or otherwise describe the content is "metadata."[18]

In general, a given piece of metadata serves one of the following purposes:

---

[18] As I write this topic I realize that it's a little odd that the primary element for holding arbitrary *meta*data is named `<data>`, but there it is.

- Identifies: associates a distinct label, name, or identifier with the content. DITA @id attributes, DITA keys, and CMS-specific object IDs are all examples of identifying metadata. Identifying metadata usually serves the needs of more-or-less direct and persistent addressing or reader recognition of objects through descriptive or well-known labels or names, such as citation strings for journal articles, digital object identifiers (DOIs), or part numbers for mechanical parts.

- Classifies: associates one or more classifying values with the data. For example, DITA keywords within `<prolog>` serve as classifiers, as do index entries. Classifying metadata generally serves the needs of search and retrieval or query-based association (as opposed to direct addressing using identifiers). Classifying metadata is often bound to taxonomies or ontologies that define the vocabulary of classification values and their relation to each other or to other taxonomies or ontologies[19]

- Describes: associates one or more descriptive properties with the content. Obvious examples are the DITA author, product, and copyright metadata elements allowed within `<prolog>`. These capture properties of the map or topic that are neither identifying nor classifying, but descriptive or associative. For example, one can think of the `<author>` element as establishing a relationship between the topic as an object and the author as an object, even though the author may not be represented literally in the DITA content other than as a string value within the `<author>` element. But in many Publishing-related systems, authors are represented by specific content, for example, author biographies and other metadata about authors as business objects within the publishing process and there is a definite business and information management requirement for there to be an explicit, not implicit, association between a map or topic and its author objects. In a real Publishing information system, just having the author value "John Brown" is not sufficient because there could be any number of John Browns who are authors of works published by the same publisher. So while we tend to think of descriptive metadata as name/value pairs, they may need to be more sophisticated.

- Annotates: associates some form of commentary with the content, such as editorial notes, historical background, etc. It is annotative metadata that is most obviously both metadata from the standpoint

---

[19] By *taxonomy* I mean a strictly or mostly hierarchical system of classifications from more general to more specific, of which the Linaean taxonomy of living things is the most obvious example. By *ontology* I mean a directed graph of relationships among classifications or "subjects." That distinction seems to be the most generally accepted and useful definitions of these terms, at least in the context of applying them to DITA-based content. I have zero patience for arguments about what is or isn't an ontology. One can, of course, argue that a taxonomy is just a degenerate form of ontology and one would be right, but so what? It's useful to distinguish the purely (or mostly) hierarchical from the very much not hierarchical. In particular, defining taxonomies and creating user interfaces that reflect them is easy. Defining ontologies and user interfaces that reflect them is hard. Note that the DITA 1.2 Subject Scheme map type is capable of representing both taxonomies and ontologies with equal ease, although the Topic Map standard is more optimized for representing ontologies (Topic Maps have no direct relationship to DITA other than coincidence of names and the fact that a DITA map could be expressed as a topic map). See *Value Lists, Taxonomies, and Ontologies: SubjectScheme Maps* on page 305.

of the thing annotated and content from the standpoint of the person interested more in the commentary than the commentary subject.

Within maps and topicrefs, metadata about the topicref as a whole or the map as a whole is held within `<topicmeta>`. Within topics, the `<prolog>` element holds metadata that applies to the topic as a whole. The `<data>` element is used for most other metadata and can occur in most contexts. Metadata on topicrefs that point to topics cascades, by default, to the referenced topic, adding to or overriding the metadata on the topic in that use context.

When used outside of `<topicmeta>`, the `<data>` element applies to the element that directly contains it. For example, if you put a `<data>` element inside a `<p>` element, then the `<data>` element is metadata for the `<p>` element. When used inside `<topicmeta>`, the `<data>` element applies to the same scope as the `<topicmeta>` element that contains it, that is, the topicref (and referenced topic, if any) or map as a whole.

By default, `<data>` is not rendered. This means that all `<data>` elements are suppressed in most outputs unless you say otherwise. You are, of course, free to render `<data>` elements if you wish to, but they should not be rendered by generic DITA processors using only default presentation rules.

Note that "not rendered" is not the same as "not processed"—processors that generate intermediate versions of DITA content as they perform DITA preprocessing (content reference resolution, link resolution, link text construction, and so forth) should pass any metadata elements through to the final rendition stage. It is the rendition processor (that is, the last stage before the data is presented to the reader) that decides what to do with each metadata element. Not carrying metadata through in earlier stages would deny rendition stages the opportunity to present some or all of the metadata if it so desires.

Because DITA's specialization mechanism does not allow you to define new attributes for individual element types (you can only define global attributes through specialization), you must use `<data>` or specializations of `<data>` where you would otherwise use element-type-specific attributes. (Attribute specializations are global because any specialization declaration syntax that allowed you to add attributes to individual elements would be prohibitively complex, at least in the context of the current attribute-based syntax.)

The use of nested `<data>` elements as though they were attributes does pose a problem for DTD-syntax content models because you cannot have a content model that both allows #PCDATA and requires specific elements before any text. You can do that with XSD schemas. However, there's no point in worrying about this because the semantics of `<data>` are, or should be, independent of where the `<data>` elements occur within the element they apply to. By convention they are usually collected at the beginning, like attributes, or at the end.

Custom processing that reflects `<data>` elements in the rendition should not depend on the elements being at any particular location within the content. Rather, processing code should treat child `<data>` elements like attributes and process them without regard to where they occur.

Note that `<data>` can contain `<data>` to any level of nesting, so you can construct sophisticated metadata structures if you need to.

It is absolutely wrong to use `<data>` to created titled hierarchies within topic bodies. That is, you must not specialize from `<data>` and then customize your processing to render the `<data>` elements simply to get around the prohibition on the nesting of sections or similar constraints. The DITA specification has an explicit statement to this effect. DITA 1.2 provides two arbitrarily-nesting content elements, `<bodydiv>` and `<sectiondiv>`, that can be used to create arbitrary *untitled* content structures without the need to abuse `<data>`.

The `<data>` element takes two attributes:

- @name specifies the name of the metadata item, for example, `<data name="clause-number">`.
- @value specifies the value of the metadata item, for example, `<data name="clause-number value="12.4.3"/>`

You can choose to put the metadata value in the @value attribute or in the content of the `<data>` element. In general, you should do one or the other, but not both, for a given element instance. In specializations you can set defaults for either or both attributes. As a matter of practice, you should always set a default for the @name attribute on specializations of `<data>` so that general-purpose processors will report it just as they would for an unspecialized `<data>` element.

The `<data-about>` element is used to associate metadata with an element by pointing at the element to which the metadata applies, rather than having the metadata literally nested. This allows you to apply metadata to existing content that you cannot or do not want to modify. This could be a handy feature, but at the time of writing I'm not aware of anyone who depends on this feature of DITA or any tools that support it, including the Open Toolkit (as of version 1.5.3).

`<data-about>` presents implementation challenges for information management, especially if you want to enable search based on metadata. To support efficient search would require you to maintain indexes to associate `<data-about>` elements with the elements they annotate. This isn't hard to implement, but it does require thought when designing your search and retrieval system.

In a sequential processing application like the Open Toolkit you could simply push `<data-about>` elements into the content of the elements they point to, changing the `<data-about>` elements into `<data>` elements, and then let subsequent processing operate as it would normally operate on nested `<data>` elements.

Another base form of metadata is index entries, represented by the `<indexterm>` element. Like `<data>`, index terms are not presented by default at the point of occurrence, but are used to construct back-of-the-book indexes or similar navigation or retrieval structures. You can put index terms either within map or topic metadata using `<keywords>` within `<metadata>` within `<topicmeta>` or`<prolog>`, or you can put them inline in content elements. Normal practice for modular content is to put index entries in topic metadata rather than inline, where they contribute to the general classifying metadata for the topic. But you can put index terms inline if you want to or where it is required, such as when topics tend to span multiple pages in printed output, meaning that entries in the topic metadata might not result in accurate page number references in a print index.

Mention Elements: Term and Keyword

DITA provides a general set of element types for capturing mentions of things that are often defined elsewhere in the information set and to which the mention may be implicitly or explicitly linked.

In pretty much all writing, but in technical documentation especially, clearly identifying the mentions of things can be very important.

By a "mentions of a thing" I mean an occurrence in the content of the name or other identifier of a specific thing, such as a person, place, part number, API construct, or any other abstract or real-world thing to which a name is or can be associated. For example, in the sentence "Use the ant command to run build scripts," "ant" is a mention of a thing. A human can tell from context that it must be a command, but a computer can't necessarily make that inference. Thus, you often need to tag mentions to indicate the kind of thing the mention is of, for example, "Use the <cmdname>ant</cmdname> command to run build scripts." The <cmdname> element identifies the string "ant" as a mention of a command name and not, for example, the name of a family of insects.

DITA provides specific markup for tagging such mentions. The main DITA elements for tagging mentions are <keyword> and <term> and their specializations, such as <cmdname> and <apiname>.[20]

The primary reasons for using mention elements include:

- Creating typographic distinctions. For example, the XML domain used in this book's source defines the <xmlelem> element, a specialization of <keyword>. It enables generation of the appropriate font and, in most renderings, the left and right angle brackets.
- Enabling you to find mentions by the type of thing mentioned. If I want to find (or more likely, index) all of the different element types mentioned in this document I can simply search for all occurrences of <xmlelem>, group them by string value, and report the list.
- Enabling implicit association between things mentioned and the definitions of those things. For example, in the documentation for a document type, you could implement automatic linking between <xmlelem> elements and their reference entries. This technique works when the names of the things mentioned are reliably unique or otherwise discriminated, but it breaks down when you can have different base names in different contexts, such as the same class name ("Element") in different Java

---

[20]   Meta note: The markup that produces the typographic distinction for the element types in this paragraph is an example of a specialized mention element, the element type <xmlelem> from the DITA for Publishers XML domain (and this footnote just used that element to mark a mention of itself. Dude. That is so wild).

libraries. In that type of case, a simple name is not sufficient to determine the correct link target (this is one reason DITA has the keyref facility).

- Enabling explicit association between things mentioned and their definitions. In DITA this is through the use of `@keyref` on `<keyword>` and `<term>`.
- Acting as classifying metadata when used in an explicit metadata context, such as within `<topicmeta>`.

Mention elements are very useful, and therefore you are likely to specialize new mention elements sooner rather than later (along with creating custom conditional attributes). If you're writing about wangdoodlers, hornswagglers, and vermitious knids you probably need corresponding specialized mention elements to distinguish mentions of specific wangdoodler instances from specific knid instances.

Fortunately, defining specialized mention elements is the second-easiest form of specialization, after attribute specialization. See *Volume 2: Element Domain Specialization Tutorial.*

Within the DITA vocabulary, the `<keyword>` element is the more general mention element, meaning essentially any mention that isn't a term. The `<term>` element is intended for words that have, or could be expected to have, a glossary definition. The distinction is essentially, `<keyword>` is for mentions of things that could or should have corresponding reference topics and `<term>` is for things that are defined terms. If you are creating specialized mention element domains you will usually specialize from `<keyword>` unless you are explicitly creating distinct forms of `<term>`, for example, to indicate different target glossaries. For example, you might specialize term into `<common-term>` and `<jargon-term>` to distinguish terms that are defined in common dictionaries (and thus not in your glossary) and terms that are specific jargon that are in your glossary. Or you might specialize `<term>` to reflect the taxonomy or ontology the term is defined in (see the footnote on taxonomies and ontologies in *Data and Metadata in DITA* on page 219).

Note that the mention element for keywords in programming languages and command line interfaces is the `<kwd>` element defined in the Technical Content software domain. Do not confuse with `<keyword>`.

I use the term "mention" because it is general to all documentation-related information structuring systems, XML and non-XML. That is, all computer-based systems for authoring and storing content with even a modicum of semantic identification have the notion of mentions, or at least the ability to represent them. Think of Microsoft Word and similar word processing systems that are limited to essentially paragraphs and inlines. As long as you can have named inline styles you have what you need to create semantically-distinct mentions, and most people who use tools like Word for anything at all sophisticated will have created mention styles in exactly the way I mean here, even if they didn't realize that was what they were doing. Thus mentions are a fundamental concept in markup design and it's useful to have a generic term for them. The DITA architecture doesn't (or didn't before DITA 1.2) use the term "mention" in a formal way, but what DITA means by `<keyword>` and `<term>` is exactly what I mean by "mention."

Sections and Divisions: Organizing Topic Body Content

Topic bodies may be organized into a single level of titled containers (sections) or contain hierarchies of untitled containers (body divisions). Sections may also contain hierarchies of untitled containers (section divisions).

A fundamental design rule for DITA is that hierarchies of arbitrarily titled components are represented using hierarchies of topics created either through maps or by directly nesting topics within topics in a single XML document. By "arbitrarily titled" we mean the title is defined in the instance by the author, rather than being an invariant title generated automatically.

Thus, within the body of a single topic it would be wrong to have more than one level of arbitrarily-titled things.

This rule is reflected in DITA by the `<section>` element.

The `<section>` element allows `<title>` as a direct child, meaning that authors can create sections with arbitrary titles. However, `<section>` does not allow `<section>` as a descendant. This is specifically so that authors cannot create a hierarchy of arbitrarily titled things within a topic's body.

If authors need to create arbitrary hierarchies of titled things, they must use topics to do so. (General discussion of designing topic and map markup hierarchies is in Volume 2 of *DITA for Practitioners*.)

Many practitioners with background in other document types often react negatively to this aspect of DITA when they first come to understand it. I certainly did—you can find in the archives of the DITA Technical Committee's mailing list a fairly long discussion between me and others as to whether sections should or should not be allowed to nest.

However, once you understand that topics are the fundamental unit of content aggregation you see that it is not only correct but necessary that sections do not nest.

The `<section>` element was intended primarily for use in reference topic types where you have a consistent set of titled containers where the titles are generated (invariant). The `<section>` element takes an attribute, `@spectitle`, which let's you specify fixed or default title text (using a text lookup key) as part of a specialization of `<section>`, so authors don't have to deal with titles if you don't want them to.

The `<section>` element was not really intended to be used in its unspecialized form by authors, and unspecialized use should be discouraged. In short, authors who use unspecialized `<section>` elements will soon realize that it doesn't nest and become frustrated when they realize that they should have been using subordinate topics all along. Then, they will have to rework their content. Don't let that happen.

DITA also provides for arbitrarily nested *untitled* structures, which serve as the specialization base for defining organizational wrapper elements or modeling complex content structures. These structures are called "divisions" and are represented by the `<bodydiv>` and `<sectiondiv>` elements. The two element types are required to ensure that you cannot indirectly put sections within sections: `<bodydiv>` allows `<section>`, `<sectiondiv>` does not.

Divisions are explicitly not titled, meaning they do not allow `<title>` in their content and are not intended to allow author-defined titles. They may have the processing effect of generating titles, but they may not have arbitrary titles, as that would violate the principle that "only topics may define title hierarchies."

8

Pointing to Things: Linking and Addressing in DITA

DITA relies heavily on the use of different kinds of links. DITA links may use direct addresses (URI references) or indirect addresses (key references).

DITA's linking and addressing capabilities are heavily influenced by IBM IDDoc, the HyTime standard, and other formal models of hyperlinking and hypertext, but they also reflect the practical recognition that linking is essential for reuse and for optimizing the usability of information. While DITA was not originally designed primarily as a hypertext application, in fact it has become a sophisticated hypertext application with a reasonably consistent linking and addressing architecture.

To talk about the hyperlinking and addressing features of DITA it is necessary to use some jargon. The following sections first explain general linking and addressing concepts and then discuss how those concepts are implemented in DITA.

Hypertext Jargon: A Twisty Maze of Passages

There is no single accepted vocabulary for talking about links. However, there is a fairly well-established vocabulary that comes out of work done on computer hypertext systems in the 1980s and early 1990s and is reflected in things like the HyTime standard. The terminology used here is the terminology I have used for the last 20 years or so in my work both applying hypertext and hyperlinking to large-scale systems of documents and as a co-editor of the HyTime standard. I can't claim that it is universally understood, but I think it's well enough established that anyone already well versed in hypertext formalisms would understand the jargon. I have presented the terminology I use as received, without bothering to qualify it, since I consider it to be common vocabulary and not jargon specific to this book. As relatively few people today give much thought to the formalisms behind hyperlinking systems, I figure both that my jargon is as good as anyone's and that you're not likely to run into anyone with a competing set of jargon and a reason to argue with my particular use of terms.

However, the jargon I use will not necessarily be reflected in other applications that do hyperlinking so you may need to work out the mapping between the general concepts and abstractions presented here and the details of any particular application or markup design. One purpose of presenting this abstract model of linking is to separate the general from the specifics of markup and implementation details so that it is in fact possible to meaningfully compare and analyze how different applications handle linking, which can be very important for generating specific interactive renditions of DITA content from DITA source.

Linking vs. Addressing

Linking establishes relationships among things, links use addresses to point to those things.

In order to understand and make best use of links in any documentation application, but especially in DITA, it is important to understand the distinction between links as abstract objects and the plumbing that makes links work.

Links as objects that represent relationships

In general terms, a *link* is a relationship among two or more things. In the context of DITA, the things that can be linked are XML elements, because XML elements are the unit of semantic structure in XML and DITA is an XML application.

When you create a topicref, which is a kind of link, you are establishing a relationship between the `<topicref>` element and the `<topic>` element that the topicref points to. Likewise, a cross-reference establishes a relationship between the `<xref>` element and the element it points to (which could be almost any type of element).

When you use @conref or @conkeyref you are establishing a use by reference relationship between the element that specifies @conref or @conkeyref and the element pointed to. In the case of topicrefs and cross-references, the element types are always links. In the case of the @conref and @conkeyref attributes, the attribute creates a link from an element that is not inherently a link.

All relationships have some sort of type that indicates the reason or purpose of the relationship, for example, "related information" (`<xref>`) or "navigation position" (`<topicref>`). Sometimes the type is generic ("navigation") and sometimes it is specific, although in most documentation contexts link types tend to be generic.

Link types are analogous to element types, in that the type allows processors to do different things for different kinds of links. In DITA you can use several different kinds of general link types (topicrefs, xrefs, reltable links, conref links, etc.) that have specific processing semantics, and you can add your own more-specific types through specialization (for example, specializations of `<topicref>`).

As an abstract object, a link simply establishes a relationship among two or more objects, the *link ends*. One of the link ends may be the link element itself, as in the case of topicrefs and cross references. Links do not inherently have directionality, meaning that, in theory, you should be able to traverse any link starting at any link end and go to any other link end.

Link ends may also be referred to as "anchors." However, the term "anchor" is problematic because it may also refer to an object that is the target of an address to which links can point but that is not itself part of a link. The HTML `<a>` element with only an `@id` or `@name` attribute is an example of this second meaning of the term "anchor."

Even links that we tend to think of as highly directional, such as cross-references, have two ends and, while you may not normally want authors to traverse from the target of the cross-reference to the reference itself, it is often useful to know that a given element is in fact a reference target and where the reference is.

This is often referred to as the "where used" problem, and it comes up particularly in the context of component management systems, which should keep track of links and provide quick answers to the "where used" question. Answering a "where used" question for a given cross-reference target or similar highly-directional link means traversing from the link end that is the target of the reference to the link end that is the reference itself.

Other links are not inherently directional. Such links are usually referred to as "bidirectional" (if there are exactly two link ends) or "multidirectional" (if there are more than two link ends). In DITA, relationship table links are not inherently directional.

A link has a type. Likewise, each end of a link has a *role*, sometimes referred to as *anchor role*. The role of each link end allows the semantic purpose of each end to be distinguished. This allows for a more complete description of the relationship and allows processors to do different things for different link ends. In DITA, for most links the roles are implicit in the link type and are not specified anywhere. In other links, such as DITA relationship table links, the roles are specified.

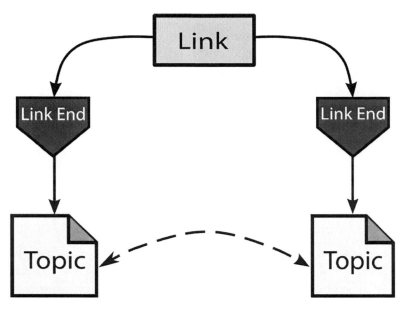

Figure 7: Abstract link model

If you think about links as representing relationships, it should be clear that some relationships are inherently directional and some are not. Thus directionality of links is a function of the semantic of the link as a relationship and of policies applied to the link regarding navigation behaviors. In some systems, such as military task support systems or educational systems, it may be important that navigation only be allowed in one direction for certain links. In most documentation systems, directionality is more likely a matter of practicality and user interface, meaning there is no need to enable direct navigation from the targets of cross-references to the original reference since doing so would clutter the presentation and create user interface challenges. Even for inherently non-directional links such as DITA relationship table links, you may define link types that are directional and therefore use processing rules to render the links with a specific directionality.

To belabor the notion of relationship directionality a bit more, some relationships are reflexive, in that you can read them in either direction without changing the link type. For example, the relationship "is married to" is reflexive in that you can read it as "husband is married to wife" and "wife is married to husband" without changing the link type. Other relationships are not reflexive, meaning that the link type is only meaningful for a particular direction. For example, the relationship "is parent of" is only meaningful when read starting at the "parent" role: "parent is parent of child." The reverse direction requires a different link type, in this case, "is child of."

Of course, all non-reflexive relationships imply an inverse as in the parent-of/child-of relationship. Thus one challenge of link relationship design is how to express the types of non-reflexive relationships in markup: do you leave one direction implicit? Do you use link types that reflect both directions? Do you use pairs of directional links? Does anyone actually care?

This last question is actually quite important: does anyone actually care about links and formal link types and anchor roles? While it's possible to formally analyze the links used in a body of documentation and work out all sorts of formal relationships, it may not add any value to do so. This raises the question of what links are really good for and when should you care about them?

The practical value of links include:

- Enabling reader navigation from one place to another in order to make best use of the information, usually in support of a task or in understanding a concept. In DITA this means cross-references and relationship table links.
- Enabling construction of complete publications from reusable component parts. In DITA this means maps, topicrefs, and content references.
- Enabling the reader to find information based on its participation in relationships, often as it relates to real-world objects or concepts. In DITA this means relationship table links, subject scheme maps, or links established outside of a DITA context, such as by taxonomies or ontologies, possibly using technologies like RDF.

The first two bullets don't really require a great deal of formalism to be useful. Simply creating new element types for `<topicref>` or `<xref>` is sufficient semantic distinction to support authoring and processing.

The last bullet is really about using links to represent facts about the world to which the information relates so that you can then navigate or find information components based on the model of the world reflected by the links. For example, documentation about a complex machine could be linked using more-specific link types that reflect the component and subcomponent structure of the machine itself (for example, subcomponent-of links, rather than simple navigation links). As a user of the information you should be able to get a view that reflects the machine as a system of components, navigate that model, and then be able to get from a specific machine component to all the relevant information about that component, distinguished by information type (for example, by topic type). It is in this type of model that link types become more important.

Another implication of this way of thinking about links is that there are all sorts of interesting ways you can create data models of the content or the information domain to which the content applies and then express those data models using formal hyperlinks. This is, for example, the focus and purpose of the Topic Map and RDF standards, which are all about using hyperlinks to represent knowledge and relating those links to specific information components. Likewise, the DITA Subject Scheme map type can be used to represent formal taxonomies and ontologies as systems of links that can be imposed onto other content. These can be very interesting, especially in the context of managing large bodies of content that cover lots of subjects, such as encyclopedias or catalogs of published works.

Because it provides appropriate linking and addressing facilities and because of its modular nature, DITA is well suited to abstract linking applications.

Links as sets of pointers

As an abstraction, a link is a relationship among objects. But to make that abstraction concrete you have to point at the objects in some way. That is, for each link end there must be a pointer to the thing or things that constitute that end of the link. These pointers are "addresses" and the act of pointing to something is "addressing."

Addressing is the plumbing that makes links work. Everyone is familiar with HTML links, which are essentially all plumbing (the `@href` attribute and the URIs it contains) and no semantics (the link type represented by the element type `<a>` is completely unspecified, given that "a" stands for "anchor" in HTML, meaning one end of the link). In fact, HTML has trained most people to confuse the address with the link and think that what is important is the address.

But the address is no more important than whether or not the pipes that deliver the water to your tap are PVC, copper, or Roman lead—as long as drinkable water comes out, you don't care how it got there.

By the same token, the pipes could be completely replaced with a different type of pipe, and as long as you got the same water, you wouldn't know or care.

So it is with addressing: as long as the address gets to the appropriate element, it doesn't matter what form of address is used. Likewise, you can always change the addressing mechanism without changing the meaning of the link as long as the ultimate target is the same.

Addresses may be implicit or explicit.

An "implicit address" is one that does not need to be specified because it is implied by some other aspect of the link. For example, in the case of elements like `<topicref>` and `<xref>`, the link element itself is one of the link ends, and therefore "this element" is the address of that link end, which clearly does not need to be further specified.

DITA does not define any other type of implicit link or address, though of course, you are free to implement implicit linking behavior for your own content. A typical example is linking based on classification metadata within topics, where, given a taxonomy that defines the classification values you can automatically relate topics to each other based on the relationships defined in the taxonomy. DITA enables this but does not define any built-in semantics for it.

An "explicit address" may be direct or indirect. In the context of XML applications like DITA, the purpose of an address is to point unambiguously at one or more XML elements or subcomponents of XML elements (attributes, text, etc.). In DITA, all addressing is to elements—DITA has no notion of addressing individual attributes of elements or individual text nodes.

For explicit linking, DITA defines two forms of address:

- Direct addressing using URIs and DITA-specific fragment identifiers.
- Indirect addressing using keys and key references.

URIs are a standard,[21] but the URI standard only defines the rules for how to address complete "resources" (for example, files). It does not define how to address things within resources. Addressing within resources is always specific to the details of the resource's data, which could be anything. The URI standard has no choice but to delegate to the different data types the rules for addressing within those data types. Thus DITA defines its own fragment identifier syntax.

Note that there is no single standard for XML fragment identifiers. This is because there are simply too many different ways that it might be useful to address XML elements. There are some standards, such as XPointer, but they are neither universally implemented nor necessarily attractive. In any case, for largely historical reasons, DITA defines its own fragment identifier syntax and does not use other standards such as XPointer.

Note too that W3C standards such as XPointer and XLink are explicitly *delivery* standards, not authoring standards. They are designed to meet the requirements of hyper-document delivery, not hyper-document authoring, and as such lack features, such as indirection, that are required for authoring but necessarily avoided for delivery. Thus, it would be inappropriate for DITA to use a standard like XPointer or XLink because those standards don't meet authoring requirements, regardless of any other technical flaws or value they may have. It is unfortunate that no general authoring-specific addressing standard has emerged, but the lack of it hasn't been a huge issue. It does mean, however, that DITA-aware processors cannot directly use any existing addressing infrastructure they may have developed for other addressing standards since DITA's addressing details are specific to DITA and not even coincidently the same as any other addressing standard.

In any case, the key point is that the form of address used for a link doesn't matter and should be changeable without affecting the semantic of the link as long as the ultimate target of each address is the same. In DITA this means that you should be able to replace any direct URI reference with the equivalent key reference and visa versa. This is important for authoring and delivery, because it means you can make direct addresses indirect (important for authoring) and indirect addresses direct (important for delivery), and you can do it without risk of breakage as long as you can prove that the ultimate target of the address is the same before and after.

Another aspect of addressing is identity, in particular, how do things like topics and elements within topics establish their identity as unique objects relative to all other existing and potential objects? Without identity you cannot unambiguously address things.

In XML generally, identity is established as follows:

1. Every XML document is, by definition, a storage object (for example, file) within some storage system. As a storage object it has identity represented by its storage location, for example, its URL within a repository: `http://example.com/mydocs/doc1/topic-01.dita`. By implication, if two documents have the same storage location they are the same document.

---

[21] Internet Request for Comment (RFC) 2396, *http://www.ietf.org/rfc/rfc2396.txt*

2. Every element within an XML document has a unique and invariant location within the tree of elements rooted at the document element. That is, every element can be unambiguously and reliably addressed by an XPath expression of the form `"/root/element()[n]/element()[n]/element()[n]"`, where n is the child number of the element at that level in the hierarchy.

Thus, every element within an XML document is inherently an object whose identity can be expressed as the combination of resource location (URI) of the containing XML document and the XPath tree location of the element.

Of course, the tree location of an element is only invariant for a specific version of the document. If the document is updated, then the tree location may be different in the new version. Therefore, it is convenient (but not absolutely necessary) to put some sort of persistent identifier on elements so they can be addressed without worrying about changes in their position over time.

Using IDs is not a complete solution to the challenge of managing pointers as documents are revised, but it works well enough that it's worth doing for convenience if nothing else.[22] A complete solution must provide some form of indirect addressing, which in DITA is provided through the key reference facility, about which more later.

For element identity DITA defines the following mechanisms:

- Topic elements require the `@id` attribute, which for `<topic>`, is declared as type "ID," (an XML ID) meaning that its value must be unique within the document that contains the `<topic>` element. This is the only place in DITA that `@id` attributes are declared as type "ID."

  Note that this does *not* require that all topics have globally unique IDs, only that topics have unique IDs within their containing XML documents. For documents that contain exactly one `<topic>` element the topic ID doesn't matter at all, as the topic can be unambiguously addressed by addressing the XML document as a whole. Any processor that either requires that topic IDs be globally unique or assumes that they are is broken.

- Almost all non-topic elements within topics may have an `@id` attribute. The value must be unique within the non-topic children of the containing topic, but there is no way in DTD or XSD to express this requirement so most editors will not enforce it. The identity of non-topic elements within topics is established by the combination of the topic ID and the element ID of the element itself.

  Note that if a topic contains a subtopic, the same element ID may be used within the subordinate topic (but of course, the topic IDs must be unique within a single XML document as that is the rule for

---

[22] To understand why it's not a complete solution, consider the case of an element with an ID getting split into two elements as a result of a revision—some of the references to the original ID will continue to be correct but some will not be; thus there is no alternative but to update the incorrect references to point to the newly-created element. At that point, it should become clear that, because it can't protect you from broken links, an ID is no better than a tree location. IDs are at best a convenience and at worst a distraction.

XML attributes of type ID). That is, each topic establishes a new ID space for all of the non-topic children within that topic (i.e., the elements within the short description, abstract, prolog, and body of the topic, but not within any nested topics nor the nested topic elements themselves).

This design was driven primarily by a desire to make it possible to combine topics together into new documents without having to rewrite IDs and pointers to them. It makes some things easier and some things harder. It's not how I would have done it, but it is how DITA was designed long before it became an OASIS standard.

Note also that concerns about what happens during processing, such as resolving conrefs or applying "chunk" rules should be of no concern because processors should always have enough information to manage addresses through the processing of content (remembering that addresses can always be changed as long as the resulting target is correct).

- Elements within maps may have an `@id` attribute. The value must be unique within the map but, for various good reasons, these `@id` attributes are not declared as type ID and therefore XSDs and DTDs cannot validate ID uniqueness within maps.

If you have a situation where you are migrating legacy content into DITA you may run into issues around capturing current IDs or multiple IDs. If your legacy content uses normal XML IDs then there should be no problem since they will be at least as unique as DITA requires as long as you're not combining things from different documents into new documents. Likewise, CMS object IDs should translate to element IDs since they are presumably also unique.

If you need to capture additional identifiers, in addition to the element ID, that is best done by using `<data>` within topic prologs or non-topic elements (if the identifiers don't apply to the topic as a whole).

Linking, Addressing, and Reuse: The Need for Indirection

Element-to-element links present inherent reuse challenges. To overcome these challenges you must use some form of indirection for addressing. Indirection lets you change the ultimate target of a link without modifying the link itself.

In the context of a publication developed and published in isolation, using links poses no particular practical challenge beyond constructing addresses (that is, setting the value of the `@href` attribute). Once created, the links will work reliably as long as files are not moved or renamed and element IDs are not changed. There are challenges managing addresses when you revise a publication, but those challenges are manageable. While indirect addressing can help in this simple case, it is not a hard requirement.

However, as soon as you introduce a second publication to the system, things get very challenging very quickly.

This issue is dependencies. A link from one topic to another makes the first topic dependent on the second; anywhere the first topic is used, the second topic must also be used.

In DITA, where topics are used by reference from maps and the same topic can be used in different maps (and therefore in different publications), you need to handle topic-to-topic dependencies. In addition, because the same topic may be used multiple times within the same map, there is a potential issue with *use context* when linking to a topic used multiple times.

The term "use context" simply means the context within which a piece of content is used or included. In DITA this ultimately means the root map that directly or indirectly includes a given topic. The focus is on topics because all content is ultimately included in topics, and it is topics that establish the addressing context for all non-topic elements. Therefore, the use context of topics establishes the use context for all non-topic content elements.

Generally speaking a given root map represents a distinct publication or processing context, which I generalize as the concept "publication." Within a publication, a given topic will be used from specific places within the map hierarchy. Each of these places is also a use context. Thus, when a topic is used multiple times within a map it has an overall use context, which is the publication, and one or more specific use contexts. Both types of use contexts may be important for referencing and reusing the topic.

Consider a topic that has a cross-reference to another topic, for example, a task topic that links to a supporting reference topic:

```
<task id="changing-toner-cartridge">
  ...
  <context>
    <figure>
      <title>Toner Cartridge Access Panel</title>
      <image
href="../images/model_PR3604/illustration-toner-cartridge-access-panel.jpg"/>

      <p>For toner cartridge specifications see
    </figure>
<xref
href="../ref/model_PR3604/PR3604_specifications.dita#specs-PR3604/toner-cartridge-specs-table"

    type="table"/>.
  </context>
  ...
</task>
```

The topic "changing-toner-cartridge" now has a dependency on the topic "PR3604_specifications.dita," and therefore, any map that includes the task "changing-toner-cartridge" must also include the reference topic "PR3604_specifications.dita."

However, consider a case where we want the "changing-toner-cartridge" task to be a generic task for any printer, and we want to reuse that task in other places. In that case, it would be incorrect to include the reference topic for this specific printer.

What to do?

Using direct addresses, as in the example above, there is no way to avoid including the linked topic except to make a copy of the task and change the reference. Making a copy of the task is obviously counter to the point of reuse.

One solution would be to move the generic parts of the task into a separate topic, leaving only the part that is specific to the target reference, namely the cross-reference, and then pull in the generic parts by conref. You would then create different versions of the task for use in different maps so you could link to different reference topics.

This works but is really complicated and requires new work for every new publication you want to use the task in. At that point it starts to look easier to just make the copies and eat the cost of keeping them in sync.

Another solution is to simply avoid using cross-references. For example, you could replace the cross-reference with a reltable link that establishes the relationship between the task and the reference topic. This works and is exactly what relationship tables were designed for, but it may not result in the best result for readers (we are probably all familiar with online help that includes 15 or 20 "related links" links at the end of a topic, with little to distinguish one link from another). In addition, there may be contexts, such as Publishing documents, where the cross-reference is required either by the original document, by editorial practice, or by the author's choice. In that case, a relationship table will not work (at least not in DITA, through 1.2, where relationship tables provide no way to reference elements inside topics; they can only reference whole topics).

The example here uses a cross-reference, but the same problem applies to conref: if you have created a content reference to a different topic you have necessarily created a dependency between the two topics. In this case, the technique of breaking up the topic into generic and use-context-specific components doesn't help since that requires the use of conref itself.

It should not take long to realize that direct addressing is the problem here: a direct address creates a "hard pointer" to a thing. A direct address is not sensitive to the use context within which the reference occurs.

If the direct address is an absolute URL, then it is clearly independent of any use context.

If the direct address is a relative URL, it is relative to the *storage* location of the XML document that contains the reference, not the use context of the document. That is, a relative URL is just a shorthand form of absolute URL where the base part of the absolute URL is determined by the URL of the containing document. In DITA terms, the location of the using map is again immaterial.

The solution then is, as in many aspects of computer systems, indirection. In particular, you need an addressing facility where the ultimate target can be determined relative to a given use context.

In DITA this means that the ultimate target of any indirect reference from a topic or submap must be defined in a map that uses the topic or submap. In this context, "map" means the compound map rooted as a particular root map, not a specific map document.

This form of indirection is often referred to as "late-bound indirection" because you can't know the ultimate target of a reference until you have established the root map you are processing. It is possible to have static, or "early bound" indirection, which simply protects initial references from changes in the details of targets but this form of indirection is not specific to the use context. DITA, through version 1.2, does not provide this form of indirection nor does any other general XML facility.[23]

As long as DITA did not provide some form of indirect addressing, reuse of topics that had hard references to elements in other XML documents was effectively impossible. Of course, people got around the problem in various ways, including defining their own addressing mechanisms, using post processing to fix the problem, or simply accepting limitations on what they could do within topics. All of these approaches have drawbacks and costs.

Therefore, late-bound, use-context-specific, indirect addressing is a hard requirement if you want unconstrained reuse of content.

With version 1.2, DITA adds late-bound indirect addressing in the form of the key reference facility. Key references allow the same reference to be bound to different targets in different use contexts (that is, in different maps). It does not, as of version 1.2, allow the same reference to be bound to different targets in different submaps. That is, within the scope of a given root map, a given key reference will always resolve to the same resource. Thus, the key reference facility is not a complete solution to the reuse and linking problem, but it goes a long way toward providing a complete solution. You can expect that the facility will be extended in future DITA versions so that it provides a more complete, if not 100% complete, solution to the linking problem.

The most important point is that as soon as you need to reuse topics in different maps, and you need to link from those topics to other topics, you will need some form of indirect addressing to make the content reusable and the addresses manageable without resorting to non-standard tricks or workarounds.

---

[23]   Some years ago I submitted a note to the W3C for such a facility, "XML Indirect," but it was largely ignored as far as I'm aware. I realize now that it was ignored because it is only of interest in authoring environments and the W3C does not do authoring standards, only delivery standards. In practice most systems avoid the need for this type of indirection by simply imposing some reasonable constraints on addressing or by simply eating the cost of breakage when things change. At the same time, few if any XML-aware content management systems actually solve the problem of versioned hyper-document management. So, perhaps XML Indirect's time will come anon.

DITA's Direct Addressing Syntax

DITA uses URIs and a DITA-specific fragment identifier syntax to directly address components of DITA documents.

XML is a Web application and as such uses URIs for addressing. As an XML application, DITA uses URIs as well. All direct references in DITA are URI references, usually URLs. Almost without exception any element that can make a direct reference does so using the `@href` attribute.

To oversimplify, a URI reference consists of two basic parts: the resource part and the fragment identifier. Both are optional, but at least one or the other must be specified. The fragment identifier is separated from the resource part by a hash sign (#), for example, `"http://example.com/mydocs/doc-01/topic-01.dita#some-topic-id"`, where `http://example.com/mydocs/doc-01/topic-01.dita` is the resource part and `some-topic-id` is the fragment identifier. For a complete definition of URIs see *RFC 2396: Uniform Resource Identifiers (URI): Generic Syntax (http://www.ietf.org/rfc/rfc2396.txt)*.

The resource part can be a uniform resource name (URN) or a uniform resource locator (URL). In most applications you will use URLs since those are, by definition, directly resolvable, while URNs are indirect and require another layer of processing to be resolved.

URLs can be absolute or relative. Relative URLs are relative to the location of the XML document that contains the reference.[24]

Note that URLs use "/" (forward slash) as the path separator, not "\" (backward slash). Any use of "\" in DITA documents is wrong and should not be supported by any processor. Some processors will interpret these as Windows filenames, but they should not since the value is not a valid URL (at least not without escaping the backslash), and other processors are not likely to honor it.

DITA fragment identifiers take one of two forms:

- For topic elements and elements within maps, the fragment identifier is the value of the target element's `@id` attribute: `href="#some-topic-id"` where `some-topic-id` is the fragment identifier.

---

[24] Technically, they are relative to the effective base URL, which can be set by the `@xml:base` attribute. DITA cannot prevent the use of `@xml:base` but its use in an authoring system would be rare since it would cause all sorts of havoc in most situations. The main reason to use `@xml:base` in an authoring environment would be to make authoring URLs of things outside the scope of the DITA content more convenient by moving the common part of the URL into a single location. Note that per the applicable standards for XML processing and URL resolution, the processing and application of `@xml:base` when it is present is mandatory and unconditional for all URI references. This means that processors are not free to apply their own processing semantics for `@xml:base` as regards the resolution of URI references.

- For non-topic elements within topics, the fragment identifier is the topic ID, a forward slash ("/"), and the element ID: `href="#some-topic-id/some-element-id"`.

  The element ID part must be an element within the non-topic children of the topic. That is, each topic establishes a separate ID namespace for all of its non-topic descendants. When you have nested topics each nested topic establishes its own ID namespace, which means that a parent topic and a nested topic may both have descendant non-topic elements with the same `@id` value.

Note that while the fragment identifier syntax for non-topic elements looks like a path, it is not path, it is always a topic-id/element-id pair. If you want to address an element within a nested topic you simply use the ID of the nested topic—you do not specify the ID of the ancestor topics. For example, given this topic with a nested topic:

```
<topic id="parent-topic">
  ...
  <topic id="child-topic-01">
    <title>Child Topic 1</title>
    <body>
     <p id="p-01">Paragraph one</p>
    </body>
  </topic>
</topic>
```

The fragment identifier for the paragraph "p-01" is `#child-topic-01/p-01` *not* `#parent-topic/child-topic-01/p-01`.

Likewise, the parent topic could also have a paragraph with the ID "p-01":

```
<topic id="parent-topic">
    <body>
     <p id="p-01">Paragraph one in parent.</p>
    </body>
  <topic id="child-topic-01">
    <title>Child Topic 1</title>
    <body>
     <p id="p-01">Paragraph one in child.</p>
    </body>
  </topic>
</topic>
```

The fragment identifier for the parent's paragraph would be `parent-topic/p-01`.

You can, of course, refer to non-DITA content from DITA documents. In that case the fragment identifier syntax is determined by the target resource and is not defined or constrained by DITA.

Keys and key references

Key references are indirect because the reference is just a key name. The key name is bound to a resource by a separate key definition within a map. In order to resolve the initial reference to the ultimate target resource, the processor must first find the correct key definition and then resolve that to a resource, which then becomes the resource to which the initial key reference resolves. The resource bound to the key name be a topic, a map, or a non-DITA resource, such as a graphic or Web page.

Indirect addressing allows you to author links that will resolve to different resources (topics, maps, graphics, or other non-DITA things) depending on the root maps that use them.

A typical example is a generic task that applies to many products but which refers to product-specific details. For example, printers often use the same print engine and toner cartridge but have different covers. The task of changing the toner cartridge is the same for all applications of the print engine but the illustrations of the specific printers that use it will be different for each printer model.

If the "change the toner cartridge" task included a reference to a printer-specific illustration you would need a separate copy of the task for each printer model, even though the text of the task is identical for all printers. By contrast, if the task could refer abstractly to the "changing the toner cartridge" illustration and let some other part of the system figure out which illustration to use for each instance, then you would only need one copy of the task.

The "other part of the system" binds key names to specific resources using key definition topicrefs within maps. In particular, the root map for a publication determines the binding of keys to resources. Different root maps can define different bindings for the same key.

Key bindings create a *global* key space for a given root map. This means that, within the context of a given root map, all references to a given key name will resolve to the same resource. When a root map includes other maps it forms a *map tree*. Key definitions may occur within any map in the map tree, and there may be multiple definitions for the same key name. When there are multiple definitions for the same key, only one can be the "effective" binding within the scope of a given root map. The rules for determining which definition of a key is the effective one are explained in *Constructing key spaces* on page 253.

For authors, the important (dare I say key) concept is that key bindings are global, not scoped by the map they are defined in. Thus it doesn't matter where a given key reference is, relative to where the effective key binding happens to be in the map tree: the binding is global and therefore all references to the key will resolve to the same resource for a given root map. This behavior is designed to allow higher maps in the map tree to determine the effective bindings for specific keys. While you might intuitively expect that key definitions within a submap would override those defined in an ancestor map, keys don't, and can't, work that way. The discussion of key space construction *Constructing key spaces* on page 253 discusses the global aspect of keys in more detail.

In the case of our toner cartridge replacement task we know that we need to always have an illustration of the printer that shows where the toner access panel is. We can assign a key name to this illustration and use it to indirectly point to the graphic. For example we could assign the key "illustration-toner-cartridge-access-panel" and then use it from an <image> element, like so:

```
<task id="changing-toner-cartridge">
  ...
  <context>
    <figure>
      <title>Toner Cartridge Access Panel</title>
      <image keyref="illustration-toner-cartridge-access-panel"/>
    </figure>
  </context>
  ...
</task>
```

Note that the <image> element uses a @keyref attribute, rather than an @href attribute. The value of the @keyref attribute is a *key name*. As the author of this task we only need to know the key name for the graphic, we don't need to know where the graphic is. In fact, because we know that this key will resolve to many different graphics in different printer-specific publications, we *can't* know for sure what graphic it will resolve to. Of course, while we're authoring we might have a particular version of this graphic, for example, the illustration for the first printer model this task is used for, or maybe a representative graphic that serves as guidance to illustrators who will create the printer-specific versions. But, as the author of this task, we don't care what graphic the key "illustration-toner-cartridge-access-panel" resolves to as long as it resolves to something in each publication.

Using the key establishes a requirement for the illustration but it's up to the author of each model-specific publication's map to bind key to the appropriate illustration.

Within a map, you create a key definition using the <topicref> element or any specialization of <topicref>. The <topicref> element uses the @keys attribute to specify the key or keys to be defined and then either points to a resource (a topic, another map, or a non-DITA resource such as a graphic) or uses subelements within <topicmeta> to define text to use as the resource (or both).

For our task example, we need to bind the key "illustration-toner-cartridge-access-panel" to the appropriate printer-specific illustration. This means that we must have a separate root map for each different printer model and then within each map, create the appropriate key definition. For example, for printer model "PR2105" you might have a root map like this:

```
<bookmap>
  <title>Printer PR2105 Operator Manual</title>
  ...
  <topicref
    keys="illustration-toner-cartridge-access-panel"
```

```
    href="graphics/PR2105-toner-cartridge-access-panel.svg"
    format="svg"
    processing-role="resource-only"
/>
...
<chapter href="maintenance.dita">
    ...
    <topicref href="common/changing-the-printer-cartridge.dita"/>
    ...
</chapter>
...
</bookmap>
```

The highlighted `<topicref>` element represents a key definition that binds the key name "illustration-toner-cartridge-access-panel" to the graphic file `graphics/PR2105-toner-cartridge-access-panel.svg`, which is the illustration for the PR2105 model.[25]

Note the `@processing-role` attribute on the `<topicref>` element. This attribute, new in DITA 1.2, indicates whether the topicref contributes to the main navigation tree of the map (the value "normal," which is the default) or serves only as a resource used by reference from elsewhere ("resource-only"). Because this graphic is not intended to be included in the result publication at this point in the map we must specify a processing role of "resource-only" to tell the processor not to do anything with the graphic other than remember that there is a key associated with it.

The example map also refers to the changing-the-printer-cartridge task topic, representing a specific use of the topic, a topic we know will be used from many different printer-specific publications.

When the task topic is processed *in the context of the PR2105 map* the effective binding of the key name "illustration-toner-cartridge-access-panel" will be to the PR2105 graphic. But when the same topic is used in different maps the binding may be different. For example, the map for the printer model PR3604 would look like this:

```
<bookmap>
  <title>Printer PR3604 Operator Manual</title>
  ...
  <topicref
    keys="illustration-toner-cartridge-access-panel"
    href="graphics/PR3604-toner-cartridge-access-panel.svg"
    format="svg"
```

---

[25] You could of course have model-specific key definitions that use selection (conditional) attributes reflecting the models to which they apply, but not for this example. However, because key bindings are global, you would still only be able to reflect a single model in given publication using conditional key definitions.

```
   processing-role="resource-only"
  />
  ...
  <chapter href="maintenance.dita">
    ...
    <topicref href="common/changing-the-printer-cartridge.dita"/>
    ...
  </chapter>
  ...
</bookmap>
```

Note that the only difference between the two model-specific maps is the filename of the illustration to use. The key name is the same and the task topic is the same.

Thus, the indirection provided by the key reference mechanism allows a single task to be used unchanged in different maps and be associated with the appropriate linked resources.

Note that this indirection separates the concern of information content (what information is required to support a specific topic) from the concern of content configuration management. The author of the topic says, as the content designer, "this topic requires an illustration that shows the toner cartridge access panel" and expresses that general requirement by using a key reference rather than a direct reference to a specific graphic. It is up to the author of the map to define the key binding to the appropriate graphic. This makes the content more flexible, but it means there have to be appropriate business processes and communication in place so the topic author and map author coordinate appropriately (and of course, somebody has to make sure the illustrations get drawn).

The example above uses <topicref> elements to define the key bindings so that it's clear that key definitions are done with topicrefs. Any topic reference can define keys. However, in most cases, you want to define keys as resource-only topicrefs and then use those keys from elsewhere. To make that easier, DITA 1.2 provides the <topicref> specialization <keydef>, which simply sets the default value for the @processing-role attribute to "resource-only." But it can also be useful to associate keys with normal (non resource-only) topicrefs, for example, to enable key-based linking to specific parts of a publication.

For example, in our printer operator guide publications it could make sense to put keys on the chapters and subsection topicrefs too, resulting in a map like this:

```
<bookmap>
  <title>Printer PR3604 Operator Manual</title>
  ...
  <topicref
    keys="illustration-toner-cartridge-access-panel"
    href="graphics/PR3604-toner-cartridge-access-panel.svg"
    format="svg"
    processing-role="resource-only"
```

```
  />
  ...
  <chapter
     keys="maintenance-chapter"
     href="maintenance.dita">
    ...
    <topicref
       keys="changing-printer-cartridge-task"
       href="common/changing-the-printer-cartridge.dita"/>
    ...
  </chapter>
  ...
</bookmap>
```

Here the navigation topicrefs now have keys that allow references to those topics by key reference. For example, you could have cross-references to the changing-the-printer-cartridge task that use the key rather than a direct href to the topic file:

```
<concept id="indicator-codes">
  <title>Indicator codes and response</title>
  <conbody>
    ...
    <dl>
      ...
      <dlentry>
        <dt>Toner low</dt>
        <dd>Change the toner cartridge.
See <xref keyref="changing-printer-cartridge-task"/>.
        </dd>
      </dlentry>
      ...
    </dl>
    ...
  </conbody>
</concept>
```

Here the author of the topic has indicated a requirement for a changing the printer cartridge task, but by using a key doesn't have to worry about the specific task topic. As for the image reference above, the key will be resolved to whatever resource is ultimately bound to the key "changing-printer-cartridge-task" in the context of a specific map. That might be the generic task or, for some printers, it might be a printer-specific task. The author of the indicator codes topic doesn't have to know or care.

Note too that a key reference to a normal-processing-role topicref establishes a link to a specific use of the target topic, not just to the topic in general. This allows you to have the same topic used multiple times in a map and have unambiguous references to a specific use of that topic, allowing processors to do the right thing.

A topicref that specifies the @keys attribute is said to be a "key-defining topicref." A key-defining topicref binds a key to a "resource," which can be any of the following:

- A topic
- A map
- A non-DITA object (technically, anything that can be addressed by URL that is not itself a DITA document)
- Subelements within the topicref element that provide replacement text for elements like <term>, <keyword>, and <xref> (See *Using Keys for Variable Text* on page 247 for more on this use of keys).

Note that a key cannot be bound directly to a non-topic element within a topic, it can only be bound to the topic. Key-based references to elements within topics still require you to specify the ID of the target element within the topic. This has the side effect that key-based references to specific elements require that the same element ID be used in all topics bound to the key in different maps.

For example, if you needed to create a cross-reference from the changing-the-toner-cartridge task to a table in another topic that must exist for each printer, but will be different for each model, that table would need to have the same @id value in each version of the topic that provides the table. This turns out not to be a problem in practice because these types of topics are usually cloned from a template or an original starting topic, but it does mean that there has to be some coordination of IDs used in these circumstances because there is no separate indirection mechanism for pointing to elements within topics (at least not in DITA 1.2—there's no technical barrier to such a facility, just a concern about complexity in order to satisfy a relatively rare use case, one for which there is a workaround).

Key-based references to elements within topics use the syntax *key-name/element-id*. For example, to create a cross-reference to a specific table in another topic you would do this:

```
<task id="changing-toner-cartridge">
  ...
  <context>
    <figure>
      <title>Toner Cartridge Access Panel</title>
      <image keyref="illustration-toner-cartridge-access-panel"/>
    <p>For toner cartridge specifications see
    </figure>
<href keyref="printer-specs-topic/toner-cartridge-specs-table"
  type="table"/>.
  </context>
  ...
</task>
```

The topics that get bound to the key "printer-specs-topic" must each have a <table> element with the ID "toner-cartridge-specs-table."

Using Keys for "Variable" Text

A key-defining topicref may both point to a resource and include subelements to use as the link text for links that refer to the key. When the key definition only has subelements, it can function as a "variable" that can have different values in different root map contexts.

A typical use of this feature of keys is for things like product names or other string values that may be different from publication to publication but have the same value throughout a given publication. It is roughly equivalent to the way that variables are used in desktop publishing systems like FrameMaker or the way text entities are often used in SGML and XML.

You can get the same effect by using content references to `<ph>` or `<text>` elements but putting the text in the key definition is more direct and therefore easier to author and maintain.

I put the term "variable" in quotes because the key-based facility is not really as flexible and complete as one might want. In particular, it does not reflect the scoping semantics that people familiar with programming languages might expect. For example, in a programming context, the same variable name may have different values in different scopes ("shadowing," in programming parlance), but because key definitions are global in DITA 1.2, a given key name can only resolve to a single value within the scope of a given root map. There is no mechanism in DITA 1.2 for having key definitions that are scoped to a subtree.

Another limitation of using keys as variables is that there's no way to define fallback text to use when a key is undefined. For example, if you put text in a `<keyword>` element that also points to a key that defines link text, the rules of DITA say that the text in the `<keyword>` element is always used as the link text, in preference to any text defined in key definitions. But for truly re-usable topics you'd like to be able to say "use the text from the key definition unless there's not one, in which case use this text." The fallback text might be a meaningful value that, for example, reflects a processor-defined default, or it might be something like `{variable foo not defined}` so reviewers can see that a required variable definition wasn't created. There is no way to do that in topics because key definitions are only defined in maps. You can, of course, define fallback definitions for the keys, but then each user of the topic has to know to include the fallback key definitions, which also have to be managed, documented, and so on.

If you need a variable that can be scoped to the map tree or to specific topics or subtopics, then there are at least two possible alternatives:

- Extend the key facility to provide for scoped key definitions. This approach is actively being discussed by the DITA TC for DITA 1.3 as of April, 2012, and it seems likely that some sort of key scoping mechanism will be defined for DITA 1.3. Note that there are other motivations for scoped keys. For example, you might want the same key name to point to different topics within different subtrees of a publication that reflects different products. Using the printer manual example, if you create a publication that combines different printer models in one master publication, the generic tasks would not be able to reflect different model-specific content without some way to scope the key definitions.

- Define an alternate variable facility that does not use keys at all. This is doable within the current DITA architecture. The DITA for Publishers project includes an experimental "variables" domain that defines markup and processing to support variables within maps, topicrefs, and topics. It also defines fallback semantics. This capability serves as an example of how a solution could work and demonstrates that it's relatively easy to implement, at least given map-driven XSLT processing, which the DITA for Publishers project also provides.

So while the DITA 1.2 key reference facility does provide a form of "variable" the mechanism is weak at best and insufficient for many use cases at worst. My personal feeling is that a key-based solution to variables is not appropriate and that a separate facility specifically for variables would be a better solution. While the DITA Technical Committee does not necessarily agree with me, it doesn't matter. One of the cool aspects of DITA is that I can define and implement the mechanism in a conforming fashion and provide it without the need to change the base DITA architecture. If my solution proves useful and people use it, the TC may then consider codifying it in the base standard, or it may not. There's no need to depend entirely on the TC to decide.

At the same time, I could be wrong about key-based variables, and the TC may in fact develop a key-based solution that satisfies all the requirements. In any case, the need for scoped keys is undeniable regardless of whether they are used as variables, too.

Elements that can make key references

Key references can be used in a number of ways:

- For topic references (`<topicref>`)
- For cross-references (`<xref>`, `<longquoteref>`, etc.)
- For image references (image)
- For inline elements to `<make>` them into links, including `<ph>`, `<keyword>`, and `<term>`.
- For content references from any element that allows the `@conref` attribute (most elements except a few like `<title>`).

Topic reference elements can use key references in place of URI references to point indirectly to topics, maps, or non-DITA resources. A key-defining topicref can itself use a key reference, which means there can be any number of levels of indirection between a key definition and its bound resource. This can be useful for example for imposing your own set of keys onto content that already uses a different set of keys, essentially creating new aliases for the pre-existing keys. It is a basic tenet of computer science that any problem can be solved with another layer of indirection, and the key reference facility lets you add as much indirection as your tools and authors will tolerate.

When elements allow both @href and @keyref, @keyref is used, unless the key reference cannot be resolved, in which case @href is used. This can happen if the key is not defined or the resource it points to cannot be retrieved.

Elements that allow @keyref but not @href, such as <ph>, <keyword>, and <term>, become links when they specify @keyref and the key is bound to a resource. If the element's content is empty then the "link text" (that is, the text rendered for the element) is taken from a <linktext> or <keyword> element contained within the <topicref> element that defined the key. This mechanism makes it easier to author links that will work in different map contexts.

If there are multiple levels of indirection (that is, a key definition points to another key definition and so forth, creating a chain of key definitions), the first definition in the chain that has link text is used for the link text. For example, consider this chain of key definitions:

```
<keydef keys="term-x"
  keyref="term-x-gloss-01"/>
<keydef keys="term-x-gloss-01
  keyref="term-x-gloss-02">
  <topicmeta>
    <linktext>Term X</linktext>
  </topicmeta>
</keydef>
<keydef keys="term-x-gloss-02
  href="topics/gloss-term-x.dita">
  <topicmeta>
    <linktext>Term Echs</linktext>
  </topicmeta>
</keydef>
```

In this case, the keyword <keyword keyref="term-x"/> will get the link text "Term X," not "Term Echs," because the first key definition in the chain from term-x to term-x-gloss-01 to term-x-gloss-02 with link text is the one that contains a <linktext> element with the contents "Term X."

First mentions of technical terms are often linked to their glossary definitions. You can do this using @keyref from <term> or <keyword> rather than a separate cross-reference. In addition, the key definition can provide the actual text of the term so you don't have to change the reference if the term changes.

For example, in the printer example it would make sense to have the printer model number defined in the map, since we know that each publication will be specific to a single printer model. Within the task you would have something like this:

```
<task id="changing-toner-cartridge">
  ...
  <context>
    <figure>
      <title><keyword keyref="printer-model-number"/>
Toner Cartridge Access Panel</title>
      <image keyref="illustration-toner-cartridge-access-panel"/>
    </figure>
    <p>For toner cartridge specifications see
    <href keyref="printer-specs-topic/toner-cartridge-specs-table"
          type="table"/>.
  </context>
  ...
</task>
```

This example adds a <keyword> element with a @keyref attribute containing the key name "printer-model-number." Note that the <keyword> element is empty.

Within the printer-specific maps we add a definition for the key name "printer-model-number":

```
<bookmap>
  <title>Printer PR3604 Operator Manual</title>
  ...
  <keydef keys="printer-model-number">
    <topicmeta>
      <linktext>PR3604</linktext>
    </topicmeta>
  </keydef>
  <topicref
    keys="illustration-toner-cartridge-access-panel"
    href="graphics/PR3604-toner-cartridge-access-panel.svg"
    format="svg"
    processing-role="resource-only"
  />
  ...
  <chapter keys="maintenance-chapter" href="maintenance.dita">
    ...
    <topicref
      keys="changing-printer-cartridge-task"
      href="common/changing-the-printer-cartridge.dita"/>
    ...
  </chapter>
  ...
</bookmap>
```

When the task topic is processed, the <keyword> element will be rendered as though the text of the <linktext> element in the key definition was its content. Because the key definition does not also point to a resource the <keyword> element will not be a link, since there's nothing to link to.

For navigation links, content references can use key references in place of, or in addition to, URI references. This allows you to have re-useable content references without having to know in advance what topic will provide the specific element referenced.

For example, say the changing-the-toner-cartridge task is generic except for one step which must be model-specific for some reason. For the illustration and the model number, you can use a @conkeyref attribute to establish the requirement for a model-specific step and let each model-specific map hook up the appropriate topic.

The conkeyref in the task topic would look like this:

```
<task id="changing-toner-cartridge">
  ...
  <context>
    <figure>
      <title><keyword keyref="printer-model-number"/>
Toner Cartridge Access Panel</title>
      <image keyref="illustration-toner-cartridge-access-panel"/>
    </figure>
    <p>For toner cartridge specifications see
<href keyref="printer-specs-topic/toner-cartridge-specs-table"
      type="table"/>.
  </context>
  <steps>
    <step conkeyref="model-specific-steps/changing-toner-cartridge-step-one"/>

    <step>
      <cmd>...</cmd>
    </step>
    ...
  </steps>
  ...
</task>
```

Here the <step> element uses the @conkeyref attribute rather than @conref. The semantic is the same (content use by reference) but the pointer is indirect rather than direct.

The topic that provides the step would be a "resource" topic, intended only as a container of steps and other elements to be used by reference. It could look something like this:

```
<task id="reusable-steps">
  <title>Task Component Resource Topic for Printer Model PR3604</title>
  <taskbody>
    <steps>
      <step id="changing-toner-cartridge-step-one">
        <cmd>Lift the handle...</cmd>
      </step>
      ...
    </steps>
  </taskbody>
</task>
```

Each model-specific version of this topic would need to use the `@id` value
"changing-toner-cartridge-step-one" for its version of that step.

Within each product-specific map you would have a key definition that binds the key name
"model-specific-steps" to the appropriate resource topic:

```
<bookmap>
  <title>Printer PR3604 Operator Manual</title>
  ...
  <keydef keys="printer-model-number">
    <topicmeta>
      <linktext>PR3604</linktext>
    </topicmeta>
  </keydef>
  <keydef keys="model-specific-steps"
          href="resources/PR3604/PR3604-reusable-steps.dita"
  />
  <keydef
    keys="illustration-toner-cartridge-access-panel"
    href="graphics/PR3604-toner-cartridge-access-panel.svg"
    format="svg"
  />
  ...
  <chapter
     keys="maintenance-chapter"
     href="maintenance.dita">
    ...
    <topicref
       keys="changing-printer-cartridge-task"
       href="common/changing-the-printer-cartridge.dita"/>
    ...
  </chapter>
  ...
</bookmap>
```

Note that this example uses `<keydef>` rather than `<topicref>` because `<keydef>` sets the `@processing-role` attribute to "resource-only" by default, which is what we want for our reusable steps topic, since it is literally a resource used from other topics. Because keys are global you can only use this technique for root maps that reflect a single model. You cannot have two different models in the same publication and use a single key to get different results in different parts of the publication, at least not in DITA 1.2.

Constructing key spaces

In the simplest case, a given root map does not include any submaps, and every key name is defined by exactly one key-defining topicref. However, this is neither the only case nor the typical case.

Most non-trivial publications involve maps and submaps, and it will often be the case that the same key name is defined more than once within the context of a given root map and its submaps. The processing challenge is to determine which key definition is the correct one.

The general design intent of the DITA 1.2 key reference facility is that a given root map establishes a *global* key space within which a given key name has at most one binding and where earlier and "higher" definitions take precedence over later and "lower" definitions.

By "higher" and "lower" I mean the position of a map within the tree of maps descending from the root map. Maps that are closer to the root map ("higher") take precedence over maps that are farther from root map ("lower"). Within a map, maps referenced earlier take precedence over maps referenced later. This design allows maps to override the key definitions in the maps they reference. If the key definition facility were not defined in this way it would be impossible for higher-level maps to control key values.

Note that because the key space defined by the root map is global, you cannot have different bindings for the same key active at different places within a map tree. This is a limitation to be sure, but without it, we would not have had time to get any indirection facility into DITA 1.2. It is likely that future versions of DITA will extend the key definition facility to provide other key scopes.

At the same time, it is likely that additional "variable" facilities will be defined to satisfy requirements for locally-scoped, dynamically-resolved values that the key reference facility cannot satisfy today. In addition, there are processing techniques that allow you to get the effect of locally-scoped keys without changing the base key processing semantics. Many of these have been discussed on the Yahoo DITA Users group.[26]

---

[26] If you have any question about the necessity of a global key space, consider the case of a topic referenced from one submap that references a key that is defined in two other submaps but not in the root map. If the key space was not global, then which of the two possible bindings to use would be undefined, and there would be no way for authors to indicate which they meant. Likewise, if keys were scoped by submaps, it would be impossible for topics in one submap to refer to a key defined in both its map scope and a different map scope. Thus, without a way of establishing the scope (key space), the only option is to have a global key space so all key references are unambiguous.

The formal definition of key space construction says that within a given map the first key definition in "document order" is the effective definition. Within the map tree, the first definition within a *breadth-first* traversal of the map tree takes precedence.

"Document order" means the order the start tags of each element in the XML document tree are encountered, technically a *depth-first* traversal of the element tree. A depth-first traversal goes from parent to child until a leaf node is reached, and only then goes to the next sibling of that leaf (or the next sibling of its nearest ancestor with a sibling) and so on down the tree. A *breadth first* traversal goes from one node to its siblings before then going to each of the siblings' children. See *Figure 8: Map Tree of Four Maps* on page 254.

Because the rule is "first in map document in document order then first in map tree in breadth-first order," when the map tree consists of exactly one map, the first definition in document order wins. When the map tree consists of two or more maps, the first definition within the map nearest the root map in breadth-first order takes precedence, with the root map always being first.

Consider a system of four maps: a root (Root Map 1), two submaps, Submap 1 and Submap 2, both referenced from the root map in the order Submap 1 followed by Submap 2, and submap Submap 3, referenced from Submap 1.

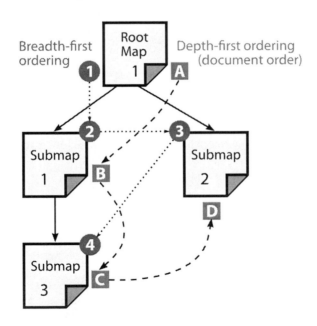

Figure 8: Map Tree of Four Maps

Any key defined in the root map will take precedence over the same key defined in any of the submaps. A key defined in Submap 1 will take precedence over the same key defined in Submap 2 because Submap 1 occurs before Submap 2 in the map tree. Finally any key defined in Submap 2 will take precedence over the same key defined in Submap 3 because Submap 2 occurs before Submap 3 in a breadth-first traversal of the map tree.

Note that the position of key references is not important: the key space is global and must be determined before any key references can be resolved.

Consider this set of key definitions in the root map:

```
<map>
  <title>Root Map 1</title>
  <topicgroup>
     <keydef keys="key-01" href="topic-1A.dita"/>
     <keydef keys="key-01" href="topic-1B.dita"/>
  </topicgroup>
  <keydef keys="key-01" href="topic-1C.dita"/>
</map>
```

Here there are three key-defining topicrefs for the key name "key-01." The effective definition is the binding to topic-1A.dita, because that is the first definition in document order (depth-first traversal of the element tree within the map document). The breadth-first rule only applies to the tree of maps, not to the tree of elements within a document.

Now consider the root map with a reference to Submap 1 added:

```
<map>
  <title>Root Map 1</title>
  <topicgroup>
    <mapref href="submap-01.ditamap"/>
  </topicgroup>
  <topicgroup>
     <keydef keys="key-01" href="topic-1A.dita"/>
     <keydef keys="key-01" href="topic-1B.dita"/>
  </topicgroup>
  <keydef keys="key-01" href="topic-1C.dita"/>
</map>
```

If Submap 1 also defines a binding for key name "key-01" it cannot be effective because, by the breadth-first map tree traversal rule, any definition in the root map takes precedence over any definitions in submaps, even though the reference to the submap happens to occur before any of the key definitions in the root map.

If we now add the reference to Submap 2 we establish the order of those maps in the map tree:

```
<map>
  <title>Root Map 1</title>
  <topicgroup>
    <mapref href="submap-01.ditamap"/>
  </topicgroup>
  <mapref href="submap-02.ditamap"/>
  <topicgroup>
    <keydef keys="key-01" href="topic-1A.dita"/>
    <keydef keys="key-01" href="topic-1B.dita"/>
  </topicgroup>
  <keydef keys="key-01" href="topic-1C.dita"/>
</map>
```

Again, it is the document (depth-first) order of the references to the maps that determines their ordering in the map tree. Thus, even though in this example the reference to Submap 2 comes first in a *breadth*-first traversal of the elements within the root map, that is not relevant because it is the document (depth-first) order that is important. Thus this markup produces the map tree shown in *Figure 8: Map Tree of Four Maps* on page 254.

To complete the map tree Submap 1 must include Submap 3:

```
<map>
  <title>Submap 1</title>
  <mapref href="submap-03.ditamap"/>
  <keydef keys="key-01" href="topic-1D.dita"/>
</map>
```

And let Submap 3 look like this:

```
<map>
  <title>Submap 3</title>
  <keydef keys="key-01" href="topic-1E.dita"/>
  <keydef keys="key-02" href="topic-2B.dita"/>
</map>
```

Finally, Submap 2 looks like this:

```
<map>
  <title>Submap 2</title>
  <keydef keys="key-01" href="topic-1F.dita"/>
  <keydef keys="key-02" href="topic-2A.dita"/>
</map>
```

The effective value of key "key-01" is set in the root map because the root map has at least one definition for that key.

The effective value of the key "key-02" is determined by its first position within the map tree because it is not defined in the root map.

In this case, key-02 is defined in two maps: Submap 2 and Submap 3. The effective definition is the definition in Submap 2 (topic-2A.dita) because Submap 2 comes first in the map tree in a breadth-first traversal.

The key space defined by this map tree can be represented by a table that has one row for each unique key and indicates at least the effective definition, as shown in *Table 2: Key space table for Root Map 1* on page 257.

Table 2: Key space table for Root Map 1

Key Name	Key Definitions (In precedence order)	Containing Map
key-01	**`<keydef keys="key-01" href="topic-1A.dita"/>`**	rootmap.ditamap
	`<keydef keys="key-01" href="topic-1B.dita"/>`	rootmap.ditamap
	`<keydef keys="key-01" href="topic-1C.dita"/>`	rootmap.ditamap
	`<keydef keys="key-01" href="topic-1D.dita"/>`	submap-01.ditamap
	`<keydef keys="key-01" href="topic-1F.dita"/>`	submap-02.ditamap
	`<keydef keys="key-01" href="topic-1E.dita"/>`	submap-03.ditamap
key-02	**`<keydef keys="key-02" href="topic-2A.dita"/>`**	submap-02.ditamap
	`<keydef keys="key-02" href="topic-2B.dita"/>`	submap-03.ditamap

In this table, the key definitions for a given key are listed in precedence order, first by document order within a single map and then by breadth-first order within the map tree. The first key definition for each key is therefore the effective one, as shown by the highlighting.

Note that the root map serves as the identifier of the key space because it is the root map that ultimately determines the effective bindings of all the keys. Different root maps represent distinct key spaces.

By the same token, you cannot resolve any key until you have established the active key space for the resolution attempt. This has important implications for authoring and component management, about which more later.

To more clearly demonstrate the fact that different root maps establish different key spaces, let us now create Root Map 2, which omits the definitions of key-01 in the root and includes Submap 1 and Submap 2, but in the reverse order from Root Map 1:

```
<map>
  <title>Root Map 2</title>
  <topicgroup>
    <mapref href="submap-02.ditamap"/>
    <mapref href="submap-01.ditamap"/>
  </topicgroup>
</map>
```

Now Submap 2 comes before Submap 1 in the map tree and that makes the effective value of key-01 the binding defined in Submap 2, namely "topic-1F.ditamap." The key space table for key space Root Map 2 looks like this:

Table 3: Key space table for Root Map 2

Key Name	Key Definitions (In precedence order)	Containing Map
key-01	`<keydef keys="key-01" href="topic-1F.dita"/>`	submap-02.ditamap
	`<keydef keys="key-01" href="topic-1E.dita"/>`	submap-03.ditamap
key-02	**`<keydef keys="key-02" href="topic-2A.dita"/>`**	submap-02.ditamap
	`<keydef keys="key-02" href="topic-2B.dita"/>`	submap-03.ditamap

Any topic that has a link to key "key-01" will link to different target topics when processed in the context of Root Map 1 than when processed in the context of Root Map 2.

You might wonder why the key space table shows all the bindings even though only one can be effective within a given key space. There are several reasons:

- For this example it makes it clear what the precedence order of the different definitions is.
- For analysis and debugging it can be useful to know all the definitions of a given key in a given keyspace. Thus, key space constructing processors should build this sort of table so users can see it on request.
- In a CMS system it may be useful to maintain repository-wide knowledge of all the key definitions in all the maps, then determine effective key spaces dynamically. A "key database," where you use the key for lookup, would resemble this table.
- When applicability (conditional processing) is in play, it may be necessary to hold all potentially effective bindings for a key and determine the effective binding in the context of a specific set of conditions. This is especially important in authoring support systems where authors may want to see a dynamic, in-editor view of the data as determined by some set of conditions. Unless the key space table includes at least all potentially-applicable key definitions, this type of dynamic view cannot be provided.
- In the future it is likely there will be a way to define the resolution scope for specific key references, which means that any definition of a key could potentially be effective based on specific processing-time or resolution-time scope settings.

Finally, note that the map tree is constructed using only directly-addressed maps. This is because you can't resolve any key-based map references until you construct the key space and you can't construct the key space until you have constructed the map tree.

This implies that there are conceptually at least two passes in the processing of the map: a first pass to construct the map tree and key space and a second pass to construct the full map tree, taking any indirect map references into account. The output of the second step would then be the input to any additional processing applied to the map.

Key definitions and applicability (conditional processing)

When all key definitions are unconditional, constructing the key space is relatively easy. However, when key definitions or map references are conditional, things can get complicated very quickly.

The issue is that the DITA specification allows processors to choose when conditional processing is applied: before or after key space construction. In addition, some processors may need to apply conditional processing as late as possible, for example, editors and component management systems that need to provide different views of the source documents reflecting different sets of active conditions.

Note that only the filtering aspect of conditional processing is relevant here—flagging is a rendition issue and does not affect key space construction in any way.

Flagging is the process of indicating in the presented content what it applies to, for example, "For Windows" or "For OSX". See *Conditional Processing: Filtering and Flagging* on page 291 for more information on flagging.

When filtering is applied before key space construction, then the key space is fixed, meaning that any excluded key definitions are eliminated before key space construction and therefore cannot be represented in the final key space.

When filtering is applied after key space construction, then the effective value for a given key cannot be completely determined except in the context of a specific set of active conditions.

For example, let's take the Root Map 1 example and define key-01 for different conditions using the @platform property. That gives us the following markup:

For example, say that the definitions of key-01 in the Root Map 1 example actually reflect the bindings appropriate for different conditions, resulting in this markup:

```
<map>
  <title>Root Map 1</title>
  <topicgroup>
    <mapref href="submap-01.ditamap"/>
  </topicgroup>
  <topicgroup>
    <keydef
      platform="platform-A"
      keys="key-01"
      href="topic-1A.dita"/>
    <keydef
      platform="platform-B"
      keys="key-01"
      href="topic-1B.dita"/>
    <keydef
      platform="platform-C"
      keys="key-01"
      href="topic-1C.dita"/>
  </topicgroup>
</map>
```

Now, each definition of the key "key-01" has a different value for the @platform property. The effective binding will depend on the setting for the platform property either at the time the key space is constructed (filtering applied first) or at the time the key reference is resolved (filtering applied after key space construction).

In serial batch processors like the Open Toolkit or DITA2Go, the result is the same either way. But for interactive systems like editors and component management systems the difference is important.

To make the example a little more interesting, let's add an unconditional definition for the key as well as a duplicate conditional definition:

```
<map>
  <title>Root Map 1</title>
  <topicgroup>
    <mapref href="submap-01.ditamap"/>
  </topicgroup>
  <topicgroup>
    <keydef
        platform="platform-A"
        keys="key-01"
        href="topic-1A.dita"/>
    <keydef
        platform="platform-A"
        keys="key-01"
        href="topic-1H.dita"/>
    <keydef
        platform="platform-B"
        keys="key-01"
        href="topic-1B.dita"/>
    <keydef
        platform="platform-C"
        keys="key-01"
        href="topic-1C.dita"/>
    <keydef
        keys="key-01"
        href="topic-1G.dita"/>
  </topicgroup>
</map>
```

Now there are four possible bindings, any one of which could be effective depending on the active value for the platform property. The binding to topic "topic-1H.dita" cannot ever be effective because it comes after a definition for the same key name with the same set of conditions (`platform = "platform-A"`). But the remaining four definitions could each be active under different sets of conditions.

Thus, if a processor needs to provide resolution-time determination of key bindings based on conditions, it needs to add a "conditions" column to the key space table, as shown in *Table 4: Key space table for Root Map 1 with applicability conditions* on page 262.

Table 4: Key space table for Root Map 1 with applicability conditions

Key Name	Key Definitions (In precedence order)	Containing Map	Applicable Conditions
key-01	`<keydef keys="key-01" href="topic-1A.dita"/>`	rootmap.ditamap	platform = platform-A
	`<keydef keys="key-01" href="topic-1B.dita"/>`	rootmap.ditamap	platform = platform-B
	`<keydef keys="key-01" href="topic-1C.dita"/>`	rootmap.ditamap	platform = platform-C
	`<keydef keys="key-01" href="topic-1D.dita"/>`	rootmap.ditamap	None
	`<keydef keys="key-01" href="topic-1D.dita"/>`	submap-01.ditamap	None
	`<keydef keys="key-01" href="topic-1F.dita"/>`	submap-02.ditamap	None
	`<keydef keys="key-01" href="topic-1E.dita"/>`	submap-03.ditamap	None
key-02	`<keydef keys="key-02" href="topic-2A.dita"/>`	submap-02.ditamap	None
	`<keydef keys="key-02" href="topic-2B.dita"/>`	submap-03.ditamap	None

Now a processor resolving "key-01" sees four potentially effective definitions, and to resolve the key reference, it needs to know the value of the `@platform` condition.

The implications for dynamic resolution are:

1. Processors must inspect the set of conditions on each key definition to determine the set of potentially applicable key definitions. For a given key, the first definition with a unique set of conditions is potentially effective, second and subsequent definitions with the same condition set cannot be potentially effective (by the precedence rules for key definitions).
2. Processors must maintain knowledge of the applicable conditions for each potentially-effective key definition.

3. Resolution requests must allow users to specify active conditions as parameters to the request. That is, given an API method like `resolveKeyReference()`, the parameters must include a set of active conditions in addition to the key space (or the identifier of the root map that establishes the key space) and the key to be resolved. Likewise, user interfaces that allow users to see the effect of resolved references must provide a way to specify active conditions. This could be either through direct specification or through prior configuration.

Key definitions and content reference resolution

Because content references may use key references, conref resolution processing cannot be fully performed until the key space has been constructed. However, processors may choose to do resolution of direct conrefs before doing key space construction. This could result in different effective key spaces in some cases, although it should be rare for key definitions to be managed in maps through conref rather than through topicref-based inclusions.

Relationship Tables

Relationship tables create extended links among topics. These links are usually rendered as "See also" links. Relationship tables are defined in maps.

When a topic is authored it is impossible to know all the possible contexts in which it might be used. Thus, it is impossible to define within a topic all the possible links it might have to other topics. Likewise, a topic used in different maps may need to link to different topics in the context of different maps.

To do this you need a link that works without modifying the topics themselves. Such a link is usually called an "extended link" to distinguish it from inline or "embedded" links like cross-references and topicrefs.

An extended link consists of two or more "anchors," where each anchor points to one or more resources. The link represents a relationship among the anchors and thus among the resources anchored. The link itself usually has a type reflecting the meaning of the relationship, for example, "married-to" or "more-information-for." Each anchor usually has a role reflecting the role it plays within the relationship, for example, "husband," "wife," "spouse," "base topic," "supporting topic," etc. Link types and roles may be more or less precise as needed. *Figure 9: Abstract Extended Link* on page 264 shows the general model for extended links.

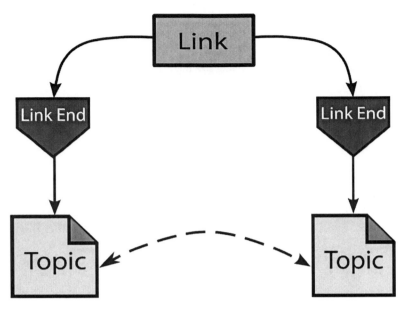

Figure 9: Abstract Extended Link

There are many ways that extended links can be modeled in XML. The DITA approach is the relationship table, which contains one or more extended links of the same type. Each row is an extended link. Each column represents one anchor role. Each cell represents an anchor for that row's extended link.

Each cell contains zero or more topicrefs that point to the resource(s) for that anchor. All the resources linked from one anchor are then linked to the resources linked from the other anchors in that row.

A typical relationship table looks like this:

```
<reltable >
  <relheader>
    <relcolspec>
      <topichead>
        <topicmeta>
          <navtitle>Concept</navtitle>
        </topicmeta>
      </topichead>
    </relcolspec>
    <relcolspec>
      <topichead>
        <topicmeta>
          <navtitle>Reference</navtitle>
        </topicmeta>
      </topichead>
```

```
      </relcolspec>
    </relheader>
    <relrow>
      <relcell>
        <topicref
          href="concept-01.dita"/>
      </relcell>
      <relcell>
        <topicref
          href="reference-01.dita"/>
      </relcell>
    </relrow>
    <relrow>
      <relcell>
        <topicref
          href="concept-01.dita"/>
        <topicref
          href="concept-02.dita"/>
      </relcell>
      <relcell>
        <topicref
          href="reference-02.dita"/>
      </relcell>
    </relrow>
  </reltable>
```

This relationship table defines two extended links. The anchor roles are "Concept" and "Reference," as defined by the navigation titles of the `<relcolspec>` elements in the `<relheader>`. In the first link, the concept anchor points to "concept-01.dita," and the reference anchor points to "reference-01.dita." In the second, the concept anchor points to the two concept topics "concept-01.dita" and "concept-02.dita," and the reference anchor points to the "reference-02.dita." The link type in this case is unspecified and is therefore the very generic "related-to" link type.

Through DITA 1.2, relationship tables do not provide a direct way to indicate the link type other than by specializing the `<reltable>` element to indicate the link type. Thus, if you need to indicate different link types, you may need to establish a convention for using the relationship table title or metadata to indicate the link type or choose roles that clearly imply the link type.

The relationship table establishes the links among the topics, creating a graph of relationships, as shown in *Figure 10: Link Graph for A Relationship Table* on page 266.

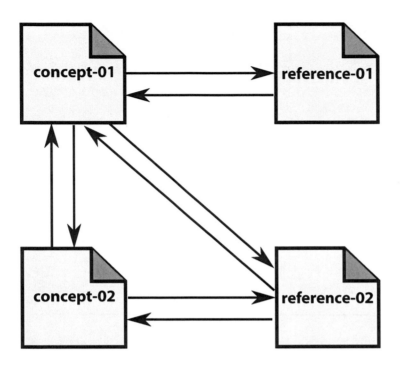

Figure 10: Link Graph for A Relationship Table

There are many ways that the links could be used for navigation and information presentation. By default, the Open Toolkit renders relationship table links as "related links" at the end of each topic to which a link applies. So in this example, "concept-01" would have two related links, one to "reference-01" and one to "reference-02." Topic "reference-01" would have one related link to "concept-01." Topic "reference-02" would have two related links, one to "concept-01" and one to "concept-02." And topic "concept-02" would have links to "concept-01" and "reference-01."

Note that there is no relationship between topics "concept-01" and "concept-02," even though they are both members of the same reltable cell. This is because there is no implicit relationship among topics referenced from the same cell in a relationship table.

Another possible presentation effect would be to present the table itself as a set of navigable links, perhaps as an alternative to the normal table of contents usually associated with a map.

In short, relationship tables can drive the same kinds of link-based interactions as technologies like RDF and XLink.

If you are familiar with RDF, for example, it should be clear that a DITA relationship table can be restated as a set of RDF relations. Likewise, it could be restated as a set of XLink extended links.

Authoring relationship tables can be a challenge simply because it's a lot of fiddly work to create the rows and then create the topicrefs for each cell. Most DITA-aware editing tools provide some support for creating the tables and links, but they may not provide maximum convenience. But for data sets where you need extensive interlinking and there is a lot of topic reuse, relationship tables are usually the only way to practically create and manage the links.

It may also be possible to auto-generate relationship tables based on knowledge held elsewhere. For example, you might be able to use a product bill of materials to generate relationship tables among the topics that reflect the individual product subcomponents. Or you might be able to use associations between metadata items or full-text queries to generate relationship tables. There are many possibilities.

Finally, note that there is no built-in way to have relationship table links generate embedded links as though they were directly-authored cross references. There are possibly ways in which that could be done, but it would depend entirely on writing and editorial conventions that will be specific to your data sets and processing tools, so DITA does not attempt to standardize such a facility, at least not today.

9

Reuse at the Element Level: The Content Reference Facility

DITA provides a powerful use-by-reference facility that allows almost any element to be used by reference from maps or topics as long as specific constraints are met. This facility is the "content reference facility" or "conref" for short.

The conref facility uses two main attributes, @conref and @conkeyref. With these attributes, you can create a link were the referenced element is processed as though it were located at the point of reference.

For example, you might manage standard <note> elements in one topic like the following:

```
<topic id="standard-notes">
  <title>Standard Notes</title>
  <body>
    <note id="dont-run-scissors">Don't
run with scissors.</note>
    <note id="hands-inside">Keep
hands inside the car when it's moving</note>
    ...
</topic>
```

Within other topics, you can create `<note>` elements that link to the standard notes:

```
<task id="making-snowflake">
  <title>Making Paper Snowflakes</title>
  <taskbody>
    <context>
     <note
      conref="standard-notes.dita#standard-notes/dont-run-scissors"/>
     ...
</task>
```

The result for each reference is that the referenced note is processed as though it had occurred in place of the referencing note. Thus, the "Making Paper Snowflakes" task will show the "Don't run with scissors" note when it's rendered. If the note text is changed, then all users of the note will reflect the next text the next time they are rendered. (Note that this example uses a direct @conref reference for simplicity. In practice you should use key references for content references.)

By *use by reference* I mean using something without copying it. Use by reference is important because it allows a single piece of content to exist in exactly one place and be used in many places.

The practical benefits of use by reference include minimizing writing effort by not having to maintain multiple copies, minimizing localization costs by allowing the same localized content to be used many times, and enabling the creation of new publications from existing content with a minimum of effort.

Use by reference is not without costs, however. Once a piece of content is used in two places you have a management challenge; you must know about all uses and coordinate changes with anyone who uses that content. This coordination is either explicit, meaning you have to communicate with users, or implicit, meaning you need business rules or component management features that help ensure that the correct thing is done when things change.

The alternative to use by reference is *use by copy*. Use by copy means literally copying something and then using the new copy in a new context, i.e., "cut and paste." Use by copy is easy to do because it doesn't require any linking or content management facilities, but it has the problem that it results in multiple copies of what is often essentially the same content, copies that then have to be kept in sync. In most cases, copies are not tracked, meaning that the knowledge of the original source of the copy is not maintained in a manageable way.

As an information management practice, use by copy is usually the wrong thing to do (although it's not always wrong). Some component management systems track copy actions, providing a record of what was copied from where and when. To create appropriate information use and reuse policies you must clearly distinguish use by copy from use by reference and define when it is appropriate to use one or the other. If you allow use by copy, you need to define record-keeping requirements to keep track of the location of any copies. DITA does not provide any built-in attributes or metadata elements for capturing use-by-copy information.

Use by reference is a form of hyperlinking and, therefore, brings with it some of the fundamental challenges of hyper-document management. A use-by-reference link establishes a dependency that has to be tracked and managed.

For example, if Topic A reflects release 1.0 of a product and re-uses by reference a paragraph from Topic B, what happens when Topic B is updated to reflect release 1.1 of the product? Topic A has to decide which version of the paragraph from Topic B it should now use: The original version? The new version? A third, yet-to-be-created version?

If you coordinated the development of topics A and B, then that may not be a problem, but if you haven't, then you need to evaluate the development and management processes that created topics A and B. The eventual answer might be "always reflect latest" or it might not be. You might realize you need to start using DITA's conditional processing features to handle the release-specific content, or you might need a component management system that provides version-aware addressing facilities.

The point is that while use by reference is powerful and can address difficult business challenges, it also introduces complexity that must be considered carefully. In more than 20 years working with and building systems for complex documents, I have found that use by reference is used much less frequently than many people expect when they first move to XML. I think this is because people find that the management cost and source data complexity outweighs the benefit or at least appears to. That is, sometimes it's easier (or appears to be easier) to just make copies and manage the copies than it is to use direct use by reference.

Your mileage will vary of course. You have to think carefully about local requirements, your tools, your authors' capabilities and enthusiasm, and your business goals and requirements. In general, if you can limit use by reference to the topic level using maps or to specific cases where the benefit is clear, such as re-used warnings or steps, then things will be easier. But allowing authors free reign to reuse anything from anywhere is probably a non-starter for most environments.

Use by reference in the world

Before diving into DITA's use-by-reference facilities, let's discuss the things DITA doesn't use and why.

The most obvious one is XML external parsed entities.

External parsed entities are an XML feature that is a hold over from SGML. External parsed entities (often informally referred to as "file entities") are fragments of XML documents that are stored as separate resources (for example, separate files) and referenced from the root XML document (directly or indirectly) using an inline entity reference. The entity's content (the "replacement text") is parsed in the context of the reference, meaning that any markup in the entity must be valid at the point of reference.

External parsed entities are not use by reference, they are use by copy. This is because entities are essentially string macros, not objects in the computer science sense. The parsing effect of an entity reference is *identical* to having cut and pasted the content of the entity at the point of reference. This means entity references are not objects in the way that XML elements are; you can't put attributes on them and parsers are not obligated to preserve them or report them to other processors. Many XML-aware repositories do not preserve entities, which means that knowledge of the original entities is lost when XML is put into the repository. This is true of the MarkLogic product, for example.

Finally, entities can only be defined using a DOCTYPE declaration. DOCTYPE declarations are not required by XML or DITA.

For all these reasons, and more, external parsed entities are not a good idea (I am on record many times as saying "entities are evil," and I stand by that statement). My greatest regret as a member of the XML Working Group is that I fought to retain entities in XML, when I should have fought to eliminate them.

External parsed entities provide the *illusion* of reuse without actually providing it, leading many people astray. DITA correctly and explicitly does not support or encourage the use of external parsed entities. DITA cannot disallow their use, but it is certainly not DITA practice to use entities, and if you are using them you should stop immediately. The DITA content reference facility is designed, in part, to satisfy the requirements that people thought external parsed entities would satisfy, but that they do not.

Another XML facility is XInclude. XInclude provides a markup-based facility that allows reference to XML content using links. It is better than external parsed entities because it is markup based (meaning it uses elements rather than something else), but it is not much better than external parsed entities because its behavior is essentially use by copy, not use by reference.

There are three reasons for this:

1. XInclude is intended to be applied during parsing, rather than after parsing, which means processing applications cannot control the results.
2. XInclude has no provision for ID and pointer rewriting, which effectively means that XML IDs must be unique across all documents being processed.
3. XInclude provides no way to constrain the location of includes or the content being included. This means you can't control how and where authors do inclusions using content model constraints, markup design, or other XML facilities.

So XInclude is no good, at least for authoring. Like other W3C standards it might be useful for delivery, but that's a pretty rare use.

Some parsers do support XInclude natively, such as the Xerces parser, but because it requires using the `<xi:include>` element in your documents, which DITA explicitly does not include in any form, it is impossible to have a valid and conforming DITA document that uses XInclude.

In fact, DITA's content reference facility predates XML and XInclude by a decade, since it reflects features that were originally designed for the IBM ID Doc document type back in the late 80's and early 90's, which were designed to overcome deficiencies in SGML's entity mechanisms. At this time, DITA probably has the most complete and general element- and link-based, use-by-reference solution of any general XML application.

If you want to determine whether or not a given content modularity feature is use by reference or use by copy the test is simple: what happens when a chunk of XML content that contains an XML ID is used twice in the same parent context?

If the answer is "the ID attributes and references to them are not modified," that is, the result is the same as if you cut and pasted the content into both locations, then you have use by copy. If the answer is "the IDs are made unique in the use context, and references to them are modified to be correct following resolution" then you have use by reference.

This test applies to *all* forms of identifiers and the addresses that use them, not just XML IDs. I use XML IDs in the statement of the test because they're obvious. But the requirement applies to any form of address whatsoever, since addresses must continue to be correct after resolving the references, whatever "correct" means. XML IDs are just an obvious way of revealing the problem.

Because managing IDs and their attendant references requires processing that understands the semantics of the content, not just its syntax, true use-by-reference facilities cannot be implemented at the syntax level, that is, at the parsing level. Both external parsed entities and XInclude fail the test because they are syntactic, not semantic. By contrast, DITA's conref facility and its map facility are semantic, being handled by a DITA-aware processor following parsing of the individual XML documents involved. That means the processors have full knowledge of both the original data content and the semantics of the identifiers and addresses and can therefore do whatever needs to be done to ensure that the resolved result is correct.

In the case of element IDs and references to them, DITA has specific rules to ensure that authors can create links and addresses that are correct as authored and that will be correct following use-by-reference resolution. This capability distinguishes DITA from essentially all other XML documentation applications, none of which have an equivalent true use-by-reference facility.

Basic Conref: Reusing Single Elements

The simplest application of conref is a single element using another single element.

A typical use case is re-using notes, cautions, warnings, and other content developed and maintained by groups, such as a Legal department, that create content authors should not be writing or modifying. The general term for notes, cautions, and warnings is *admonitions*, although this is not a term used in the DITA standard.

To use conref you need two things:

1. A topic that contains the element to be used by reference. Elements to be used by reference must have @id attributes so they can be addressed using normal DITA addressing syntax.
2. An element of the same, *or less specialized,* type that points to the element to be reused. Any constraints on the two elements must be compatible, meaning that the element to be reused must be at least as constrained as the referencing element. See *Content Reference Constraints* on page 281 for details.

For this example we have a topic containing a set of admonitions intended to be used by reference:

```
<?xml version="1.0"?>
<!DOCTYPE topic PUBLIC "urn:my:local:topic:shell" "topic.dtd">
<topic id="admonitions">
  <title>Common Admonitions for Tasks</title>
  <body>
    <note id="note-01" type="caution">This is note one.</note>
    <note id="note-02" type="danger">This is note two.</note>
    <note id="note-03" type="warning">This is note three.</note>
  </body>
</task>
```

Because this topic only exists to hold elements for reuse, topicrefs that reference it should set @processing-role to "resource-only, ", for example:

```
<map>
  ...
  <topicgroup>
    <topicref
       href="common/tasks/admonition-set-01.dita"
       processing-role="resource-only"
    />
    ...
  </topicgroup>
  ...
</map>
```

If you will have a number of such resource topics, you can make the map simpler by moving the @processing-role attribute to an ancestor <topicgroup> or <topichead> element:

```
<map>
  ...
  <topicgroup
    processing-role="resource-only"
  >
    <topicref
      href="common/tasks/admonition-set-01.dita"
    />
    ...
  </topicgroup>
  ...
</map>
```

The attributes of the ancestor element cascade to the descendant elements, so this example sets the effective value of @processing-role to "resource-only" for all the topicrefs under the topic group.

To use one of the notes within a real task, you simply use a `<note>` element with the `@conref` attribute:

```
<task id="task-id">
  <title>Do Something Useful</title>
  <taskbody>
    <context>
      <note
conref="../../common/tasks/admonition-set-01.dita#admonitions/note-01"/>
      ...
    </context>
    <steps>
      ...
    </steps>
  </taskbody>
</task>
```

Normally, the processor will render the referenced note at the point where the `<note>` element with the `@conref` attribute occurs.

I say "normally" because content reference processing is not 100% mandatory—you could implement a processor that did something else. That's possible because conref processing is semantic, meaning it occurs after the XML data has been parsed. It is not a function of the XML parsing like handling entities or XInclude is.

For example, you might implement a processor that produces a "conref report" that shows what the references are rather than resolving them. The DITA Open Toolkit resolves conrefs during pre-processing, so later processing steps normally see data that has had any conrefs resolved. But that's simply an implementation choice—the order in which conref processing is applied is not mandated by the DITA standard.

Conkeyref

In the preceding example, the `@conref` attribute is a direct pointer to the admonition set topic. As discussed in the section on linking and addressing, this establishes a hard dependency between the using task and the admonition set task. In addition, the reference depends on all the files being in the correct relative location.

A more flexible approach is to replace `@conref` with `@conkeyref`. We can quickly rework the example to use keys by adding a `@keys` attribute to the topicref for the admonition set topic and replacing `@conref` with `@conkeyref` on the `<note>` element:

```
<map>
  ...
  <topicgroup>
    <topicref
        keys="admonition-set-01"
        href="common/tasks/admonition-set-01.dita"
        processing-role="resource-only"
     />
    ...
  </topicgroup>
  ...
</map>
```

And in the using topic:

```
<task id="task-id">
  <title>Do Something Useful</title>
  <taskbody>
    <context>
      <note conkeyref="admonition-set-01/note-01"/>
      ...
    </context>
    <steps>
      ...
    </steps>
  </taskbody>
</task>
```

Now the conref is not sensitive to the specific location of the admonition set topic. In addition, different root maps could provide different sets of admonitions for different purposes, for example, different regulatory environments, national languages, or product versions.

Note that the value of the @conkeyref attribute is the key name, a slash, and the element ID of the target note. There is no need to specify the ID of the topic element in the @conkeyref because the key-defining topicref already addresses the appropriate topic.

In this example the ID of the note is just "note-01," but in practice you would probably give specific elements IDs that reflect their purpose, for example, "dont-run-with-scissors" for the "Don't run with scissors" danger admonition.

Because keyref requires topics to use the actual ID value of the referenced element, it makes sense to assign meaningful IDs that clearly identify the purpose of the element, regardless of whether it's intended for use by reference or as the target of cross references or other navigation links.

Conref for maps and topics

The DITA content reference facility applies to all DITA content, not just topics. This means you can use conref in maps as well as in topics.

As far as I can tell it's fairly rare for people to use conref within maps for the simple reason that DITA already provides good facilities for constructing compound maps using topicrefs. Nevertheless, you can use conref with maps, and there may be information management challenges that are best met using conref in maps (although I have not encountered any in my own work). Certainly all conforming DITA processors must be prepared to apply conref resolution processing to maps.

The main caveat for conref within maps is that you cannot reliably use conref to configure or create key definitions, because you cannot resolve key-based conrefs without first having constructed the key space. If you used key-based conrefs to construct key-defining topicrefs, those topicrefs can have no effect on the key space. While a processor could choose to first resolve all direct conrefs, then build the key space, and then resolve all key-based conrefs, DITA does not require processors to work that way. So any map construction scheme that relied on some interaction between conref and key definitions would be dicey at best.

When doing conref within maps, keep in mind that the fragment identifiers for map elements are simply bare `@id` values, because each map document is a single ID namespace (as though all `@id` attributes had been declared as type ID).

Within topics you could use conref to nest topics within other topics without using a map. However, there's little obvious reason to do this instead of using maps to create hierarchies of topics. Because you can create submaps and re-use them from other maps, you can create small maps that combine a few topics to form a single unit of re-use. For example, you could create a map to combine a task, one or more supporting concepts, and one or more supporting reference topics. [Citation to original IBM paper on this subject]

Note that you cannot use `<topicref>` within `<topic>`, where you might have expected it to be allowed. Topicrefs occur only within maps.

Attribute Merging

The attributes on the referencing element and referenced elements are merged according to strict rules.

When an element uses another element by reference the attributes of the referencing element and the referenced element are merged, and the attributes of the referencing element take precedence over the attributes of the referenced element.

In the re-used note example, the referenced `<note>` specifies the `@type` attribute with the value "caution." Because the referencing element does not also specify `@type`, the effective value of `@type` following conref resolution will be "caution."

But if the referencing element specified a different value, that value would take precedence. For example, this use results in an effective `@type` value of "danger":

```
<task id="task-id">
  <title>Do Something Useful</title>
  <taskbody>
    <context>
      <note conkeyref="admonition-set-01/note-01"
            type="danger"/>
      . . .
    </context>
    <steps>
      . . .
    </steps>
  </taskbody>
</task>
```

The default attribute merge behavior can be reversed by using the value "-dita-use-conref-target" for that attribute on the referencing element. This is needed for attributes that are declared as an enumerated set of values with a default. In that case the attribute will always have some value on the referencing element (because of the default), so authors need a way to explicitly indicate that the referenced element's attribute should be used in preference to the referencing element's value.

For example, in a specialization or constraint module you can declare the `@type` attribute to use a subset of the values allowed by the base vocabulary and set a default value of say "note." Then, the original example would result in `@type` having the value "note," rather than the value set on the referenced element, because the default attribute on the referencing element would override the value on the referenced element. In this case, authors would need to specify "-dita-use-conref-target" on the referencing element:

```
<task id="task-id">
  <title>Do Something Useful</title>
  <taskbody>
    <context>
      <note conkeyref="admonition-set-01/note-01"
            type="-dita-use-conref-target"/>
      . . .
    </context>
    <steps>
      . . .
    </steps>
  </taskbody>
</task>
```

This may seem like something of an edge case but in fact it's probably quite likely, because the DITA 1.2 constraint facility makes it easy to tune content models and attribute declarations to match local editorial rules and to make things easier for authors. But having done that, in particular having set defaults on attributes that do not normally have a default value, you must be aware of the implications for conref and train authors appropriately, as the typical author would never figure out why they weren't getting the note type they expected.

Linking to Referencing Elements

You link to the result of conref resolution by linking to the referencing element in the content as authored.

Sometimes you need to create a cross-reference to an element that is itself a conref to another element. For example, within a task you might need to create a reference to a step where the step is used by reference.

In this case, the referencing element must have an @id attribute and the cross-reference must point to that ID, *not* the ID of the content reference target.

For example, given this set of steps:

```
<task id="task-id">
  <title>Do Something Useful</title>
  <taskbody>
    <context>
      <note conkeyref="admonition/note-01"
        type="-dita-use-conref-target"
      />
      ...
    </context>
    <steps>
      <step conkeyref="common-steps/remove-access-cover-step"/>
      ...
      <step>
        <cmd>...</cmd>
        <info>
         <p>You must have performed Step 1.
         </p>
        </info>
      </step>
      ...
    </steps>
  </taskbody>
</task>
```

Where you want to replace the literal text "Step 1" with a cross-reference, you would first put an ID on the referencing element and then refer to that element:

```
<task id="task-id">
  <title>Do Something Useful</title>
  <taskbody>
    <context>
      <note conkeyref="admonition/note-01"
        type="-dita-use-conref-target"
      />
      ...
    </context>
    <steps>
      <step id="step-01"
        conkeyref="common-steps/remove-access-cover-step"/>
      ...
      <step>
        <cmd>...</cmd>
        <info>
         <p>You must have performed
         <xref href="#task-id/step-01" type="step"/>.
         </p>
        </info>
      </step>
      ...
    </steps>
  </taskbody>
</task>
```

This reflects the general principle that all addresses in the source data should reflect the data *as authored*, not as rendered. By pointing to the referencing element, the author's intent is clear, and there is enough information for the processor to do the right thing. By the rules of attribute merging, the @id attribute of the referencing element will be the effective value following conref resolution.

Or said another way: the IDs of referenced elements are only useful for creating conref links, they should have no effect on the content reference result. If you need to create a link to the conref result, you must put an ID on the referencing element. If you don't need to link to the conref result, the effective value of the @id attribute following conref resolution has no effect on anything because nothing points to it (other than the original referencing element). Because the referencing element has no ID, there is no way to author a link to it, and therefore the fact that the effective element might have an effective @id value after conref resolution is irrelevant—the link cannot be authored with respect to the content as it exists in the source. Likewise, any conref processor that handles IDs correctly *must* be prepared to rewrite IDs in the resolved result so that two uses of the same element in the same topic or map don't result in duplicate IDs in the resolved result.

Content Reference Constraints

The content reference facility imposes some constraints on the referencing and referenced elements.

The intent of these constraints is to ensure that the resolved result is consistent with the content model rules that apply to the referencing element. In particular, authors should not be able to subvert content model rules by referencing elements that are less constrained.

The basic rule is that an element can only create a conref to an element of the same type or a *more specialized* type. You cannot create a conref from a more-specialized element to a less-specialized element. This rule takes advantage of the DITA requirement that specialized elements must be at least as constrained as their base element. That is, specializations can never add anything that would be invalid if the more-specialized elements were transformed into their less-specialized ancestor types.

The *element* you're using by reference must be the same as or more specialized than the element making the reference. However, the topic that contains the referenced element may be less specialized than the topic that contains the reference. For example, you can use a generic `<topic>` element to contain re-usable `<note>` elements but still use those notes from `<task>` topics. The rule about the used element being the same or more specialized is only checked for the elements involved, not the topics that contain those elements. However, the two topics must use compatible constraint modules, as explained below.

As an example of using more-specialized types from less-specialized elements, say we create a new "admonition" domain that creates distinct element types for the note types "caution," "warning," and "danger," resulting in elements like the following:

```
<warning class="+ topic/note admon-d/warning ">This is a warning</warning>
<danger class="+ topic/note admon-d/danger ">This is a danger</danger>
```

In the DTD, we assign the `<warning>` element's `@type` attribute value to be "warning" and the `<danger>` element's `@type` to be "danger." We then use this domain to create a set of re-usable admonitions similar to the original re-used note example above, but using our specializations of `<note>`. From a topic that needs to use one these admonitions by reference, we can use either `<note>` or the specialization as the referencing element:

```
<task id="task-id">
  ...
  <context>
    <note conkeyref="admonition-set-02/warning-01"/>
    <warning conkeyref="admonition-set-02/warning-02"/>
  </context>
  ...
</task>
```

Both forms of conref are valid. If `<note>` is the referencing element, the referenced element is a more-specialized note (`<warning>`). If `<warning>` is the referencing element, the referenced element is the same element type.

However, it would not be valid to create a conref from a `<warning>` element to one of the `<note>` elements from the original example, because the `<note>` elements in that topic are *less* specialized than `<warning>`.

There is an additional rule involving the use of constraint modules: the constraints used in the referencing document must be consistent with the constraints used in the referenced document, which means the referenced document must not be less constrained than the referencing document.

This is why you cannot conref from a DITA 1.1-style constrained task to elements in a DITA 1.2 general task: the general task in DITA 1.2 uses a constraint module that makes it match the DITA 1.1 task model. Because general task does not use this constraint module, it is less constrained. You can, however, use elements from constrained tasks by reference from unconstrained tasks because in that case the referenced elements are more constrained than the referencing elements.

For example, suppose you defined a constraint module that removes `<object>` from the content model for `<note>`. If that constraint module were integrated with the task shell for the referencing task, but not with the task shell for the admonition set task, then it would not be possible to conref from the referencing task to the admonition set task because the referencing task is more constrained than the referenced task. On the other hand, if the admonition set topic used the constraint module and the referencing task did not, the conref would be fine because the referenced topic is more constrained than the referencing topic.

Processors determine whether or not two DITA documents have consistent constraints by examining the value of the `@domains` attribute on the root elements of the documents involved. The `@domains` attribute lists all domain and constraint modules used by the document (and should list all structural modules used, but that is not required in DITA 1.2). By comparing their `@domains` values a processor can determine if two documents use the same set of domains and constraints or, in the case where one domain is a specialization of another domain, that the referenced document's domains are all the same as or more specialized than the referencing element's. See *Vocabulary Modules and DITA Document Types* on page 184 for more about how DITA constraint module usage is declared.

Note that for constraint modules, the referenced document must use the same or more constraints. For domain modules, the referenced document must use the same or fewer domains. This is because constraint modules limit what can be used, but domain modules extend what can be used, so fewer domain modules means more constrained (fewer things allowed).

Note also that processors do not direct analyze content models on an element-type basis, they only compare the set of vocabulary and constraint modules used by the two documents involved in the conref relationship. This means that a processor might disallow a conref because the domain and constraint modules are not consistent, even though a human can inspect the content models of the elements involved and determine that the content models of those particular elements are consistent.

In practice you should be working in an environment where all the topic and map types are managed as a whole, and therefore, whoever defines the document type shells can ensure that all the topic and map types use exactly the same domains and constraints or that map and topic types intended to hold reusable elements are as or more constrained than any map or topic type that would use those elements. In the second case, this might mean you need to create topic or map types that use the intersection of all domains used by the different topic or map types that might use those elements.

Finally, note that many DITA-aware tools do not actually check or validate conref constraints, even though they should. This puts the burden on the people setting up DITA environments to ensure that the conref constraints will not violated by the references authors are likely to create and to train authors to understand what the constraints are. That way, authors will be less likely (or simply unable) to create content references that will be rejected by tools that do validate conref constraints.

Reusing a Range of Elements: conref range

You can reuse sequences of elements using the conref range facility.

There are times when you want to re-use a sequence of elements as a unit, for example, a set of steps. You could, of course, create one conref for each element in the sequence, but that's tedious and hard to maintain. DITA 1.2 adds the "conref range" feature, which allows you to use a single element to reuse a sequence of elements. A conref range is not just a sequence of elements but a sequence of sibling nodes, meaning that the conref result will include any text or processing instruction nodes that occur between the start element and the end element, not just element nodes.

You specify a conref range by pointing to the start of the range, as you would for a single-element conref, using @conref or @conkeyref. You then use @conrefend to specify the ID of the last element in the range.

For example, the following topic contains steps to be used by reference, bound to the key "step-set-01":

```
<task id="reusable-steps">
  <title>Reusable Steps</title>
  <taskbody>
    <steps>
      <step id="step-01">...</step>
      <step id="step-02">...</step>
      <step id="step-03">...</step>
      <step id="step-04">...</step>
    </steps>
  </taskbody>
</task>
```

You could pull in two or more of the steps like so:

```
<task id="task-id">
  ...
  <steps>
    <step conkeyref="step-set-01/step-01"
          conrefend="dontcare.dita#topicid/step-03"
    />
  </steps>
  ...
</task>
```

Note that the value of @conrefend is a direct DITA URI reference complete with fragment identifier. However, the only part of the reference that is actually relevant is the ID component, "step-03."

That's because when you use @conkeyref the key reference determines the topic context for the conref end, meaning that everything except the element ID part of the @conrefend value is ignored.

If you are using @conref and @conrefend, then the address used in @conrefend must point to the same topic as the address in @conref.

Of course, you cannot just refer to random sequences of elements willy-nilly. You must observe some constraints:

1. The first and last elements of the range must have the same parent element.
2. The parent element of the referencing element must be the same as or more specialized than the parent of the referenced elements.
3. The first and last elements in the range must be of the same or more specialized types than the referencing element.

This means you can pull sequences of list items into lists or steps into steps or paragraphs into a topic body. But, for example, you couldn't use conref range to pull multiple notes from the admonition-set-01 document into a <context> element, because the parent element of the <note> elements is <body> in that example.

While the start and end elements of a range must be of the same or more specialized types, that is not true of intermediate elements, so you could have a range of steps that includes one or more <stepsection> elements between the first and last <step> elements. Or you could use a <p> element to point to a range of elements bracketed by two <p> elements, but including between them anything valid in the parent element type.

Note that one could construct specialized or constrained content models that would allow referenced ranges to be invalid. It would be a challenge to do so but it could happen. For example, if the content model were (a, b, a, c, a, d), meaning a sequence of required elements that alternated the element type a with other types, you could reference the sequence (a, b, a), from the second a in the referencing topic, resulting in the effective element sequence (a, b, a, b, a), which would not be schema valid.

There are no content models of this form in the base DITA vocabulary, but nothing prevents someone from defining one in a specialization or constraint module. But it is highly unlikely anyone would define something like this except for the most specialized and task-specific applications.

Also, remember that validity doesn't just mean what the DTD or schema enforces, it means what the processors that operate on the data do or don't accept. If trapping this case and reporting is important, you can always check using a separate validation application like Schematron or custom code.

The rules for attribute merging are a bit more complicated. Attributes specified on the referencing element get merged to all the sibling elements in the referenced range (but not to descendants of the elements in the range). In a conref processor that creates a literal result document, it is up to the processor to rewrite IDs and references in the referenced elements to ensure that all addresses in the resolved result are correct and unambiguous.

Unilateral Change: Conref Push (`@conaction` attribute)

The conref push feature lets you replace elements in, or impose additional elements into, topics or maps, allowing you to change or extend content you can't or shouldn't modify directly.

Because DITA enables true blind interchange, it means you might be in a situation where you get content from a third party, such as a publisher, a supplier of product subcomponents, or another business unit in your company. You can easily integrate this content into your publications using maps. What you can't, or shouldn't, do is modify the content after you get it.

However, there is often a need to change or extend third-party content to reflect your use of it, perhaps to add commentary to regulations or to add use-context-specific or product-specific information to otherwise generic topics.

This requirement is addressed by the DITA 1.2 conref push facility, expressed through the `@conaction` attribute. Conref push lets you point into a map or a topic and link elements before or after an element, making them effectively part of the topic or map linked to. You can also replace elements in the referenced context with pushed elements.

For example, given a generic task for a common subcomponent of a larger product, you could use conref push to add product-specific steps to the generic task or to replace generic steps or context information with product-specific information.

You create a push conref by creating a topic that holds the content to be pushed and that points at the topic to be pushed to. Within the topic to be pushed to, the elements that serve as the push targets must have IDs, just as for any other use of conref. You then include both topics in your map. Normally you would include the pushing topic with a processing role of "resource-only" since its only purpose is to push content to another topic that is, presumably, in the main navigation flow of the publication.

The possible actions for conref push are "pushreplace," "pushbefore," and "pushafter," and they mean exactly what their names suggest.

The "pushreplace" action completely replaces the referenced element with the referencing element.

The "pushbefore" and "pushafter" actions put the referencing element before or after the referenced element, respectively. For pushes, the same constraints as for conref range hold: the pushed element must be the same type or more specialized than the referenced element and both elements must have the same type of parent or the pushed element's parent must be more specialized than the referenced element's parent. This helps ensure that the result of the push is schema valid.

When you use a @conaction of "pushbefore" or "pushafter" you must also create an instance of the same element type as the pushing element that uses a @conaction value of "mark." Effectively the "marker" element serves as a local proxy for the target element you're pushing relative to and helps ensure that the resolved result will be schema valid. The marker element points to the same element as the pushing element.

Because the "marker" element serves as a proxy for the target of the push, it goes in the same position relative to the pushing element as the pushed element will be relative to the referenced element. Thus, for an action of "push after", the marker element goes before the pushing element, and for an action of "push before," the marker element goes after the pushing element. Both cases are shown in the example below. Consider this task topic, bound to the key "generic-task-01":

```
<task id="generic-task">
  <title><ph id="title-text">Some Generic Task</ph></title>
  <taskbody>
    <context id="context">
     <p>This is the generic context.</p>
    </context>
    <steps>
      <step id="step-first">
        <cmd>The first thing you do.</cmd>
      </step>
      ...
      <step id="step-last">
        <cmd>The last thing you do.</cmd>
      </step>
    </steps>
  </taskbody>
</task>
```

You could use conref push to both replace the `<context>` element with a product-specific one and insert new steps before or after the first or last steps. You do this by creating a separate task topic:

```
<task id="push-to-generic">
  <title>Conref push task</title>
  <taskbody>
[1]  <context
        conkeyref="generic-task-01/context"
        conaction="pushreplace"
     >
      <p>This is product-specific context.</p>
     </context>
     <steps>
[2]    <step
          conkeyref="generic-task-01/step-first"
          conaction="pushbefore"
        >
          <cmd>Do this before you do anything else.</cmd>
       </step>
[3]  <step
          conkeyref="generic-task-01/step-first"
          conaction="mark">
          <!-- Required marker element for the push-before action.

               Goes after the pushing element (same relative position
               as the referenced element).
            -->
          <cmd/></step>
[4]    <step
          conkeyref="generic-task-01/step-last"
          conaction="mark">
          <!-- Required marker element for the push-after action

               Goes before the pushing element (same relative position
               as the referenced element).
            -->
          <cmd/></step>
[5]    <step
          conkeyref="generic-task-01/step-last"
          conaction="pushafter"
        >
          <cmd>Do this after you do everything else.</cmd>
       </step>
     </steps>
  </taskbody>
</task>
```

In this topic, note the following key bits:

[1]   A push that replaces the referenced topic's `<context>` element with this element.

[2]   A step that is pushed before the step with the id "step-first" in the referenced topic

[3]   The required marker element for the push-before. It occurs in the same position relative to the pushing element as the referenced element will be relative to the pushing element, after is pushed. This requirement ensures that the pushed element will be valid in the location it is pushed into.

The marker <step> elements have empty <cmd> elements. This is because the content model for <step> requires <cmd>, so it has to be there in order for the document to be schema valid even though the element's content is ignored.

[4]   The required marker element for the push-after.

[5]   A step that is pushed after the last step in the referenced topic. Note that it must occur *after* its corresponding marker element.

You would then include both topics in a map like so:

```
<map>
 <topicgroup
   processing-role="resource-only">
   <topicref
      href="prod-specific/tasks/push-to-generic-task-01.dita"

   >
 </topicgroup>
 ...
 <topichead>
   <topicmeta>
     <navtitle>Product-Specific Manual</navtitle>
   </topicmeta>
   ...
   <topicref
     keys="generic-task-01"
     href="common/tasks/generic-task-01.dita"
   />
   ...
 </topichead>
</map>
```

The first topicref in the map pulls in the pushing task as a resource. This makes the topic available to the processor but doesn't include it in the main navigation hierarchy of the map. Note that the @processing-role attribute on the containing <topicgroup> makes all the topicrefs within the <topicgroup> into resource-only topicrefs, which is what we want for the reference to the pushing topic.

The second topicref pulls in the generic task with the (default) processing role of "normal," which includes it in the main navigation hierarchy. The topicref also binds the key "generic-task-01" to the topic.

The processing result is that the rendered result of processing `generic-task-01.dita` at that location in the map will reflect the replacement of the original `<context>` element with the one from the pushing task, the insertion of a new step before step "step-first" and a new step after step "step-last." The result will be the equivalent of the following task:

```
<task id="generic-task">
  <title><ph id="title-text">Some Generic Task</ph></title>
  <taskbody>
    <context id="context"
      >
      <p>This is product-specific context.</p>
    </context>
    <steps>
      <step
        >
        <cmd>Do this before you do anything else.</cmd>
      </step>
      <step id="step-first">
        <cmd>The first thing you do.</cmd>
      </step>
      ...
      <step id="step-last">
        <cmd>The last thing you do.</cmd>
      </step>
      <step
        >
        <cmd>Do this after you do everything else.</cmd>
      </step>
    </steps>
  </taskbody>
</task>
```

Finally, note that in DITA 1.2 conref push can only be used for single elements, not for ranges. This restriction is to avoid cases where the resolved result would not be schema valid.

It might seem that if you wanted to generate two different versions of the same generic topic in the same use context, you could create two different keys pointing to that topic, then push different content by creating two referencing elements, each using one of the keys. However, the DITA TC has ruled that no matter how many times you try to push into a given topic, there will only be one result topic. In the case where two topics push into the same topic, the result is undefined.

Content Reference Data Management Strategies

Management of conref references requires you to follow a few general practices.

To recap the general practices for making conref manageable:

- Use keys and `@conkeyref` to avoid hard topic-to-topic dependencies and to make your content more flexible.
- Use meaningful and consistent IDs on elements that are intended to be or may be the targets of conref links.
- Establish clear business rules and policies for what *must* be used by reference, what *may* be used by reference, and what *should not* be used by reference. In general, do not allow arbitrary use by reference.
- Organize content to be used by reference into specific areas on the file system or within your content repository.
- Use domain and constraint modules consistently to ensure that all allowed or appropriate referencing and referenced documents satisfy the content reference constraint rules for consistency of vocabulary and constraint use.
- To enable conref push, put `@id` attributes on useful push targets. Note that putting IDs on elements effectively establishes extension points in your content. If your content is intended for or likely to be used by third parties who will want to extend it, you should document your policies and practices for enabling conref push.

10

Conditional Processing: Filtering and Flagging

DITA provides a general facility for binding elements to specific conditions to which they apply. This facility enables filtering and flagging of elements during processing.

Filtering means information components are either filtered out (suppressed or removed) or filtered in (allowed to be processed).

Flagging means information components are differentiated in the rendered output based on a condition. The rendered output could be differentiated using techniques such as setting a text or background color, generating a change indicator, or generating an effectivity statement.

In DITA, conditional processing is enabled through globally-available attributes that let you associate any number of distinct conditions with elements. At processing time you specify which condition values should result in filtering out (exclusion), filtering in (inclusion), or flagging. For flagging, you also define the flagging details for each condition.

Other XML standards may use different terminology for their conditional processing features—applicability, profiling, effectivity—but they are all different expressions of the same basic requirement and the same basic facility.

I prefer the term *applicability* for what DITA calls variously "conditional processing" and "selection" because applicability is a more general term and better separates the properties of elements from they way processors might use those properties.

Applicability vs. Effectivity

Associating an element with selection properties is *applicability*. Using those properties to generate a specific statement or visual indicator is *effectivity*.

Some well-known XML applications, such as ATA 2100 and S1000D, use the term *effectivity* to mean "conditions for which an element is *effective*," and this use is usually reflected by the generation of *effectivity statements* in the published content with statements like "For use at high altitudes" or "For GE engines."

The key distinction here is that applicability is a property of the elements in the source and is independent of any particular processing or rendition of that content. For example, an element's content either applies to high altitude conditions or it does not.

Effectivity is an aspect of rendition that reflects applicability plus processor-specific configuration for how a given applicability value or set of values should be represented in the output. Effectivity is a property of the rendition, and different renditions of the same content can produce different effectivity representations for the same applicability.

For example, if you published a high-altitude-specific version of the manual that only included content that is applicable to high-altitude applications, there would be no need for the effectivity statement "For use at high altitudes" on individual elements because the whole rendition is for high altitudes.

DITA makes a clear separation between applicability, which is a property of the content as authored, and effectivity, which is a function of renderers. DITA supports applicability through the select attributes, which include @props and its specializations, as well as several built-in select attributes, which are not specialized from @props.

Effectivity is fundamentally an implementation issue, and therefore, DITA does not fully standardize it. It does provide a method for defining filtering and flagging configurations, the DITAVAL document type, but the use of DITAVAL is not required by DITA-aware processors, and the DITAVAL facility is not necessarily complete for all possible ways that effectivity could be implemented.

The DITA Conditional Processing Attributes

DITA provides a built-in set of applicability attributes as well as a general attribute, @props, from which you can create specialized applicability attributes.

By defining specific attributes for conditional processing, DITA makes an architectural distinction between element metadata in general and metadata specifically intended to enable conditional processing.

This is an important distinction because there are many places where it's important for a general processor to know whether a given element is conditional, and if so, what conditions apply to that element. An example of such processing is key space construction, where you may need to construct a provisional key space that reflects all potentially-applicable definitions of each key name. In this case, the processor needs to know which key definitions and map references are conditional and what the conditions are so it can determine the set of potentially-applicable and potentially-effective keys for a give name. It's not doing actual filtering or flagging, it's just collecting data, but that data collection depends on knowing which attributes of each element are or are not conditional processing attributes.

While processors could use any property of any element to do conditional processing, you should avoid doing this if interchange is a requirement or you need to use a general-purpose DITA-aware processor. DITA codifies the concept of conditional attributes specifically so that generalized processors can do the right thing for all DITA documents.

The DITA conditional processing attributes are:

@audience   Specifies the audience to which the element applies, for example, "expert," "novice," etc.

@platform   Specifies the platform to which the element applies. For software this normally means the operating system, but DITA doesn't mandate a specific meaning for "platform."

@product   The product to which the element applies.

@rev   The revision to which the element applies. Here "revision" normally means revision of the content, but it could also be used to reflect revisions of the thing being documented. The @rev attribute is used only for flagging, not filtering. It's designed to enable generation of change bars or equivalent revision marking or highlighting.

@otherprops   A catch-all attribute that allows you to specify your own selection property names and values. It is effectively obsolete. It predates DITA 1.1, which introduced the ability to specialize from the @props attribute, which is the better way to define custom select attributes. You can specify arbitrary values in @otherprops, but they won't be associated with a meaningful condition name (the condition is effectively "otherprops").

@props   The base attribute for creating custom select attributes through specialization. Specializing from @props is the easiest specialization to do, and it allows you unbounded freedom to create whatever conditional properties you need to address your business and information requirements.

While @props is intended primarily as a base for specialization, you are allowed to author @props directly in content. The main danger with direct-authoring of @props is consistency in the names for the properties you are using—there's no easy way for XML editors to assist in setting @props values correctly because of its syntax rules. So for production use you should always specialize. But for casual use or to do something in advance of getting a proper @props specialization in place, you can specify @props directly.

The value of @props when directly authored is a sequence of one or more parenthesized property name/value pairs, for example, (platform windows). You can specify any property name and any value name, for example, (myprop somevalue), where myprop is a property name you just made up. If you were to create the equivalent specialization of @props, the attribute name would be @myprop. You can specify multiple parenthesized groups, for example:

```
<p props="(myprop somevalue) (yourprop anothervalue)">...</p>
```

You can think of @audience, @platform, and @product as a starter set of conditional properties, sufficient for many computer documentation requirements but clearly not sufficient for all possible users.

This means that you should expect to specialize from @props early in your production use of DITA, if not immediately. Fortunately, specializing from @props is about as easy as specialization can be. See *Custom Conditional Processing Attributes* on page 299 and *Volume 2: Attribute Specialization Tutorial* for details. If you specialize from props as described there, you can use your specialized attributes in the same way you use the built-in attributes.

DITA doesn't define values for any of these attributes. That's because the set of potentially useful values is unbounded and will always be specific to a given user, information set, and documentation subject.

You will probably want to define values for each of the conditional attributes your authors need. There are a number of different ways you can do this, including creating constraint modules that set the values for each select attribute, using editor-specific features, and using subject scheme maps to define sets of values for specific attributes.

Using constraint modules is the most general approach because it uses normal DTD or schema features that all XML editors should support. However, this requires either that all documents use the same sets of values or that you have different constraint modules and different document type shells for each set of documents that needs a different value set.

Because conditional attributes usually reflect details of the things being documented, it is often the case that different sets of authors or different product groups will need different sets of values and those values are likely to change over time. Thus, having the values baked into DTDs or even constraint modules can be bad. Addressing the need for more flexible value lists is one of the motivations for the Subject Scheme map type as well as for similar facilities for managing lists of values, such as the genericode standard (another OASIS specification, *http://www.genericode.org/*). See *Value Lists, Taxonomies, and Ontologies: SubjectScheme Maps* on page 305.

Select attributes take blank-delimited lists of keywords as their values, where each keyword reflects a distinct value for the property represented by the attribute, for example `audience="expert trainee"`. This means that the element applies to both the expert audience and the trainee audience, that is, a logical OR ("expert or trainee").

You might expect that there would be some way to express more complicated boolean expressions such as "not beginner," but there is not, for the simple reason that you would quickly end up with a full boolean expression language and all the complexity that entails.

So if you need things like "not x" you need to define property values that mean "not x," for example, `audience="notBeginner"`, and then do the right thing in your processing configuration to get the appropriate result.

Using DITAVAL you can also negate all instances of a given attribute by default. See *Filtering and Flagging During Processing (DITAVAL)* on page 295.

Filtering and Flagging During Processing (DITAVAL)

The DITAVAL facility provides a standard way to configure and control how filtering and flagging is done for a given processing instance.

When you place a conditional processing attribute on an element and specify a value or values for that attribute, you effectively bind the element to a set of conditions. You are saying "this element applies to the value *x* for condition *y*."

At processing time a processor can choose to exclude or include the element (filtering), or it can choose to highlight or otherwise make the element visually or behaviorally distinct (flagging).

When evaluating elements to determine if they are included or excluded, you need to look at all of the conditional attributes on that element. If any single conditional attribute on an element evaluates to "exclude" then the element is excluded. That is, it is only necessary for one of the element's conditional attributes to evaluate to "exclude" for the element to be excluded. If this weren't the case, then to exclude an element, you'd have to configure your filtering such that all possible conditional attributes evaluated to "exclude," which is clearly not going to work.

To determine whether a particular conditional attribute evaluates to "exclude," you need to look at the list of values assigned to that attribute. If all of those values evaluate to exclude, then the attribute evaluates to "exclude."

So, within a given attribute instance, all of the values must be set to "exclude" for that attribute to evaluate to "exclude," but once any attribute does evaluate to "exclude" the element is excluded.

To apply the appropriate filtering or flagging, the processor must be told what processing to perform for each property/value pair. The meaning of DITA's conditional attributes is always the same, but the implementation is processor specific.

DITA provides a general-purpose facility for configuring filtering and flagging: the DITAVAL document type. Conforming DITA processors are not required to support DITAVAL, but they should if DITAVAL is at all close to matching their filtering and flagging semantics.

The DITAVAL document type is used to create XML documents that serve as configuration specifications for processors. DITAVAL documents are not "DITA documents" in the sense that maps and topics are. They are not intended to be included in maps. Although it might be useful to be able to specify DITAVAL documents from maps, where a given map reflects an invariant filtering and flagging configuration, DITA 1.2 does not provide such a feature, though you could create a private implementation.

A typical DITAVAL document looks like this:

```
<?xml version="1.0" encoding="UTF-8"?>
<val>
  <prop action="exclude" att="platform"/>
  <prop action="exclude" att="audience"/>
  <prop action="include" att="audience" val="expert"/>
  <prop action="flag" att="platform" val="windows" color="red" >
    <startflag><alt-text>[Win]</alt-text></startflag>
  </prop>
  <prop action="flag" att="platform" val="osx" color="blue" >
    <startflag><alt-text>[OSX]</alt-text></startflag>
  </prop>
</val>
```

A DITVAL document has a root element type of `<val>` and contains zero or more `<prop>` elements.

Each `<prop>` element takes the following attributes:

@action   Specifies the action to apply for the specified condition and value. The `@action` attribute is required.

@att   Specifies the property (condition attribute) to which the `<prop>` element applies, for example, "audience," "platform," etc. This can also be used for property names used in `@props` and `@otherprops`. For example, if you have `props=" (mycondition value1) "`, then you would specify "mycondition" as the value of the `@att` attribute. If `@att` is not specified, then the `<prop>` element applies to all properties.

@val   Specifies the value of the condition to which the `<prop>` element applies. If not specified, then the `<prop>` element applies to all values of the property specified by the `@att` attribute, thus setting the default action. The `@val` attribute should only be specified if `@att` is also specified.

You should have at most one <prop> element for a given combination of @att and @val values, meaning at most one <prop> with only an @action attribute, at most one @prop with a given @att attribute value and no @val attribute, and at most one <prop> for a given @att and @val pair.

A <prop> element with only an @action attribute defines the global default value for all properties. A <prop> element with @action and @att attributes, but no @val attribute, defines the default value for the property named by the @att attribute. And a <prop> element with all three attributes defines the value for the property named by the @att attribute with the value named by the @val attribute.

The possible values for @action are:

include   The element is included. This is the default for all properties and values.

exclude   The element is excluded. You can make this the default for all properties by specifying `<prop action="exclude"/>`. You can make this the default for a particular property by specifying `<prop action="exclude" att="property"/>`.

flag   The element is flagged according to the settings defined on the <prop> element.

passthrough   The element is included in the output preserving the conditional attribute so that a processor applied to the output can itself do filtering or flagging. How the value is preserved is specific to a given output type and processor.

The DITAVAL configuration works as follows:

- For a given attribute value you can either filter on it (include or exclude) or you can flag on it, as in the example above. Setting the action to "flag" implies "include."
- Any value that is not explicitly defined as excluded by the DITAVAL document is included. For elements that specify multiple values for a given attribute, if any of those values are *included* then the element is included. That is, an element is excluded if and only if all of the values for at least one of its conditional attributes are set to "exclude." The default setting for all attributes is "include," so by default all content is included.
- You can set the default behavior on a per *attribute* basis by setting @action to "exclude" and omitting @val. In the sample DITAVAL file above, @audience and @platform have been set to "exclude," meaning that any value specified for @audience or @platform means "exclude" unless explicitly set to "include" or "flag" (which implies inclusion) in another <props> element. In the example, the only time the @audience attribute will evaluate to "include" is if the value is "expert."

  You normally use this to include only a subset of possible values without having to define both explicit positive keywords and explicit negative keywords for the same property values. For example, using the sample DITAVAL file again, if you have a variety of possible audiences, you can filter to produce output reflecting any subset of those audiences. To do this, you set the default for the @audience property to "exclude," then add a <prop> element with @action set to "include" for each of the audiences you want to include. The result is that any element that includes the @audience attribute will be included if the value of that attribute is given an action of "include." Otherwise it will be excluded. In the example, the only value that would be included is "expert."

Looking at the preceding example DITAVAL document, it is saying the following:

- The value "windows" for @platform is flagged using the color "red" and the text "[Win]".
- The value "osx" for @platform is flagged using the color "blue" and the text "[OSX]".
- Any value for @platform other than "windows" or "osx" should be excluded. This is the implication of the first <prop> element, which sets the default action for @platform to "exclude".
- Any value for @audience other than "expert" will be excluded because the second <prop> element sets the default action for @audience to "exclude".

For flagging, you can specify foreground and background colors for the flagged text using the @color and @backcolor attributes of the <prop> element, and you can also specify a text style:

```
<prop att="platform" val="linux"
  action="flag"
  color="red"
  backcolor="yellow"
  style="double-underline"
/>
```

The possible style values are "underline," "double-underline," "italics," "overline," or "bold." The color values should either be HTML color names or 6-digit hexadecimal color numbers of the form "#aabbcc."

You can also add graphic or text indicators before or after the flagged element using the <startflag> and <endflag> subelements of <prop>. Both elements can point to a graphic, define text, or both. Normally you would use a small icon for a graphic, although the rendering details are processor-specific. Use the @imageref attribute to specify the URI of the graphic. Use the <alt-text> subelement to contain the alt text. For example, to flag the platform with icons rather than text, you could do something like this:

```
<?xml version="1.0" encoding="UTF-8"?>
<val>
  <prop action="exclude" att="platform"/>
  <prop action="flag" att="platform" val="windows" color="red" >
    <startflag imageref="icons/windows-icon.jpg"
      ><alt-text>[Win]</alt-text></startflag>
  </prop>
  <prop action="flag" att="platform" val="osx" color="blue" >
    <startflag imageref="icons/osx-icon.jpg"
      ><alt-text>[OSX]</alt-text></startflag>
  </prop>
</val>
```

If both @imageref and <alt-text> are present, then the image is used and the value of <alt-text> becomes the alternate text for the image. If only <alt-text> is present, then the text is used as the flag. Relative image reference URLs are relative to the location of the DITAVAL file.

For revision flagging you use the <revprop> element instead of <prop>. The <revprop> element lets you specify change bars or their functional equivalent based on the value of the @rev attribute. (Note: not all DITA processors or rendition types support the generation of change bars.) In addition to the attributes allowed on <prop> you can specify the @changebar attribute, where the value of @changebar is a processor-specific specification of the character, color, or style to use for the change bar. For example, to flag different revisions you can do something like this:

```
<val>
    <prop action="exclude" att="platform"/>
    <prop action="flag" att="platform" val="osx">
      <startflag imageref="graphics/osx-icon.jpg">
         <alt-text>[OSX]</alt-text>
      </startflag>
    </prop>
  <revprop action="flag"
    val="1.0"
    changebar="1"
  />
  <revprop action="flag"
    val="1.1"
    changebar="2"
  />
  <revprop action="flag"
    val="1.2"
    changebar="3"
    color="red"
    style="underline"
  />
</val>
```

Note that the DITA specification specifically disallows the use of @rev for filtering. This is because @rev is supposed to represent logical revision identifiers, normally reflecting product releases or similar revision labels, not literal revisions of the source. Trying to use @rev and DITA for version-specific configuration management would be madness. Version management is best done with versioning component management systems and code control systems.

Custom Conditional Processing Attributes

You can define your own applicability attributes by specializing from the @props attribute.

See *Volume 2: Attribute Specialization Tutorial* for a complete tutorial on creating attribute specializations.

The built-in set of conditional processing attributes is small and tailored to the needs of primarily software documentation. Thus it's highly likely that you will require additional conditional processing attributes that reflect the details of your content and business processes. Even if the base DITA vocabulary provided a long list of conditional processing attributes you would still likely need your own because everyone's business processes are different.

Conditional processing is one place where the details of business processes and the nature of what you're documenting or writing about intrude on your markup. Another is classifying metadata. You should therefore expect to need to specialize for both custom conditional processing attributes and custom classifying metadata, even if you otherwise have no need for specialized markup.

I have heard many people say "we don't need specialization." What they really mean is "we don't need specialized markup for our content." But everybody needs specialized conditional processing attributes or classifying metadata sooner or later.

Fortunately both are easy to define.

The @props attribute is the base for all specialized conditional processing attributes. You specialize from it by creating an attribute domain module.

An attribute domain module defines exactly one attribute, which must be specialized from either @base or @props. The @base attribute is used for attributes that are not conditional processing attributes. Attributes specialized from @props are by definition conditional processing attributes, and all specialization-aware DITA-aware processors should recognize them as such.

All specializations of @base and @props must be global, meaning that they are allowed on all element types. The only exception is that you can use constraint modules to remove global attributes from specific element types.

An attribute domain module consists of a single file named "*attname*AttDomain.ent", where *attname* is the name of your specialized attribute. For example, to create a new attribute named @region for selecting content based on geographical region, you would create the module file `regionAttDomain.ent`.

The module contains two declarations: a parameter entity declaration for the attribute itself and a general text entity that provides the @domains attribute contribution:

```
<!-- @props attribute specialization module for attribute "region" -->

<!ENTITY % regionAtt-d-attribute "region   CDATA #IMPLIED">

<!ENTITY regionAtt-d-att        "a(props region)"  >

<!-- End of module -->
```

That's the entire attribute module declaration file, just two declarations and some comments. I know it looks like it's too little, but that's all you need. The parameter entity `%regionAtt-d-attribute;` contains the attribute list declaration fragment that is used to add the new attribute to the attribute list declarations for all element types (remember that specialized attributes are always global).

The general entity "regionAtt-d-att" contains the `@domains` contribution for this attribute. The leading "a" before the left parenthesis indicates an attribute specialization. The keyword "props" indicates a specialization of `@props` and "region" is the name of the specialized attribute. This declaration tells processors that `@region` is a conditional processing attribute. If you don't have this declaration properly integrated, processors will not see your attribute as a conditional processing attribute.

You integrate your specialized attributes into shell DTDs by including the module file, adding a reference to the parameter entity to the `%props-attribute-extensions;` parameter entity in the shell, and adding a reference to the `@domains` contribution general entity in the included-domains general entity declaration:

```
...
<!-- ============================================================= -->
<!--                  DOMAIN ATTRIBUTE DECLARATIONS                -->
<!-- ============================================================= -->

<!ENTITY % regionAtt-d-dec PUBLIC
    "urn:example.org:dita:vocabulary:props:region"
    "regionAttDomain.ent"
>%regionAtt-d-dec;
...


<!-- ============================================================= -->
<!--                  DOMAIN ATTRIBUTE EXTENSIONS                  -->
<!-- ============================================================= -->

<!ENTITY % props-attribute-extensions   "
%regionAtt-d-attribute;
" >
<!ENTITY % base-attribute-extensions    "" >
...


<!-- ============================================================= -->
<!--                  DOMAINS ATTRIBUTE OVERRIDE                   -->
<!-- ============================================================= -->

<!ENTITY included-domains
    "&hi-d-att;
     &regionAtt-d-att;
    "
>
...
```

The highlighted text shows the three integration components for the region attribute domain:

- An external parameter entity declaration and reference for the .ent file that is the attribute specialization module.
- A reference to the `%regionAtt-d-attribute;` parameter entity within the `%props-attribute-extensions;` parameter entity, which adds the entity declaration to the global attribute list declaration for all element types.
- A reference to the "regionAtt-d-att" general entity within the "included-domains" general entity, which adds the `@domains` attribute contribution for the new attribute.

That's all there is to it. Once you have created the .ent module and integrated it into your shells, you should be able to refer to your new attribute in DITAVAL files or in the equivalent tool-specific conditional processing configuration mechanism for whatever tool you're using.

When an element has multiple specializations of `@props` specified on it, those multiple attributes can be generalized to a single `@props` attribute, with each specialized attribute/value pair replaced by a parenthesized group of `(propname value)`. For example, if you have two specializations of `@props`, `@prop-a` and `@prop-b` and they are both used on an element:

```
<p prop-a="cond-one" prop-b="cond-two"/>
```

Then if the `<p>` element was generalized, the result would be:

```
<p props="(prop-a cond-one) (prop-b cond-two)">
```

DITA-aware processors should process both the specialized attributes and the `@props` attribute in exactly the same way, so that the filtering or flagging result should be the same for both ways of specifying the conditions.

Processing Implications Of Filtering

The timing of when filtering is applied relative to other processing, such as content reference resolution and key space construction, can affect processing results.

DITA 1.x does not mandate when a processor must perform filtering relative to other DITA processing such as content reference resolution and key space construction. In particular, this means that processors can choose to do filtering before or after conref resolution.

The order in which these operations are performed can change the result of content references. In particular, because the attributes of referencing elements take precedence over the attributes of referenced elements by default, you can have a situation where an element would be included if conref resolution is done before filtering but excluded if conref resolution is done after filtering.

Consider these two elements:

```
<p id="para-01"
   platform="osx"
   conref="#topicid/para-02"/>
<p id="para-02"
   platform="linux"
>This happens to be true for linux and OSX</p>
```

The first element, paragraph "para-01," makes a content reference to paragraph "para-02." These two paragraphs have different values for the @platform selection attribute.

If the filtering specification is set to include platform "osx" and exclude platform "linux," then if filtering is done first the target of the conref gets filtered out *before* the conref is resolved, meaning that the conref target doesn't exist when conrefs are being resolved. This should result in an error message like, "cannot find conref target topicid/para-02." [27]

However, if conref resolution is done first, then the effective value of paragraph "para-01" is:

```
<p id="para-01"
    platform="osx"
>This happens to be true for linux and OSX</p>
```

And subsequent filtering will cause this paragraph to be included.

As of version 1.5.3, the Open Toolkit performs filtering *first* by default, although you can change that by reworking the Open Toolkit Ant scripts. Other processors may do filtering before or after conref resolution or give you a way to control the behavior.

My own analysis is that conref processing should *always* be performed first, otherwise, because of the attribute merging precedence rules, it is impossible for a processor to correctly reflect the intent of the author. However, the Toolkit performs it second for historical reasons that may have made sense in the deep mists of time but are no longer necessary or appropriate. However, because large communities of Toolkit users depend on this behavior, it cannot be changed.

---

[27] This is something of an artificial example. In real life, it might be that the two paragraphs are in different topics and the @platform attribute on para-02 was added after the initial content reference from paragraph para-01 was created.

11

Value Lists, Taxonomies, and Ontologies: SubjectScheme Maps

The SubjectScheme map specialization provides general facilities for defining enumerated lists for attribute values, classification taxonomies, and ontologies.

A general challenge in XML is the management of enumerated lists of values, usually for use in attributes. While it is possible to declare attributes with enumerated value lists, often the lists of values either change frequently or need to be different for different authors or uses of the XML. For example, for conditional processing attributes, such as @product, the set of possible values is both specific to your local set of products and may be different for different groups within the same enterprise or even department. Likewise, the set of products changes constantly over time. It would be impossible to have a single DTD that provided value lists for different sets of users and difficult at best to keep the DTD up to date as the set of products changed over time.

The general solution is to have a separate definition of the values and a means to use that definition within editors. DITA provides the subject scheme map specialization for defining enumerated value lists and associating them with attributes. DITA-aware editors may use such maps to provide value lists for attribute editing. A typical use is to define the values for conditional attributes. Subject scheme maps can also define taxonomies and ontologies. The subject scheme map vocabulary is documented in the "Classification elements" section of the *DITA Language Reference*. Please read that for a complete discussion of subject scheme maps with many more examples than I can provide here.

For this discussion I define *taxonomy* as a hierarchical organization of subjects from general to specific, usually used for classification, and *ontology* as a graph of relationships among subjects. These are not universally-accepted definitions, but this is not a treatise on knowledge representation, so these definitions will work for our purposes here.

The Linnaean taxonomy for biological classification is the textbook example of a taxonomy. Taxonomies are often used in documentation as subject classification schemes, website structures for online stores, or for faceted searching within a website. For example, an online bookstore may have an organizing taxonomy to classify the books they sell.

An example of an ontology would be the sort of graphs popular in knowledge representation where you have entities like "Shakespeare," "Richard III," and "Play" and then use associations to say Richard III is a Play written by Shakespeare.

Subject scheme maps can represent simple enumeration definitions, strict taxonomies, and ontologies. Although subject scheme maps can represent ontologies, the DITA architects are not trying to replicate or compete with other ontology and knowledge representation schemes such as RDF and topic maps. There is nothing that prevents you from using RDF, topic maps, or any other scheme for your knowledge representation needs. By the same token, it is possible to generate RDF assertions or topic maps from subject scheme maps, for example, to serve websites or other information systems.

Defining and Using Attribute Value Lists

To define attribute value lists you create a subject scheme map and use the `<subjectdef>` element to define the values to use. You bind lists of values to attributes using `<enumerationdef>` within the subject scheme map. You can define the values for an attribute globally or for a specific element type.

Editors provide different ways for authors to indicate which subject scheme to use. For example, the OxygenXML editor uses the currently-selected map as the source for values used in the attribute editor. This means you could either have a standalone subject scheme map or include the subject scheme map into a publication's map, whichever makes more sense.

You define the set of values as a subject definition and point to the subject set from `<enumerationdef>` to bind the list to a specific attribute or element/attribute pair. A set of values is represented by a single

`<subjectdef>` element that contains zero or more child `<subjectdef>` elements, one for each value. The @keys value used on each child `<subjectdef>` defines the value to use in attributes:

```
<subjectScheme>
  <title>Product Attribute Value Lists</title>
  <subjectdef keys="product-set-01">
    <subjectdef keys="prod-A"/>
    <subjectdef keys="prod-B"/>
    <subjectdef keys="prod-C"/>
  </subjectdef>
  <enumerationdef>
    <attributedef name="product"/>
    <subjectdef keyref="product-set-01"/>
  </enumerationdef>
</subjectScheme>
```

The values of the @keys attributes on the `<subjectdef>` elements are used as the allowed values for the attribute @product, for example, "prod-A," "prod-B," and "prod-C." The key associated with the parent `<subjectdef>` is used to refer to the list as a unit from the `<enumerationdef>` element.

This is a very simple example but it demonstrates the principle. If a `<subjectdef>` has no child `<subjectdef>` elements, then it defines an empty list, meaning that attributes that use that list do not allow any value to be specified.

In practice you would likely have one map that defines sets of values for different purposes and other maps that use `<enumerationdef>` to bind attributes to value sets as needed. For example, the example above could be refactored into two maps:

Value-list-defining map value-lists.ditamap:

```
<subjectScheme>
  <title>Product Attribute Value Lists</title>
  <subjectdef keys="product-set-01">
    <subjectdef keys="prod-A"/>
    <subjectdef keys="prod-B"/>
    <subjectdef keys="prod-C"/>
  </subjectdef>
  <subjectdef keys="product-set-02">
    <subjectdef keyref="prod-A"/>
    <subjectdef keys="prod-D"/>
    <subjectdef keys="prod-E"/>
  </subjectdef>
</subjectScheme>
```

Enumeration-defining map:

```
<subjectScheme>
  <title>My Product List Bindings</title>
  <schemaref href="value-lists.ditamap"/>
  <enumerationdef>
    <attributedef name="product"/>
    <subjectdef keyref="product-set-01"/>
  </enumerationdef>
</subjectScheme>
```

The value-lists.ditamap now defines two different value lists from which separate subject scheme maps can choose as needed. Note that the second set, product-set-02, reuses the subject "prod-A" by making a key reference to the key "prod-A." You have to do this because if you had a second `<subjectdef>` element with the key "prod-A," that key would never be effective because the first definition of key within a map always wins. So the second `<subjectdef>` would effectively be invisible. Thus, you must use `@keyref` to point to any subject already defined elsewhere in the map.

That is, for a given subject identified by a given key name, that subject definition can occur exactly once in the subject scheme map and must be used by reference in all the other places where it is needed.

You can define the default value for an attribute using `<defaultSubject>` within `<enumerationdef>`:

```
<subjectScheme>
  <title>My Product List Bindings</title>
  <schemaref href="value-lists.ditamap"/>
  <enumerationdef>
    <attributedef name="product"/>
    <subjectdef keyref="product-set-01"/>
    <defaultSubject href="prod-B"/>
  </enumerationdef>
</subjectScheme>
```

The default specified in a subject scheme enumeration is used if there is no default specified in the governing DTD or schema and there is no value specified in the document instance. In DITA, most potentially-enumerable attributes, such as the selection attributes, do not have DTD- or schema-defined defaults, meaning that defaults defined in subject-scheme maps should take effect in processors that support the use of subject scheme maps.

The enumeration definition shown above applies to all uses of the `@product` attribute. However, you can limit it to a specific element type by using `<elementdef>` within `<enumerationdef>`. For example, to use the list product-set-01 only on `<table>` elements, you would do this:

```
<subjectScheme>
  <title>My Product List Bindings</title>
  <schemaref href="value-lists.ditamap"/>
  <enumerationdef>
    <elementdef name="table"/>
    <attributedef name="product"/>
    <subjectdef keyref="product-set-01"/>
    <defaultSubject href="prod-B"/>
  </enumerationdef>
</subjectScheme>
```

Note that `<elementdef>` only applies to the element type named, not to specializations of it.

When defining sets of subjects to use as values, you can nest `<subjectdef>` elements to create a hierarchy. At least for the purposes of doing DITA-defined filtering, the implication of the hierarchy is that lower (more-specific) values match to higher (more-general) values as specified in a DITAVAL document or similar run-time conditional processing specification.

For example, you might have products and variants within a given main product, where anything that applies to a product's variant also applies to the product. You could model that like so:

```
...
<subjectdef keys="product-set-01">
  <subjectdef keys="prod-A">
    <subjectdef keys="prod-A-community"/>
    <subjectdef keys="prod-A-enterprise"/>
    <subjectdef keys="prod-A-pro"/>
  </subjectdef>
  <subjectdef keys="prod-B"/>
  <subjectdef keys="prod-C"/>
</subjectdef>
...
```

For the purposes of setting attribute values, the hierarchy is treated as a flat list, for example, "prod-A," "prod-A-community," "prod-A-enterprise," etc.

For conditional processing, if the `@product` value "prod-A" is set to "include" and "prod-B" and "prod-C" are set to "exclude," then you would expect a subject-scheme-aware processor to include elements with a `@product` value of "prod-A-community, ""prod-A-enterprise," or "prod-A-pro" in addition to those with a value of "prod-A." Or said another way, by explicitly setting "prod-A" to "include" you implicitly set all the subordinate values of subject "prod-A" to "include." This ability to have hierarchical subject lists can make it much easier to manage and use complex conditional processing values.

Defining General Taxonomies

Subject scheme maps are not limited to defining enumerated attribute values. They can be used to represent general taxonomies, whether for use with DITA-based content or as a convenient XML markup for taxonomies. Because `<subjectdef>` elements are specializations of `<topicref>`, they can point to topics or other resources. This lets you bind the definition of a subject within the taxonomy to supporting information, such as the documentation of the subject itself. For example, you might have a set of glossary entry topics that define the terms within a given classification taxonomy. You can create a subject scheme map to define the taxonomy and link each `<subjectdef>` to its corresponding glossary entry.

In the case of the DITA language itself, there are reference entries for each topic type defined by the DITA standard. These topic types exist in a specialization hierarchy that reflects the taxonomic relationships of the topic types as they apply to technical documentation or instructional design practice. This means we can define a subject scheme map that formally defines the topic type hierarchy and literally links to the reference entries for each topic:

```
<subjectScheme>
  <title>DITA Topic Type Taxonomy</title>
  <subjectHead>
    <subjectHeadMeta>
      <navtitle>DITA Topic Types</navtitle>
    </subjectHeadMeta>
  </subjectHead>
  <mapref href="urn:dita:language-reference:key-definitions"/>
  <subjectdef keys="topic" keyref="topic-refentry">
    <subjectdef keys="concept" keyref="concept-refentry">
      <subjectdef keys="glossentry" keyref="glossentry-refentry"/>
    </subjectdef>
    <subjectdef keys="reference" keyref="reference-refentry"/>
    <subjectdef keys="task" keyref="task-refentry">
    </subjectdef>
    <subjectdef keys="learningBase" keyref="learningBase-refentry">
      <subjectdef keys="learningAssessment"
                  keyref="learningAssessment-refentry"/>
      <subjectdef keys="learningContent"
                  keyref="learningContent-refentry"/>
      <subjectdef keys="learningOverview"
                  keyref="learningOverview-refentry"/>
      <subjectdef keys="learningPlan"
                  keyref="learningPlan-refentry"/>
      <subjectdef keys="learningOverview"
                  keyref="learningOverview-refentry"/>
    </subjectdef>
  </subjectdef>
</subjectScheme>
```

Note the `<mapref>` element that represents inclusion of the key definitions for the DITA language reference. Here I'm using a URN to make the point that these are coming from somewhere else and I'm avoiding the issue of where that is for this example.

In this example, each `<subjectdef>` defines the subjects "topic," "reference," "task," etc., and also pointing to the reference entry topics for the topic types. Given the correct key bindings for the reference entries, this map can be processed like any other map, and the result will be those topics formatted the same as a generic map.

Note that, by default, `<subjectdef>` topic references have a processing role of "normal," so normal map processing applied to this map will treat the `<subjectdef>` elements as if they were generic `<topicref>` elements.

Because the `<subjectdef>` elements are normal topicrefs, they can have the usual topicref metadata, including a navigation title and a short description. For many taxonomies the `@keys` value will be some more-or-less opaque ID, so you can include navigation titles to provide a human-understandable representation of the taxonomy item.

For example, the *HIPAA Health Care Provider Taxonomy Codes* (*http://www.adldata.com/Downloads/Provider-Taxonomy.html*) is a taxonomy with opaque codes and human-readable values. A bit of that taxonomy could be represented in a subject scheme map like so:

```
<subjectScheme>
  <title>HIPAA Health Care Provider Taxonomy Codes</title>
  <topicmeta>

<source>http://www.adldata.com/Downloads/Glossaries/taxonomy_80.pdf</source>

  </topicmeta>
  <subjectdef keys="193000000X">
    <topicmeta>
      <navtitle>Group</navtitle>
      <shortdesc>A business entity under which one or more
individuals practice.</shortdesc>
    </topicmeta>
    <subjectdef keys="193200000X">
      <topicmeta>
        <navtitle>Multi-Specialty</navtitle>
        <shortdesc>A business group of one or more
individual practitioners, who practice with different
areas of specialization.</shortdesc>
      </topicmeta>
    </subjectdef>
    <subjectdef keys="193400000X">
      <topicmeta>
        <navtitle>Single-Specialty</navtitle>
        <shortdesc>A business group of one or more
```

```
individual practitioners, who all practice with the same
area of specialization.</shortdesc>
      </topicmeta>
    </subjectdef>
  </subjectdef>
  <subjectdef keys="201000000X">
    <topicmeta>
      <navtitle>Allopathic &amp; Osteopathic Physicians</navtitle>
      <shortdesc>A broad category grouping state licensed providers
in allopathic or osteopathic medicine whose scope of practice is
determined by education.</shortdesc>
      </topicmeta>
    <subjectdef keys="207K00000X">
      <topicmeta>
        <navtitle>Allergy &amp; Immunology</navtitle>
        <shortdesc>An allergist-immunologist is....</shortdesc>
      </topicmeta>
    </subjectdef>
    <subjectdef keys="207L00000X">
      <topicmeta>
        <navtitle>Anesthesiology</navtitle>
        <shortdesc>An anesthesiologist is trained....</shortdesc>
      </topicmeta>
    </subjectdef>
    ...
  </subjectdef>
  ...
</subjectScheme>
```

Here, each @keys value is the taxonomic code value, the navigation title is the label, and the short
description is the formal definition of the code. It's hard to see it by just looking at the raw markup, but
the taxonomy defined is:

- Group

  - Multi-specialty
  - Single-specialty

- Allopathic & Osteopathic Physicians

  - Allergy & Immunology
  - Anesthesiology

Because each subject in the taxonomy has a key, you can use references to those keys to build up a complete
taxonomy from separate taxonomies. For example, one subject scheme map can include another map
and augment existing subjects by adding additional subjects to them or by including them in new subjects.

The DITA specification's discussion of the subject scheme map type has many good examples and much more detail on the subject of combining schemas.

Defining Ontologies with Subject Scheme Maps

For this discussion I define *ontology* as a graph of typed relationships among subjects. That is, more generally, the representation of knowledge about things using typed relationships. Subject scheme maps are capable of representing graphs of relationships of typed links and therefore of representing ontologies.

This is not to say that subject scheme maps are necessarily capable of complete knowledge representation, whatever that might mean. Knowledge representation was not the main design goal for subject scheme maps, and they are not an attempt to replicate or replace other knowledge representation approaches such as RDF/OWL or topic maps.

However, subject scheme maps do provide a DITA-specific and convenient format for reasonably complete knowledge representation that can be processed using the normal DITA processing infrastructure. So if you don't already have some other knowledge representation system in place, subject scheme maps may be just the thing. At a minimum, they provide a way to bring knowledge represented in other ways into a DITA context, for example, to enable navigation of topics through associations using normal DITA navigation and presentation tools.

If we take `<subjectdef>` elements as defining "subjects" in the knowledge representation sense, that is, named things we want to talk about, such as people, places, ideas, or components of a product, then a subject scheme map does two things:

- it defines a set of subjects, and
- it establishes relationships among those subjects.

In the taxonomy examples shown in *Defining General Taxonomies* on page 310, the relationships among subjects are all implicitly "is-a" relationships, as taxonomies define type or class hierarchies where each child subject is implicitly a more specialized instance of its parent type (for example, "concept" is a "topic"). But of course there is an unbounded set of possible relationship types that might exist between any two subjects.

For the purposes of general data modeling there is a well-understood set of relationship types, and the subject scheme map vocabulary provides markup for them. Each of these elements represents a relationship type that applies down the hierarchy of subjects it contains, such that the relationship type applies to each parent/child pair in the subject tree descending from the relationship-defining element. This markup approach avoids the need to explicitly state each relationship among a large number of subjects.

For example, the topic-type taxonomy example can be refined by adding the `<hasKind>` relationship-type-defining element as a wrapper around the original taxonomy-defining subjects:

```
<subjectScheme>
  <title>DITA Topic Type Taxonomy</title>
  <subjectHead>
    <subjectHeadMeta>
      <navtitle>DITA Topic Types</navtitle>
    </subjectHeadMeta>
  </subjectHead>
  <mapref href="urn:dita:language-reference:key-definitions"/>
  <hasKind>
    <subjectdef keys="topic" keyref="topic-refentry">
      <subjectdef keys="concept" keyref="concept-refentry">
        <subjectdef keys="glossentry" keyref="glossentry-refentry"/>
      </subjectdef>
      <subjectdef keys="reference" keyref="reference-refentry"/>
      <subjectdef keys="task" keyref="task-refentry">
      </subjectdef>
      <subjectdef keys="learningBase" keyref="learningBase-refentry">
        <subjectdef keys="learningAssessment"
                    keyref="learningAssessment-refentry"/>
        <subjectdef keys="learningContent"
                    keyref="learningContent-refentry"/>
        <subjectdef keys="learningOverview"
                    keyref="learningOverview-refentry"/>
        <subjectdef keys="learningPlan"
                    keyref="learningPlan-refentry"/>
        <subjectdef keys="learningOverview"
                    keyref="learningOverview-refentry"/>
      </subjectdef>
    </subjectdef>
  </hasKind>
</subjectScheme>
```

The addition of the `<hasKind>` element makes it explicit that each descendant of the "topic" subject is a specialization of (is a kind of) topic.

The relationship type elements are:

`<hasKind>`   Indicates that the child subjects of the containing subjects are types of (kinds of) the containing subject, as shown in the topic type taxonomy example above, for example, "topic" has-kind "concept." The has-kind relationship is transitive and the inverse is "is a ,"that is, for a has-kind hierarchy you can read up the tree as "is-a" relationships, for example, "concept" is a "topic."

`<hasInstance>` Indicates that the child subjects of the containing subjects are instances of the containing subject. For example:

```
<hasInstance>
  <subjectdef keys="vampire">
    <subjectdef keys="Lestat"/>
    <subjectdef keys="Dracula"/>
    <subjectdef keys="Mr-Burns"/>
  </subjectdef>
  <subjectdef keys="werewolf">
    <subjectdef keys="LonChaney"/>
    <subjectdef keys="EddieMuster"/>
    <subjectdef keys="DavidNaughton"/>
    <subjectdef keys="DelphineAngua"/>
  </subjectdef>
</hasInstance>
```

That is, Dracula is a vampire and Delphine Angua is a werewolf.

`<hasNarrower>` The contained subjects are "narrower" than the containing subjects. The DITA standard does not say what "narrower" means. One use might be to indicate that a topic about Shakespeare plays is narrower than a subject on plays in general.

`<hasPart>` Indicates that the child subjects are parts of the containing subjects. The has-part relationship is transitive and the inverse is "is part of." For example, the structural rules for topics could be expressed as:

```
<hasPart>
  <subject keys="topic">
    <subject keyref="title"/>
    <subject keyref="titlealts"/>
    <subject keyref="abstract"/>
    <subject keyref="shortdesc"/>
    <subject keyref="prolog"/>
    <subject keyref="body"/>
    <subject keyref="related-links"/>
    <subject keyref="topic"/>
  </subject>
</hasPart>
```

`<hasRelated>` Represents a typed relationship among the containing and contained subjects. The relationship type is defined by the `@keys` attribute value or the subject referenced via key reference. You can use `<hasRelated>` to establish any relationships you might need. For example, you could define marriage relationships like so:

```
...
  <hasKind>
   <subjectdef keys="relationship-type">
    <subjectdef keys="married-to">
      <topicmeta>
       <navtitle>is-married-to</navtitle>
       <shortdesc>A transitive relationship between two parties,
each of which plays the
role "spouse".</shortdesc>
      </topicmeta>
    </subjectdef>
   </subjectdef>
  </hasKind>
  ...
  <hasRelated keyref="married-to">
    <subjectdef keyref="SamuelVimes">
     <subjectdef keyref="SybilDeidreOlgivannaVimes"/>
    </subjectdef>
  </hasRelated>
  ...
```

Note that in this example I've formally defined the relationship "married-to" within a "kind-of" hierarchy to make my intent a bit more explicit. In this context, the `<hasRelated>` relationship functions like an RDF predicate in that it is making a formal assertion about two other subjects. By taking this idea as far as you need you could clearly use subject scheme maps to represent knowledge to pretty much any level of detail. However, as DITA maps were not designed specifically for that purpose, you would need to define markup specializations and metadata conventions to fully represent all the details that go into representing knowledge with appropriate precision and clarity.

Subject scheme maps are maps, which means they can contain relationship tables. You would naturally expect to be able to also use relationship tables to establish relationships among subjects, and you can. The subject scheme map vocabulary includes a specialization of `<reltable>`, `<subjectRelTable>`, that is intended specifically to establish arbitrary *n*-ary relationships among subjects. There is nothing special about `<subjectRelTable>`, except that it uses the subject scheme map elements exclusively. See *Relationship Tables* on page 263 for a general discussion of relationship tables. See the "Classification elements" section in the *DITA Language Reference* for a detailed discussion of subject relationship tables.

Appendix A

Character Encodings, or What Does "UTF-8" Really Mean?

While this book assumes you have a basic working understanding of XML, there is one aspect of XML that still trips up a lot of people (maybe most people), and that is encodings.

I see a lot of terminology in casual use like "UTF-8 characters" or "special character entities" or simply confusion about what encodings in XML are all about. It bugs me. Thus this discussion.

By the definition of the XML standard, an XML document consists of Unicode characters. Unicode (ISO/IEC 10646) is a character set that defines a huge number of characters, enough for all human languages in current use and many that are no longer used.

A *character set* is exactly that, a set of characters, where each character has one or more unique identifiers, such as a numeric code. A character is an abstraction that represents the idea of, for example, the letter "A" or the ideograph "大" ("da4" in Pin Yin, meaning "big" in English).

What the XML standard means by saying that all XML documents consist of Unicode characters is that the output of an XML parser is a sequence of Unicode characters. In pretty much all modern programming languages, the internal representation of strings of characters is Unicode characters.

An *encoding* is a scheme for storing characters as sequences of bytes, for example, in a file on disk.

When an XML document held in some processing system (an editor, an XSLT transform, a DOM in a Java program) is written out it is said to be *serialized*, meaning the markup and content are converted from the objects held in memory to a sequence of characters and as a sequence of bytes. When you serialize an XML document you determine the details of how the markup is represented as a sequence of Unicode characters and then what encoding is used to store those characters as a sequence of bytes.

The Unicode standard defines a number of different encoding schemes, including UTF-8 and UTF-16. The UTF-8 encoding scheme uses one byte per character through character 128. After that it uses three or four bytes depending on the character. By contrast, UTF-16 uses two bytes for each character through \uFFFF, after which it uses 4 bytes.

This means that the same *character* can be written to disk as bytes in any number of ways. For example, the character "大" becomes the three bytes "0xE5 0xA4 0xA7" in UTF-8, but in UTF-16 it becomes the bytes "0x59 0x27" or "0x27 0x59."

It is the XML parser's job to determine the encoding used in the data file and translate the byte sequences back into characters. It is a serializer's job to do the reverse.

While the XML standard mandates that all conforming XML processors must support at least UTF-8 encoding, it allows documents to be stored in any encoding. However, not all encodings are equivalent to Unicode, meaning that some may not have a way to represent all Unicode characters. For example, there are numerous 8-bit encodings based on the ASCII standard, for example, ISO-8859. Such encodings cannot directly represent Unicode characters above 255.

XML solves this problem by providing a way to represent arbitrary characters using an escaping scheme that uses only ASCII characters (that is, characters below 128). This escaping mechanism is *numeric character references*, for example, " " (decimal value) or " " (hex value) (in both cases, the non-breaking space character). As far as XML parsers are concerned numeric character references are exactly equivalent to the corresponding literal character. For example, you could represent an entire XML document on disk as a sequence of numeric character references if you wanted to.

If an XML document does not say otherwise, it is assumed to be stored in UTF-8 encoding. However, some encodings, such as UTF-16 are self describing through byte order marks, which in the case of UTF-16 indicate whether the high-order byte is first or second in each character's byte pair. So some parsers may detect or attempt to detect the encoding if it is not specified.

XML documents can also specify the encoding in the XML declaration, the processing instruction that can be the first thing in the document, for example:

```
<?xml version="1.0" encoding="UTF-8"?>
<topic id="topicid">
   . . .
```

In fact, the presence of the XML declaration helps enable encoding detection because the first 5 characters are always "<?xml" so if you know how different encodings represent those characters as a sequence of bytes you can make an educated guess as to the encoding.

It is very important that if a document has an encoding declaration that it accurately reflect the actual encoding used. The XML standard requires parsers to respect the encoding declaration if present, even if the true encoding is reliably detectable. However, not all processors do this, so if the encoding and encoding declaration do not match, you may get different results from different processors.

The practical implications of encodings have to do with the details of how documents are authored and stored and the potential for error committed by tools that generate XML documents without proper attention to encoding.

As a matter of practice you should store all the documents in a given document set or management environment in the same encoding, simply to avoid error and confusion. For content that is mostly or entirely in Latin or Eastern European scripts, UTF-8 is the obvious best choice. For content that is mostly or entirely in Asian scripts, particularly Chinese, Japanese, Korean, Thai, and the various scripts used in South Asia, UTF-16 will be more efficient because it uses two bytes where UTF-8 would require three or four.

For XML documents there should never be a requirement to store them in a non-Unicode encoding. This is because all conforming XML processors must support at least UTF-8. However, some non-conforming tools may require the use of ASCII or ISO-8859, in which case you may have no choice. Likewise, if your content is managed in a storage system that doesn't understand Unicode encodings, such as CVS, it may be safer to use an ASCII-based encoding so you avoid any potential corruption of non-ASCII characters. More modern source code control systems, such as Subversion and GIT, support Unicode fully.

If your documents are stored in a Unicode encoding, i.e., UTF-8 or UTF-16, then there is no particular need to represent any character as a numeric character reference. However, it may be convenient to use numeric character references for characters that can't be easily typed. For example, this document as authored uses a numeric character reference for character \u5927 because it's easy to look up the Unicode code point but harder to find the character. Likewise, characters that are invisible or look like spaces may be easier to work with as numeric character references. But the point is it doesn't matter as long as the encoding used to store the documents is a Unicode encoding.

If the document is stored in any other non-Unicode encoding, then you must escape all characters for which there is no correspondence in the target encoding.

Another implication of all this is that the encoding a document is stored in is largely immaterial to overall processing—as long as the characters are correctly encoded or escaped, the XML document is the same regardless of the encoding used, meaning you can change the encoding used without any risk of injury to the XML nature of the document.

For example, a document original encoded in ISO-8859-0 might be stored in UTF-8 in an XML repository and might be exported back out in UTF-16 by a particular export process. The document is the same in all three cases.

It should be clear from this discussion that the term "UTF-8 character" is particularly meaningless because UTF-8 is not a character set but an encoding scheme. As far as XML is concerned, there are only "Unicode characters" and "ASCII characters," meaning that subset of the Unicode character set that is identical to ASCII, namely the characters 0 to 128.

Likewise, the term "special character entity" is meaningless, unless you happen to be using a DTD that declares a bunch of internal general entities that resolve to single characters. But of course that old SGML practice is no longer needed in XML and is actively discouraged by DITA because DITA goes out of its way to avoid the need for entities of any sort (other than parameter entities in DTDs). What most people mean by "special character entity" is "numeric character reference." Please use the correct term.

In the case of the DITA Open Toolkit, you can use any encoding or encodings supported by the XML parser the Toolkit uses, which is normally the Apache Xerces parser, which supports just about every encoding there is.

Another important aspect of character sets and encodings is the relationship between characters and *glyphs*. A glyph is a specific representation of a character within a particular font. For example, the character "A" rendered in a serif font looks very different from the character in a sans-serif font and very, very different from the character rendered in a dingbat font like Wingdings. For a given font there is a correspondence between the characters in a character set and the glyphs in the font. For "Unicode fonts," that correspondence is simple; the code for a given glyph is the same as the corresponding character's code. Many older fonts, such as Postscript Type 1 fonts and older True Type fonts, are ASCII fonts, not Unicode fonts, meaning that they only have at most 255 glyphs. Use of these fonts with XML is challenging because of the mapping issues for non-ASCII characters.

A "Unicode font" does not necessarily have glyphs for all the Unicode characters, it simply has glyphs for that part of Unicode it supports. For example, a Devanagari font may only have glyphs for Devanagari characters, but those glyphs will be at the Unicode code points for those characters.

There are a few fonts that do, or at least attempt to, cover the entire Unicode range, at least through the first 65,000 characters (the "base multilingual plane" of Unicode), but these fonts are only a convenience and are not usually intended for production typography. In particular, ideographic content needs to be rendered in a locale-specific font. Many Asian languages, such as Japanese and Chinese, use the same ideographic characters but different glyphs. It is important not to render ideographic characters in a Japanese document using Simplified Chinese glyphs, for example.

Finally, an invaluable tool for working with different character sets and character encodings is the SC Unipad editor (Windows only). It is a free open-source editor that handles almost all encodings and lets you see exactly what's going on in your data and manipulate it at the encoding or character level.

Another useful trick on Windows is to use the Textpad editor to open XML documents in binary mode, which lets you see the specific bytes of the document.

Encoding issues can be very subtle. The characters above 128 in Unicode are stored in UTF-8 as multi-byte sequences but the individual bytes are usually also ASCII characters. If a tool tries to guess at a document's encoding and guesses ASCII when it's really UTF-8, it is possible for characters to get corrupted. Because this involves characters that may appear to be sensible characters even after corruption, you may miss the problem.

Another common problem is programs that write out XML as byte sequences without applying the right encoding. This is typified by the programming mistake in Java of writing a Java String object to disk by calling the getBytes() method on the String. The result of writing those bytes to disk is almost good UTF-16, but not quite. If you get files that don't work in some tools and are twice as big as they should be, use a binary viewer to see if the file is a sequence of zero bytes and non-zero bytes.

Another potential encoding problem is documents created on non-Western computers where the operating system's native encoding is not a Unicode encoding, for example, GB-2312 on Chinese computers. If a document is created in one of these encodings, but either lies about its encoding in the encoding declaration or doesn't have an encoding declaration, you may get character corruption or encoding errors from the parser. A tool like Unipad can help in this situation. Java also comes with command-line tools for manipulating encodings.

Finally, an important feature of XSLT 2 is character maps, which let you specify how a given Unicode character should be represented in the result of the XSLT process. This lets you explicitly use numeric character references or entity references for specific characters or even map characters to markup in the output. You can also use trivial XSLT transforms to transform a document into a specific encoding as long as the output encoding is supported by the XSLT engine. The Saxon XSLT engine, for example, provides non-standard output options that configure how or if numeric character references are used in the serialized output.

Appendix B

Bookmap: An Unfortunate Design

The Bookmap map type is the standard map type for representing print-primary publications but unfortunately it suffers from some design flaws that limit its usefulness.

I partially blame myself for Bookmap because I was on the DITA TC when the Bookmap proposal was made as part of the DITA 1.1 revision, and I wasn't paying close enough attention, and therefore, I didn't object to the design before it became part of the standard. I say that to make the point that my critiques of Bookmap are not intended to be Monday-morning quarterbacking, and I want to be clear that even though I had nothing to do directly with the design of Bookmap, I accept some responsibility for not having done anything about it when something could have been done. At the same time, my understanding of map design considerations has certainly evolved since the DITA 1.1 timeframe, so there's no guarantee I would have even realized the problems I now identify in the Bookmap design. Much of my thinking was driven by my understanding of the Learning and Training learning map design, which I consider to be innovative in ways that I now consider to be best practice.

The Bookmap map type is intended to represent typical technical documents, in particular those that reflect IBM's practice, at least as it was at the start of the 21st century, when DITA 1.1 was developed. It provides unique publication metadata and unique print-specific topicref types, such as `<part>` and `<chapter>`, which let you represent a typical print publication.

However, Bookmap has several design flaws that limit its utility. These flaws are:

- It is defined as a map *type* not a map *domain*.

  This means that you cannot extend the content models it defines nor can you use just parts of its design in the context of other map types. In particular, the publication metadata and publication topicref structures can only be used together. There is no way to swap in a different metadata design or use just the Bookmap metadata elements in a different map type. Likewise, any specialization of Bookmap must accept the structural constraints imposed on the publication structure.

  By contrast, the DITA 1.2 Learning and Training design avoided this by creating a learning-specific map domain that allows the learning-specific topicref types to be used with any map type. It also defines a separate domain for learning-specific metadata. The Learning and Training vocabulary does include a Learning map type as well, but it really just serves as a convenience and an example of how to integrate the various Learning and Training map domains together to form a working map type.

- The structural constraints imposed by the Bookmap design disallow a number of reasonable and, in the case of Publishing applications, common structures.

  For example, having used a `<part>` topicref you cannot have a `<chapter>` topicref following or between parts. However, this structure does occur on occasion. In addition, there is no option to have a common wrapper around all the body topicrefs (that is, the topicrefs between the end of the frontmatter and the start of the appendixes or backmatter). That markup pattern (having a sequence of containers) is a common best practice that many prefer, but Bookmap does not allow it.

- The publication metadata is not sufficient for Publishing applications and barely sufficient for technical documents.

  For example, it only provides one element for holding an ISBN number, but many publications have multiple ISBNs, including both ISBN-10 and ISBN-13, print and electronic ISBNs, and so on. The Bookmap metadata assumes that the publication will copyrighted and has no provision for other licensing terms such as Creative Commons licenses.

- The map design has no formal provision for references to or markup for submaps.

  For example, it is common practice to use a separate map for each part or chapter of a publication. While you can use the `<part>` or `<chapter>` topicrefs to refer to maps, it is often clearer to have distinct topicref types for making map-to-map references, analogous to the DITA 1.2 `<mapref>` convenience specialization of `<topicref>`, but constrained to the appropriate location in the map. Many authors find it clearer to have a separate topicref type for map references that has the same base semantic as the corresponding topicref type, for example, `<chapter>` and `<chapter-mapref>`.

  Likewise, it can be useful to have specific root elements for publication-component submaps, for example, `<chaptermap>` or `<partmap>`, that make it clearer to authors that what they are creating is a subordinate map that is not intended to be used as a standalone publication. Because Bookmap doesn't provide these other map types, and because it is not a map domain, there is no way to create, for example, a map type that only allows `<part>` or `<chapter>` as its first or only child, which is what you would want in order to have a Bookmap-specific submap.

For all of these reasons, the Bookmap map type is not suitable for general Publishing use and I explicitly recommend against its use. It may be suitable for general technical documentation use, as long as you can live within its constraints. But because the design is so fundamentally broken, I generally recommend against its use in any context.

I have tried to avoid these issues in the design of the DITA for Publishers Publication Map (Pubmap) map domains (one for publication metadata and one for publication structure topicrefs). The Pubmap design is specifically driven by the requirements of publishers, but as a side effect it also satisfies the needs of technical documents as technical documentation requirements are a subset of publishing requirements. Using the Pubmap domains as a base it would be relatively easy to define a new map type or set of map domains that looked structurally very much like Bookmap but without the limitations or missing features.

Index